THE LAW KILLERS

By the same author:

LAWLESS

THE LAW KILLERS

ALEXANDER McGREGOR

BLACK & WHITE PUBLISHING

First published 2005
This updated edition first published 2013
by Black & White Publishing Ltd
29 Ocean Drive, Edinburgh EH6 6JL

1 3 5 7 9 10 8 6 4 2   13 14 15 16

ISBN: 978 1 84502 724 7

Typeset by RefineCatch Ltd, Bungay, Suffolk
Printed and bound by Grafica Veneta S.p.A. Italy

For Christine
who gave me some of the words and all of the time.

ACKNOWLEDGEMENTS

Where to begin? So many people, knowingly or not, have assisted in the compilation of these pages that it is not practical to list them all. A large proportion of them were former police officers who generously shared their time and experiences with me and I am extremely grateful for their recollections. Among them was ex-Detective Inspector Bob Donaldson who helped me locate these invaluable people.

I am also deeply indebted to D.C. Thomson & Co. Ltd for their considerable cooperation, not least of which was the unrestricted access they allowed me to their extensive cuttings and photographic libraries. Many of the photographs used belong to them. In particular, I would like to thank Gwen Kissock and Anne Swadel for their encyclopaedic knowledge and willingness to help. Others who assisted were Gordon Robbie, Gus Proctor, Colin Stewart, Jackie Laing and Susan Dailly.

Special thanks are due to respected sports journalist John Mann, who took a break from some of the violence of the football field to research a 19th century poisoning, the results of which he very kindly passed to me and which were central to the preparation of one of the chapters.

My gratitude also to the staff of Dundee Central Library and the Scottish Prison Service.

Thanks too – I think – to author Norman Watson, a journalistic colleague, who enthusiastically prodded me into this, but who neglected to inform me how much work would be involved.

Most of all, I would like to record how grateful I am to the countless journalists who contributed indirectly to this book through their reports of the crimes and coverage of the trials of those responsible.

Reporters are a much-maligned breed and they do not always receive the recognition they deserve. It is not generally appreciated that the words they write in today's newspapers form the basis of tomorrow's history books.

Alexander McGregor

CONTENTS

INTRODUCTION

Murder is a funny old game. The end result is the same but the journey to that hellish destination is always different. The route can sometimes be straightforward enough, uncomplicated and not too difficult to understand why some people travelled in that direction. At other times, the trip can be as complex and unfathomable as the travellers themselves.

Some of the leading players are, in truth, not so different from the rest of us. They have committed the ultimate crime in a moment of insanity, a solitary out-of-character act which changes lives forever. It is instantly regretted but as irreversible and final as the last breath of the person who perished. It is a route they are unlikely to take again. Their meandering journey through life has merely sent them down the wrong path on the wrong day, perhaps when they stopped off along the way for one drink too many.

Sometimes it is just the chemistry between two people which is wrong, incompatibility being resolved by the most extreme of actions. If fate had not introduced the leading players, they would never have figured in the logbook of death. Others commit murder in the furtherance of another crime – an impulsive act during a robbery or to cold-bloodedly silence the victim/witness of a rape or the depraved assault of a child.

Then there are the monsters, the ones who sit beside us on the bus or are behind us in the checkout queue and whose faces we only see when they stare out at us from newspapers, after some unspeakable act of slaughter. They kill for no other reason than the pleasure it gives them. These largely untreatable people are indiscriminate and unpredictable. They could do the same again next week or next year and are only likely to desist in their murderous activities if traced and detained, or if overtaken by death themselves.

So those who assume the role of God come in many guises. The only thing they have in common is the corpse they leave behind. It is this diverse range of motives, unmatched in the criminal compendium, which makes murder the easiest or most difficult of offences to detect. When perpetrator and victim are closely connected, as they frequently are, the police are rarely troubled for long: there is usually evidence in abundance. It is the random slaying, when there is no prior link with the victim, which can launch the murder hunt that may have no conclusion.

Just as homicide does not respect age or gender or predictability, it also takes no account of geography. The malevolence which lurks in one degree or another in nearly all of us arrives wherever we live. Those who kill need not be the inhabitants of the largest cities or the places with the most violent reputations. Stick a pin in a map and you are liable to stumble upon them anywhere. In this case, it landed on the city of Dundee in Scotland. It is an average-sized town with average-type people living there and it seemed a suitable place to peel back the civilised layers and reveal what festers in all communities making up our 'orderly' society. It is no better and no worse a place than any other when it comes to murder. What goes on there happens with just the same amount of wickedness and suffering – and regret – as it does elsewhere.

Those you will read about fascinate and repel in equal measure, but there is no single reason why any of them found their way into this book. With no particular period or type of murder under consideration, there was a lot to choose from. In the end, the chapters were selected because they contained elements that were intriguing or unusual enough to make them stand out from the rest.

Some of the killings were, and will remain, among the most notorious in the dark history of homicide. Others did not attract international headlines but are absorbing for the complexities of the people who carried them out, or for the reasons they were committed. It also seemed important to try to produce a representative selection of the types of killers and their crimes from the wide spectrum available. Most categories are covered, though others might have chosen differently.

The following pages contain some material which is not for the faint-hearted. Murder is a messy business, however it happens, so there are passages you are unlikely to read in a romantic novel. Nothing has been included for gratuitous purposes and in some instances the content has been diluted to avoid offence – but not so severely that distortion occurs. To understand the act, it is necessary to acknowledge the detail. For the same reason, there has been no real painting on of false moustaches to disguise identities, except perhaps by omission and only then in the interests of fairness. The only chapter containing a significant deviation is 'Babes in the House', where the names of all those involved have been changed. They were made public at the time but, in the current spirit of protecting juvenile offenders, it seemed preferable to omit them from this account. Otherwise, the circumstances are just as they occurred.

Few attempts were made to form judgements about the main players or to analyse the reasons for their extreme conduct, but in any volume of this kind it would be impossible to avoid the occasional passing comment of some sort. None of that should prevent readers from arriving at their own conclusions or from trying to have a better understanding of what takes place in the dark corners of the places where we live. Or – and perhaps a more difficult point – to endeavour to make sense of the some of the unfathomable people who dwell within in our midst.

The true stories that lie ahead happen to be about a specific city. They could have occurred anywhere.

1

MURDER ON
A MONDAY MORNING

Cities come awake slowly. Like the people who inhabit them, they blink uncertainly in the light of the new day and move unhurriedly through a well-practised routine. It is a gentle and gradual process. Responses are automatic and no one pays too much attention to anyone else – especially when it is Monday.

The morning brings not just a new day but a new week and the city, as it stirs, is at its most disinterested. It is the perfect time for those with murder in mind.

So it was in Dundee on the morning of 8 May 1989.

Like every other day, Gordon Johnston alighted from a bus in High Street at 8.45 a.m. and walked, limping slightly, past City Square and along Nethergate before turning into Union Street and opening up Gow's Gunshop, where he worked, at the top of the street. It was a familiar scenario. He had done it for most of the thirty-seven years he had been employed in the shop, where he had started as a 16-year-old trainee gunsmith before becoming manager. That morning, after fifteen minutes in the premises, he closed up again and departed to pay a gas bill and make a purchase in a nearby store. Then he returned to Gow's and at 9.20 a.m. passers-by noted that he had stopped at the shop entrance to speak to two men. Several customers called at the gunshop over the next twenty minutes, but all found the door locked and the lights on.

That was how it stayed for the rest of the day. Late in the afternoon an anxious customer called the police and at 5 p.m. officers forced their way into the shop. They were ill prepared for what they found. Lying dead in a pool of blood at the foot of the stairs leading to the basement area was 53-year-old Mr Johnston. He was in a crouched foetal position and had been savagely attacked to the head, body and arms. His back pocket had been turned out, the till drawer had been opened and the safe ransacked. The badly damaged watch on the victim's wrist was stopped, indicating that a struggle had taken place at 9.21 a.m. Bloody footprints led from the basement back up the stairs.

Within minutes of the grisly discovery, Union Street was awash with police and teams of officers had started to interview nearby shopkeepers and commuters heading for home at the end of the day. It was a process that was to be repeated many times in the days ahead.

A post-mortem revealed that Mr Johnston had been hacked to death under an onslaught of forty-eight blows, almost all of them delivered by an axe. The motive appeared to be robbery. It seemed that £100, a jacket, knives – and more ominously – firearms and ammunition had been taken by whoever had wielded the lethal blade.

Because the raid had been carried out on a Monday morning, it was clear that cash had not been the main target since there was unlikely to have been much held in the shop. Nor was it probable that the objective was fishing tackle. There seemed to be little doubt that the sole aim of the robbery had been to acquire some of the guns held on the premises. But for what purpose? It was a question that would exercise – and deeply trouble – the minds of senior detectives again and again. Anyone who could carry out such a sustained and bloody assault in the pursuit of firearms almost certainly required them for violent reasons. It was even possible that the weapons had been taken for an attack on Prime Minister Margaret Thatcher or members of her cabinet, who were due to attend the Scottish Conservative Party conference in nearby

Perth later in the month. However, that occasion came and went without incident and, as the weeks passed, police made little progress in apprehending the killer or killers. And still there was no hint as to why the guns had been taken.

The investigation was one of the biggest ever undertaken in the city. Scores of extra officers were drafted in and new overtime rosters scheduled to run until Christmas were put in place. Everyone who had been in or near Union Street that day was interviewed and a £12,000 reward was offered by the owners of the gunshop. The strongest piece of evidence to emerge was the sighting of a young man with pointed features apparently leaving Gow's at 9.50 a.m. On the way out of the shop he fumbled with the door handle before walking backwards out of the doorway into the path of pedestrians, pulling up his jacket hood over his head as he departed. Then he ran off down Union Street, carrying two gun cases.

Police considered it possible that the person or persons they sought could have left the city by train, the station being only a few hundred yards from the scene of the crime. Hundreds of rail commuters were questioned and travellers who had used credit cards or cheques to purchase tickets that day were traced. Others who had operated automatic cash dispensers at nearby banks were also tracked down and interviewed. Every new initiative drew a blank. Video film from a security camera in a jeweller's shop opposite Gow's was minutely examined frame by frame, but that too seemed to be just another brick wall.

Police turned to the BBC's *Crimewatch* programme in the hope that national coverage would yield fresh clues. It brought almost a hundred calls offering information and possible identities. Every one of the tip-offs was followed up but none produced the slightest hint as to who had been responsible for the murderous attack on the man who was father to two young boys. After three months, over 7,000 people had been interviewed and 5,000 statements logged in the special major inquiry computer system developed by the Home Office. Still there were no significant results.

Then, on 25 July, more than three months after the mild-mannered Gordon Johnston had been so viciously put to death, police received a brief phone call which brought the moribund inquiry dramatically back to life. A male caller who would not identify himself spoke softly and said haltingly that he knew who had been responsible for the murder. Before he could be questioned further, he added quickly that one of the killers was his relative. Then he rang off.

Such calls are not unusual in major investigations, particularly when large rewards are on offer. Most come from cranks. This one had a ring of truth to it and senior officers were convinced it was genuine. Although the caller had declined to give his name, he had imparted enough information to enable a team of detectives to begin to piece the clues together. After a week they thought they knew the caller's identity. Cautious approaches were made and finally they arranged to interview him.

An extraordinary story unfolded. The man traced was 43-year-old Lucio Mario Ianetta. He confessed that he had placed the anonymous call because he could no longer endure the strain of reading daily press reports in *The Courier* and *The Evening Telegraph* detailing how the police hunt had reached stalemate, when he knew who had been responsible. Everywhere he went, he said, he seemed to be confronted by posters asking for information about the murder. Staring out at him, he said, was Mr Johnston – 'God bless him' – who seemed to be saying to him, 'You know something about this. What are you going to do about it?' He could stand it no longer, he explained, so he wanted to unburden himself. Then he recounted how his 21-year-old nephew Ryan Monks had arrived at his home, at 10.30 on the morning of the gunshop raid, in an agitated state and clutching a bag of clothing. Monks had thrown the bag on the floor and pleaded, 'It went wrong – burn them.' Uncle Lucio told senior members of the murder team that he had pressed his nephew for an explanation of what he was referring to and Monks had finally blurted out: 'The boy in the gunshop. He was wasted.'

Mr Ianetta described how, without asking many more questions, he had thrown a jacket, a pair of jeans and trainer shoes – which had been in the bag – onto his living-room fire. 'I was in a total panic,' he anxiously explained. 'You try to help your own.'

It was only later that evening, when he was in a Broughty Ferry pub and saw the evening news on TV, that he realised Monks had been involved in the gunshop killing. He was particularly shocked because, by coincidence, he had known the victim through his father, who had previously been a customer at the shop when he had bought cartridges and gunpowder to take to Italy. Finally, Mr Ianetta told the detectives, who were hanging on his every word, that his nephew's accomplice on the raid on Gow's was a young man named Paul who had hired a red Rover car as the getaway vehicle.

At seven o'clock the following morning two teams of armed officers simultaneously raided the Dundee homes of Monks and his 21-year-old friend Paul Mill. What they found stunned even the most experienced of the detectives. The robbery at the gunshop had merely been a means to an end. A thorough search of both houses produced clear evidence of a complex plot to abduct the elderly mother of well-known Dundee bakery owner Robert Brown and hold her to ransom for £200,000. Monks had once worked for Mr Brown's firm of Rough & Fraser in Kinghorne Road and had intimate knowledge of the Brown family and their habits. The surprised policemen found grubby pieces of paper detailing precisely how and when the kidnap plot would be enacted. Several ransom notes – some purporting to be from an IRA active service unit and typed in red ink – had been prepared, setting out death threats and demands to Mr Brown for cash. Failure to comply, Mr Brown was to be informed, meant he would be told 'where to find your mother's corpse'.

The blackmail scheme had its roots in the popular Clint Eastwood film *Dirty Harry*. Just as in the movie, the extortion victim would be instructed to wait at a particular payphone, where he would receive instructions for the handover of the ransom, leading to the eventual release of the hostage. That call box was to be the first in a chain of twelve stretching across Dundee on a route meticulously mapped out by Monks and Mill. The pair had noted the time it would take to travel between each box and the route had been designed to throw off any possible police tail. After arriving at the final destination, Mr Brown was to be handcuffed and hooded and locked in the boot of his own car.

Monks and Mill had a video of *Dirty Harry* and had studied it at length. But this was not the only high-profile crime that the two former schoolmates at Lawside Academy had hatched. Police also found scraps of paper detailing the movement of Post Office cash delivery vans and, by piecing the jigsaw together, discovered that the pair intended to hijack a postal van one Friday morning when it stopped outside a sub-post office in St Giles Terrace – just a few yards from Monks's home. The driver was to be seized and the van driven by the robbers to either Templeton Woods, on the outskirts of the city, or Monks's lock-up garage, where the cash would be separated from the rest of the mail.

The raid on the gunshop had been the means to an end for both of these elaborate plans, providing the would-be big-time criminals with the necessary fire power. Given the onslaught on Mr Johnston in Gow's three months earlier, there seemed little doubt the pair had the inclination to go through with their plans. In addition to the painstaking notes they had prepared, Monks and Mill had assembled a range of other accessories to help them carry out their deadly plots. Police found two sawn-off shotguns, cartridges, camouflage and combat-style clothing, a gas mask, balaclavas, handcuffs, a forged Tayside Police warrant card and an aerosol can. Under the attic floorboards of Monks's parents' house, detectives discovered the barrels of shotguns encased in concrete and the butts cut into small pieces. Passport application forms, a map of Dundee (with various locations marked in ink) and numerous magazines about guns and survival were also seized by the murder squad. Several days before the gunshop killing, Monks and Mill had hired a car, a red Rover, and fitted it with false plates, which they duly returned after the ghastly events of that May Monday morning.

It is difficult to know who was most surprised by the sudden conclusion to the murder hunt. After three months, with the inquiry leading nowhere, police had overnight rounded up two men for murder and robbery and had apparently foiled a kidnap attempt on an elderly woman, as well as an armed raid on a Post Office cash delivery van.

Monks and Mill were just as taken aback. With each passing day, they had grown more confident they would never be linked with the frenzied attack on the gentle Mr Johnston. Without the phone call from the conscience-stricken Lucio Ianetta, that state of affairs might have gone on indefinitely. There was nothing to link them with the murder-robbery and, unlike the usual suspects in that type of crime, they had no police records. They were improbable criminals, far less killers. Both came from respectable families and both were in stable relationships with decent young women. Monks had two children – the youngest born just two weeks after the death of Mr Johnston – and Mill was a father-to-be. There wasn't even that much to connect them to each other. Although they had been schoolmates, they had drifted together only in the lead-up to the Gow's raid after each became jobless. Neither was known as drinkers and they spent most of their time together in each other's homes. Bored, they watched videos of crime films such as *Dirty Harry* and discussed guns and survival techniques. Then, for thrills, they started to turn their fantasies into reality by plotting their own series of crimes.

By the time the case came to trial, however, their friendship appeared to have evaporated. Each claimed they had simply been the driver of the getaway car, waiting outside the gunshop while the other had entered to carry out the relentless axe attack on the unfortunate Mr Johnston. They told how they had gone to the shop equipped with two-way radios and had devised a series of 'bleep' codes to let the other know when to bring the car to the scene and to indicate when the coast was clear for the one who had entered the shop to leave. Their stories were fundamentally the same, only each put himself in the car and the other at the murder scene. During the fifteen days they spent sitting together in the dock at the High Court in Perth, Monks and Mill never spoke and studiously ignored each other, consistent with their pleas that the other was the killer.

Part of the Crown case against the men was a video film the police had acquired from the closed-circuit television security system of the jeweller's shop opposite Gow's. Forensic officers had used special computerised enhancement facilities at Dundee Institute of Technology and the Scottish Police College to improve the images which showed a Rover car, similar to the one the pair had hired, passing the gunshop during the crucial period. It revealed two men in the vehicle but did not distinguish which of them had been driving. In the end, it did not appear particularly to matter to the jury. They took the view Monks and Mill had acted in concert, each guilty in law for the actions of the other. After an absence of just over two hours, they returned to find both men guilty of all charges.

Jailing each of them for life, Lord Mayfield told the two young killers that their crimes had amounted to 'a cruel and sadistic atrocity'. Monks and Mill listened in silence, then, as they turned away to begin their terms, the eyes of the ashen-faced pair met for the first time since they had sought to incriminate each other. It was the closest they had come to communicating in public, but they would share many words in the long years that lay ahead.

Although the jury did not distinguish between the young killers, the parole board did. Mill was released on licence after serving thirteen years. Monks was detained for a year longer before being allowed back into the community.

Lucio Ianetta, the uncle who said he wilted under the un-wavering gaze of a dead man pictured on a poster, never claimed the £12,000 reward.

2

BETRAYAL

In downtown Dundee the clubs were coming out, drunks were quarrelling at the taxi ranks and the peace was being breached at the takeaways. In the housing estates, wives were falling out with abusive husbands and contemplating calling for help. In dark corners, the odd housebreaker was considering the opportunities. It was the usual mildly lawless weekend and Sergeant Fiona Cameron expected more disturbances before her Saturday-night-Sunday-morning mobile patrol shift would draw to a close. The paperwork would be irritating but keeping order was why she had joined Tayside Police. And it was good to be busy.

When the message came in from headquarters, it sounded routine at first. She should attend a house fire at 39 Clepington Court, a block of modern flats not far from the centre of town and close to the football grounds of the city's two senior football clubs. At least it would make a change from the drunks, she thought.

But then she was told something that would make that day in November 1993 one she would remember for the rest of her life. Firefighters at the scene had discovered a body in the burning house. Even then she was unprepared for what she found when she entered the flat.

The burned corpse was that of the female occupant, and she recognised her at once. She was 27-year-old Irene Martin, a policewoman colleague and her death was not a result of the blaze. She lay in a pool of blood and the smoke-covered walls and bed clothing were blood-splattered. Later, Sergeant Cameron was to learn from medical examiners that the attractive constable had suffered 30 stab and cut wounds, some of them on her hands and arms as she had attempted to fight off her attacker. Others were to her brain and vital neck arteries. The indiscriminate slashes had also severed her voice box.

What had started as an early morning house fire had become a major murder hunt for an unknown, vicious killer – one who had taken his weapon away with him because there was no sign of anything in the house which could have caused the savage injuries.

Despite the hour and the staffing complications of it being a weekend, the area quickly swarmed with detectives and scenes-of-crime experts. Forensic science specialists, who had known the tragic victim, fought to stifle their emotions during the minute examination of her body and the damaged flat. Out in the street, uniformed colleagues manned roadblocks erected in the immediate vicinity.

Shortly after 5 a.m., several hours after the body of the policewoman had been discovered, a car was halted at one of the roadblocks as it attempted to turn into the street. PC Graeme Waghorn explained to the driver of the Ford Sierra that vehicles were being kept out of the area because of a 'major incident'. He asked the man behind the wheel what his intended destination was in the street. 'I'm here to pick up my girlfriend to go on holiday,' was the reply. Then he told the constable that he might even know her because she was a fellow officer, Irene Martin.

After identifying himself as Angus Elliott, a 30-year-old council job-training supervisor, who had been romantically involved with Irene for almost three years, he was quietly invited by the constable to accompany him to police headquarters. For the next two hours, the victim's boyfriend told a heartbreaking story of how they were supposed to be going on holiday to Cyprus that day, where they were to become engaged. On the Saturday afternoon, they had gone to a travel agent's in the city centre to collect traveller's cheques then returned to the Clepington Street flat. They had parted around 6 p.m., with Irene promising to pick him up at his home in Forfar in the early hours of the next day, in plenty of time to catch their flight to the sunshine island.

He then explained that the woman he hoped to marry had been expecting a visitor that evening, a man she had never met and did not know, but who had responded to a newspaper advertisement placed by Irene, seeking a flatmate to help defray mortgage costs. Angus Elliott added that Irene had revealed that, a day earlier, she had received a call from the man, whom she had said was well-spoken, before she departed for a pre-holiday visit to her mother and stepfather in Fife. Elliott had thought it odd that the intended lodger had called when he did because it had been three weeks earlier that the advert had appeared in two newspapers. Helpfully, he added that police would find the stranger's telephone number on a pad on a table in the lounge. He would be easy to trace. It seemed to offer a possible logical explanation for the unexplained slaying of the young policewoman and the availability of the mystery man's telephone number would mean he could be quickly located for interrogation.

There was only one problem. The table in the lounge had been one of the few pieces of furniture destroyed in the fire. There was no pad, no telephone number.

Something else was missing. When interviewed at police headquarters by Detective Sergeant Andrew Allan, who informed him of Irene's death, Angus Elliott displayed no feeling at what should have been devastating news. 'There was no emotion, there was very little reaction, there was nothing,' the detective sergeant was to recount later.

There was, however, something present that was even more intriguing than what was absent. The hands of the man seated opposite Sergeant Allan were cut and bruised. Some of the wounds were still bleeding, a fact completely at odds with Angus Elliott's explanation that they had been caused by an accident at work when a pane of glass had fallen on him.

Sergeant Allan, who had examined the murder scene, had

formed the impression that there had been a struggle in the room where Irene Martin's body had been found. He was also aware that a neighbour had spoken of being awoken in the early hours by screams and 'thuds' – a time which was hardly consistent with a 'mystery man' calling in the evening to discuss the let of the flat's spare room. It was curious, too, that Elliott had made a point of saying he did not have a key to the flat of the woman he had hoped to marry, especially since they'd enjoyed a long relationship and had previously lived together in Forfar. Was that a likely proposition? If he was not telling the truth, what was he trying to prove?

Most improbable of all was the story he had told PC Waghorn at the barrier when he tried to drive into Clepington Court. Elliott had explained that he'd called to collect Irene so they could make the 5 a.m. check-in at Glasgow Airport for their 7 a.m. flight to Cyprus. Yet at the time he said it, it was already 5.15 a.m. Not only would they have missed the check-in, they would have missed the flight as well.

Presented with such an accumulation of facts, his highly suspicious injuries, and in the absence of any evidence except Elliott's word about an unknown man's supposed visit to the house to discuss room-letting arrangements, police wasted no time in arresting the still-protesting 30-year-old. He continued to deny any knowledge of the killing during formal taped interviews, stating emphatically at one stage – after being asked if he was responsible for Irene's death – 'Definitely not'.

Several hours later, when visited in his cell by Detective Sergeant Alexander McGregor who had gone to tell Elliott his solicitor had not yet arrived, the accused man had a dramatic change of heart. 'I'm no denying it,' he told the surprised officer, adding that he wanted independent legal advice.

Four months later, at the High Court in Kirkcaldy, Angus Elliott denied the murder of Irene Martin, the woman he wanted as his wife, but was prepared to admit to the lesser offence of culpable homicide. It was not a plea the Crown found acceptable and for five days the jury heard a familiar tale of jealousy and passion, of tangled romantic relationships and the explosion of fury that culminated in the death of a young policewoman, who tragically became the victim of the most serious crime of all.

Far from leaving the flat at Clepington Court at 6 p.m. the previous evening, as he had originally claimed, Elliott had spent the night there with Irene so they could depart in the early hours for the airport and the Mediterranean holiday they had both been looking forward to. But, as they dressed in preparation for the trip, an argument broke out about the relationship Elliott still had with a previous girlfriend, the woman he had been living with in Forfar when he and Irene had met. It was a topic the couple had squabbled over on previous occasions and with growing intensity.

In the heat of the row, the distraught policewoman took an American Forces combat knife from a bedside table where she kept it for protection. It was a weapon that Elliott, a martial arts enthusiast, had given her after she'd said she was afraid Dundee 'neds' might sometime follow her home. She pointed it towards him, ordering him to leave the flat. More angry words flew between them. They grappled in a ferocious bed-top struggle. Despite her self-defence training, it was a contest the slender Irene could not win. The powerful ex-soldier – a part-time nightclub bouncer and a karate black belt – quickly seized possession of the commando dagger being thrust towards him. The control he'd been taught in the army abandoned Elliott and the knife began to flash. Reason only returned after he had swung it 30 times and Irene lay dead, her blood splattering the walls and forming pools beneath her.

The unexpected killer thought quickly. He had to flee the scene but not in the blood-soaked clothes he stood up in because tell-tale stains would be left in his car. He removed his trousers, bagged them, then dressed in a pair of Irene's uniform trousers and coat. But before departing there was something else he needed to do. To conceal the cause of Irene's death, he would set fires throughout the flat so that the resulting blaze would leave no evidence for the forensic experts. Meticulously, he set about covering his tracks. Then he slipped out of the house, but not before ensuring all the internal doors were closed in the hope the flames could do their job.

He drove quickly away from the city and back to his own flat in Forfar, where he washed and changed clothes once more. Finally, he loaded the lethal dagger, Irene's coat and trousers and his own blood-stained clothes into a bag and sped off once again, this time travelling only a short distance to another house, one he knew would be empty because the occupant had told him she would be in Edinburgh. It was the home of his former girlfriend, the one the argument had been about, and he used his own key to enter and secrete the items he knew would send him to prison if they were discovered. All the bases seemed to have been covered. He would be in the clear, he reasoned. Moments later, he drove away, heading back towards Dundee for the Oscar-winning performance he knew he would be bound to give. As he set off on the 15-mile drive to Dundee, he quietly congratulated himself on his brilliance.

Although Elliott seemed happy to ignore the fresh cuts and bruises on his arms, which proved just how courageously Irene had battled for her life, it was far from his only oversight. He had left himself so short of time that he did not reappear in Dundee until such an hour that his story of checking-in for the Cyprus flight was clearly false. But his biggest mistake of all was the scrupulous care he took to close all the doors inside the flat in the belief the flames would erupt and spread more quickly. As any firefighter could have told him, the reverse would be the case; the shut doors significantly stalling and not accelerating the advance of the fire. When Elliott turned his Ford Sierra into the street, his heart must have dropped like a stone when he saw that the flat was still largely intact and the outbreak long since extinguished. Although Irene's body had been affected by the fire, it was obvious the burn marks had been caused after death and that she had perished as a result of a frenzied knife attack.

During the trial, it emerged that Elliott found himself on a murder charge as a result of circumstances that were far from unique. He had joined a long line of men who were driven to taking a life simply because he could not choose between two women. When the ladies' man met Irene at the Brechin nightclub where he was a bouncer, he was already engaged and had lived in Forfar for seven years with his fiancée, a pretty waitress the same age as the police-woman. Although he broke off the engagement and moved out, the relationship never quite ended and the court learned how the former lovers still met. On one occasion, when Irene arrived at unexpectedly at Elliott's home, the ex-fiancée, who had been sun-bathing in the garden with Elliott, was forced to hide in a garden shed to avoid detection by the Tayside constable.

Elliott had even been with his former girlfriend on the day before he and Irene were due to depart for Cyprus on holiday. On that occasion, the upset waitress, who was departing for a week-end in Edinburgh, gave him an ultimatum – finish with Irene or I will finish with you for good.

Irene was aware of the ex-fiancée's continued contact with Elliott, if not the full extent of it, and reacted accordingly by challenging him regularly about the relationship. The final con-frontation began as the two would-be holidaymakers dressed to go to the airport and Irene openly accused the man she hoped to marry of still sleeping with his one-time partner.

Elliott claimed in court the row had broken out because he had 'jokingly' said he was calling off the Cyprus holiday and that, dur-ing her 'tantrum', Irene produced the combat dagger and started to lash out at him, ordering him out of the house. In the ensuing struggle, he fell from the bed to the floor and knocked his head. After that, he had little recollection of events and could not recall stabbing Irene or setting the fires in the flat afterwards. His only memory was of 'arms moving about in the air, striking one another.'

Weeping, he told the jury, 'I could hear her voice saying, "Gus, I love you. I want to marry you." I saw her lying on the floor. There was blood everywhere.' He accepted having possession of the knife and that he must have inflicted the wounds, but claimed he had no intention of killing the agitated Irene. He also claimed that there had been nothing between himself and his ex-fiancée, beyond friendship, after he and Irene had met. The suspicious policewoman would not believe that, he said, and the trouble between them was because she was possessive.

Curiously, that was the same word some witnesses used to describe Elliott himself in his relationship with Irene. A senior police officer later used another term. Describing how calm the martial arts expert had been under questioning, he said, 'He is the most controlling person I have ever met in life.'

The jury seemed to share that view. After an absence of only 35 minutes they filed back into court to return a unanimous verdict of guilty to murder and not culpable homicide as Elliott had hoped.

The man who found himself at the heart of one of mankind's oldest and most deadly triangles was emotionless when Lord Sutherland told him the only sentence he could pass was one of life imprisonment. But as he disappeared from the dock to begin his bleak term behind bars, a single gasp of anguish sounded in the courtroom. In the public benches Angus Elliott's former fiancée, the woman who formed the other side of the fatal triangle and who had sat through the trial, slumped forward in her seat and wept.

3

FAMILY TIES

When the newly wed teenagers walked arm-in-arm down the aisle of the picturesque village church in Longforgan that April day in 1973, it seemed to the women gathered outside with their confetti that Cupid had struck again. He was only 17 and she a year older, no more than bairns really – but they were in love and that would see them through, as it always did, thought the well-wishers.

In fact, it was a marriage which probably should never have taken place. The bride was pregnant and had gone to the altar with some reluctance after finally deciding against having an abortion. But these were the days when unmarried mothers were still stigmatised and, if a termination was ruled out, a wedding was the next option for respectable people. So Helen Maxwell, the pretty Dundee hairdresser, and baby-faced Jimmy Wilkie, an apprentice fitter whose home was in the village, were there that spring afternoon to do the right thing. She could not have looked more radiant and he was dressed in his best dark suit and new blue tie, an adornment he wore through necessity rather than choice, for they had never been his favourite item of clothing.

To the surprise of no one who knew them well, the marriage started to founder almost from the first few weeks after the simple honeymoon. The new Mrs Wilkie confided in a long-time family friend that she had walked in on her husband to discover him engaged in sex with another woman. When she had later tried to discuss it with him, she said, he had reacted by assaulting her – although by then she was mid-way through her pregnancy – as he had already done on other occasions.

Jimmy had no monopoly on unfaithfulness, however. Helen resumed a liaison with a previous boyfriend and the two met at regular intervals after her wedding in Longforgan. Her former lover, aged 19 and himself married, would visit her at her home and at the hairdressing salon where she worked. Their sexual relationship was rekindled.

The doomed marriage stumbled along amidst a series of disputes and rows, a number of them in public, and Helen made no secret of her unhappiness. But they remained together, though no one was certain whether that had more to do with impending parenthood or an underlying passion that bound them however much they might clash over other matters.

On 3 February 1974, Jimmy Wilkie had another occasion to wear his wedding day suit and blue tie, this time for the christening of their months-old son – a day which saw the consumption of much alcohol by some of those who attended the celebration in a small hotel near the family home at Hill Street in Dundee, a narrow thoroughfare of tall tenements on the slopes of the Law.

Although the day had started well, with Helen in a buoyant mood, it led, almost inevitably, to yet more friction between the couple. That evening, after dropping their newly baptised son off at Longforgan to be looked after by Jimmy's mother, the couple went out for the evening, going first of all to the Golden Fry restaurant in Dundee city centre. They never got as far as eating. An argument broke out over Helen's demands for more drink on top of the not insignificant amount she had already consumed. She stormed out of the Union Street bistro, somehow finishing with a bloody nose, apparently after stumbling on the stairs leading up to the street.

Two days later Helen Wilkie, the 19-year-old mother and reluctant bride, was reported to the police as a missing person.

The call was made by her father, James Maxwell, a prominent businessman in the city who had links with leading local Dundee councillors. He said he and his wife, also Helen, had not seen their daughter since the evening of the christening. They only became aware she was missing at midnight that day when Jimmy's mother had phoned from her home in Longforgan to enquire if Helen was there. The Maxwells learned that their daughter and her husband had had yet another public row, in a restaurant, and that she had seemingly walked out, never to be seen again.

Police treated the disappearance as a routine missing-person case and began their inquiry by gathering statements. In his interview, Jimmy Wilkie told how he and his wife had fallen out in the Golden Fry after a dispute about her wanting more liquor when he felt too much had already been taken at the christening. Describing the earlier festivities at the reception in the hotel, he said, 'I was the only sober one there and got the job of driving everyone home.' He described how his wife had attempted to walk out on him from the restaurant but had tripped on the stairs, falling forward with her nose starting to bleed. 'Helen had blood all over her clothes,' he explained, adding that they had then returned home where she changed into a wine-coloured dress. Later they went to another restaurant for a meal, then drove into town in the hope that Jimmy might see his sister. When this was unsuccessful, they headed in the direction of Longforgan to collect their newly baptised son, but on the way another argument developed over Helen's continuing demands for yet more alcohol.

In Perth Road, Jimmy said, he stopped to visit public toilets at the top of Riverside Drive. When he returned to the car, Helen had gone.

'I waited ten minutes then checked the ladies' toilets and she wasn't there,' he told the detective sergeant handling the missing-person inquiry. 'I doubled back into town, suspecting she had jumped on a bus. I didn't go to anyone's house and didn't find her. I went to the house in Hill Street, then back into town. Then I went back to Longforgan and asked my mother if she was there. I haven't seen her since.'

The day after the baffling disappearance of his wife, life apparently continued much as normal for Jimmy Wilkie. In the morning he dropped his son off at his in-laws, then went to work. That evening he returned to have tea with the Maxwells and discuss his wife's possible whereabouts but there had been no fresh developments. And that was how it remained as the following days merged into weeks and then months. Very little happened.

The Maxwells took over the care of their grandson, later adopting him, and Jimmy Wilkie eventually moved out of town to live and work, forming a new relationship with a young woman. Together they lived in Canada for a brief period.

Meanwhile, in Dundee, there was inevitable gossip and speculation about the fate of the attractive hairdresser who had apparently abandoned the baby son she doted on. Her father, an enterprising entrepreneur in business with a wide range of contacts, mounted his own enquiries and vague reports trickled through that his daughter had been sighted in London, Dundee and other parts of Scotland.

The next Christmas the postman delivered a card to Mrs Wilkie Sr in Longforgan. Bearing the greeting 'Wishing You All the Best', it was signed 'Helen' and had been posted in Dundee. That Festive Season, Jimmy Wilkie had been living in Canada.

The police never launched a major search for the missing woman, which in hindsight seems inexplicable considering her devotion to her son and the closeness of her relationship with her parents and the absence of any contact from her. Yet where would any hunt have been concentrated? And there had been the apparent sightings, even if unconfirmed. Then there was the Christmas card . . . It was a puzzle with no obvious solution. Helen Wilkie had evidently vanished off the face of the earth and no one seemed to know why, where to, or with whom.

The months slipped by. The baby boy of the absent mother became the centre-piece of his grandparents' family and Jimmy Wilkie had a fresh life in Murcar, Aberdeen. A new routine was in place and there were few people in Dundee – apart from Helen's family, friends and a few former hairdressing customers – who were particularly aware of the mystery in their midst, for the disappearance of the young mother had, perhaps surprisingly, had little publicity generated by the police.

Four years and forty-one days after the christening party – on 15 March 1978 – all of that abruptly and dramatically changed.

Workmen preparing to erect a Dutch barn at Littleton Farm, near Longforgan, had gone to a nearby den beside a quarry to collect stones for the foundations and were using a mechanical digger to scoop loads of the rocks into a lorry. When one pile was being tipped at the farm, driver John Merchant spotted an unusual object tumbling from the vehicle in the middle of the tons of stones. Work was at once halted and closer examination revealed it, unmistakably and alarmingly, as a skull. The police were alerted and at CID headquarters seven miles away in Dundee, Chief Inspector David Fotheringham summoned two colleagues. Together they hurried to the scene of picturesque Littleton Den on the slopes of the Carse of Gowrie. As they left the squad room, and without really knowing why, Fotheringham called over his shoulder to other detectives, 'You'd better look out the file on Helen Wilkie.'

His instincts did not let him down. The grim find had been made around lunchtime and there was still enough light left in the day for a full excavation to be made in the section of the den where the stones had been gathered. Within a short time they had unearthed a shallow grave about twenty yards from the Knapp Road, shielded by a copse of trees. It contained a headless skeleton, the remnants of a wine-coloured dress, jewellery, and a single fashionable ladies' boot. Round the neck was an unexpectedly well-preserved blue tie which had been wound round three times and knotted tightly at the rear. It did not take long to establish that the body was indeed that of Helen Wilkie and she had died as a result of being strangled by the tie. Dr Donald Rushton, the forensic scientist who would roast coffee beans during his post-mortem examinations to mask unpleasant odours, also concluded that the body had not been hurriedly dumped at the scene but had been carefully placed in a grave and covered by many of the stones littering the area.

Other officers went to Jimmy Wilkie's new home, a caravan in Murcar which he shared with his girlfriend Donna McKenzie (known as Wilkie), to inform him of the gruesome find. He asked two questions: 'Where did you get her?' and 'How did she die?'

After Jimmy had been brought to Dundee, ostensibly to identify the body, Chief Inspector Fotheringham showed him the jewellery which had been found beside the body. Wilkie said it had belonged to Helen and asked if her handbag had also been found. Told it hadn't, he asked, 'Did you find anything else?'

Chief Inspector Fotheringham, a shrewd and skilled interviewer, explained that all the clothing at the scene appeared to be Helen's, except for a tie, which Jimmy then asked to see. The chief inspector held it out in his hands, but with the knots concealed.

'Oh, that's my tie,' replied Jimmy at once, adding that he had taken if off at the christening and given it to his wife to put in her handbag.

'It wasn't found in her handbag, but tied round her neck,' said the detective gently.

Apprehensive but composed, and sitting tall in his seat in front of the murder investigators, Jimmy responded that whoever had killed his wife must have taken the tie from her bag and throttled her with it, quickly adding, 'I hope you don't think it was me.' A few hours later he was charged with her murder.

In June that year he sat in the dock at the High Court in Dundee and for three days listened intently as a number of witnesses described his short but turbulent marriage. They spoke of drink-fuelled arguments, of seeing bruises on Helen and him throwing objects at her. Friends of the couple said they had witnessed the two of them grappling together in their home, had seen Jimmy Wilkie presenting a knife at Helen in a restaurant and how he had kicked her while she was pregnant.

The former boyfriend who had resumed a relationship with Helen after her marriage, told the court of the day they had been walking in the street outside her home, pushing a pram with her baby in it, when Wilkie drove his car at them. They had to dive for safety when the vehicle mounted the pavement and headed straight for them. He revealed that Helen had seemed on the verge of a mental breakdown and had wanted to leave town because she hoped to escape her marriage. One acquaintance said Helen had shown him a rope looped over the door of her home with which Wilkie had tried to hang himself after an argument.

Not everyone considered the marriage to be particularly stormy. The accused man's mother, Amy, said that as far as she was aware they had 'got on fine' and there had never been any trouble between them. She told how, on the night of the christening, her son had arrived alone at Longforgan at around midnight and had explained that following an argument, Helen had run off while he was visiting the Perth Road public toilets.

Mrs Wilkie added that while they were talking she heard a car outside: 'Jimmy jumped up and went outside, saying, "That'll be Helen." But it was his sister.'

The accused man's mother also explained to the jury that she had lent her son her car on the night of the christening and the next day she noticed blood on the back door of the vehicle and on its window.

'Jimmy said it must have come from Helen's hands. He had told me the previous night that she had fallen on the stairs in the Golden Fry and banged her nose.'

She described how, at Christmas 1974, ten months after her daughter-in-law had gone missing and while her son was in Canada, she had received the card apparently signed by Helen in writing she did not recognise. Mrs Wilkie concluded her evidence by proclaiming that she believed the young couple had been happy together.

It was not a view shared by her husband. When he came to give evidence and was asked the same questions about the relationship, he had responded by saying he thought his son was 'pretty unhappy with his marriage . . . Everything went wrong from the start, I think.'

Journalists covering the hearing they had headlined the 'Body in the Den' trial jerked to life when one of the accused man's friends went into the box to speak of a drink the two had shared after the disappearance of the teenage mother. Robert Milne said that when he had asked about Helen's whereabouts, Jimmy Wilkie had answered, 'I don't think they will find her. She's well buried.' The accused had not elaborated, he said, but the following day, he asked Jimmy Wilkie if he could recall the conversation of the night before. He had replied that he had no recollection of what they had spoken about.

Another witness, Mrs Alice Tindall, who knew the young couple and Helen's parents, said that some time in 1975 she had gone into a Dundee café and spotted Wilkie sitting by himself. A short time later another man came in and joined him. She eavesdropped on the pair and heard the stranger ask Wilkie if he was away from his wife and what kind of 'pad' he had. Wilkie had told him, 'My wife's at Ninewells, six feet under.'

There was another flurry of excitement in the packed courtroom when a young woman who knew Helen Wilkie well and had baby-sat for her, said that some two or three weeks after she had been reported as having disappeared, she believed she saw the missing woman coming out of a restaurant in the centre of town.

When Jimmy Wilkie moved from the dock to the witness-box to give evidence on his own behalf, he spoke easily and with an apparent good memory for the events of the day of the christening, explaining how he and his wife had gone from the reception to the Golden Fry restaurant for a meal. But they had fallen out after Helen had shouted a drinks order to a waitress and he had then called out to cancel it.

'Helen was annoyed and kept on saying she was wanting a drink. I kept on refusing and she got up and said, "To hell with you." She got about three-quarters up the stairs and stumbled and fell forward. Helen had blood on her clothes and hands. I cleaned one of her hands while she wiped her face,' he told the jury.

Jimmy Wilkie later related how they had returned home for Helen to change her clothes, then went back into town and drove around in the hope he would see his sister. When there was no sign of her, and because it was getting late, he decided they should go out to Longforgan to collect their newly christened son. On the way there, another row flared up.

'Helen kept saying she wanted a drink and I kept saying she'd had enough. We stopped at the toilets at the top of Riverside Drive. When I came back Helen wasn't in the car.' Wilkie went on to recount how he had searched the ladies' lavatory and had then driven around searching for her. After finally going to his mother's to collect the baby, he drove back to his own home, fully expecting her to be there. When she wasn't, he fed the baby then went to bed.

Asked whether there had been any occasion when he thought he had seen Helen since her disappearance, he replied that he believed he had done so once, adding that he had asked around many times if anyone knew her whereabouts. When he was questioned about showing ill will towards her, he replied, 'I may have slapped her and grabbed her on the arms, but never with a clenched fist or anything like that.'

He disputed the interpretation that had been put on his comments about his missing wife being 'well buried', explaining that what he had probably said was something to the effect that if police had not found her by then they were unlikely to do so after such a passage of time. At the time of the conversation he and Mr Milne, whom he had made the comment to, 'had a drink on them' and he was getting fed up with people asking him if he had done anything to Helen.

When the jury retired after three days of evidence, experienced court journalists and even some of the police involved in the murder inquiry agreed that the case against the accused man was slender. There was plenty of room for suspicion and sufficient evidence that the teenage couple had had a fiery relationship, which more than once had provoked violence, but there was no overwhelming proof linking Wilkie to the actual act of murder. Without the existence of the tie used to strangle the unfortunate young mother and, more importantly, its admitted ownership by her husband, it is even possible that the case might never have arrived in court.

No one was more surprised than the speculators gathered in the corridors of the court-house when the jury of nine men and six women returned after an absence of only seventy minutes.

Jimmy Wilkie was brought back and sat in the dock, pale-faced and impassive between his police escorts, as he waited for the verdict. Without looking at him, the jury foreman rose to say they had found him guilty of the murder – by a majority.

Lord Robertson told the accused man, 'You have been found guilty by a jury of what can only be described as a horrible crime and there is only one sentence I can impose.' When the life term was ordered, Wilkie slowly bowed his head and he was then led back down the cells. In the public gallery, his girlfriend Donna was visibly upset. His mother wept.

In the following months, life once more returned to as near normal as possible for the principal players in the murder melodrama – apart from the convicted man himself, who was struggling to come to terms with the bleak regime of prison life and facing a sentence of indeterminate length. And that is how it all might have continued . . . except that a short time later Chief Inspector Fotheringham, whose skilful investigation had secured the slim conviction, received an extraordinary phone call from the Procurator Fiscal in Dundee. He heard in disbelief that a new witness had suddenly come forward to say she had been visited at her home by Helen Wilkie on 18 May 1974 – more than three months after she had disappeared after supposedly being murdered by her husband.

The woman, Mrs Valerie McCabe, who had lived at the time in the same tenement block as the Wilkies at 43 Hill Street, had related how she had been at home that evening when the doorbell rang and Mrs Wilkie was on the doorstep to say Mrs McCabe's husband Norman had just phoned the Wilkies' flat. The McCabes had no telephone themselves and the call had been to inform Valerie, a woman in her early 20s, that her husband's bus had broken down on the way home from the Scotland–England football match at Hampden that afternoon and that he would be late in returning home.

The stunned chief inspector went at once to see the belated new witness, whose first-floor home was above the ground floor flat of the Wilkies. During a lengthy interview, Mrs McCabe disclosed that she had read reports of the trial in the newspapers and had become very anxious about the verdict because she 'knew for certain' that Helen Wilkie had been in her house on the day of the football international in May. They had spent a long time chatting, she said.

The chief inspector questioned and probed, suggesting that a few years had passed and that people's memories could play tricks. But Mrs McCabe was emphatic about her identification and stressed that because of the football match she had absolutely no doubt of the date of the visit. She became indignant that her word was being doubted and asked angrily if the policeman was calling her a liar or thought she was stupid. Chief Inspector Fotheringham responded that neither was the case, but he believed it might have been a case of mistaken identity: maybe the visitor was not Mrs Wilkie, but someone else who might have been co-habiting with Jimmy Wilkie.

Later, back at headquarters, the detective learned that by coincidence a young police constable and his wife, who bore an uncanny resemblance to the missing Helen, had separated and that she had taken up with Wilkie. The chief inspector collected a colour photograph of the young woman from her estranged husband and it was subsequently shown to Mrs McCabe, who agreed it looked like Mrs Wilkie – but it had not been her who had visited that evening in May.

In January 1979, seven months after the original trial, Scottish criminal history was made when the appeal court in Edinburgh allowed new evidence to be heard in a concluded case – the first time there had been such an occurrence since the controversial case in 1927 of Oscar Slater, who was ultimately freed after being cleared of a murder for which he had served eighteen years.

Jimmy Wilkie was less fortunate. Lord Emslie, the Lord Justice General, one of three judges to consider the appeal, dismissed the plea that there had been a miscarriage of justice, saying that they were far from convinced that if Mrs McCabe's evidence had been heard at the original trial there would have been a different verdict. His Lordship said there was no reason to doubt that a woman had called at Mrs McCabe's home on the day of the football match, but the critical question was what weight and reliability should be attached to that evidence.

'In my opinion, indeed, it is the highest degree likely that an intelligent jury would have reached the conclusion without much difficulty that Mrs McCabe, although an honest witness, was quite mistaken in saying that she saw Helen Wilkie alive on the evening of 18 May 1974,' said Lord Emslie.

Then, in a devastating dismissal of the defence case, and with surgical precision, the country's leading judge demolished the supposed new evidence point by point. He said her supposed visit simply could not fit with the statements of the accused man himself two days after she vanished – and in further interviews with police, and in his own evidence – that she had never been seen again and had never returned to the flat. Nor was it consistent with the evidence of Mrs Wilkie's friends that they had not seen or heard from her, or that she failed to contact her parents or go to visit her son to whom she was devoted, after 3 February. All this evidence and the inability of the police to trace Mrs Wilkie presented a clear picture of a young woman who, if she had been alive after 3 February, had deliberately and successfully abandoned her husband, child, family and friends and had dropped completely from sight – someone who was quite determined she should not be traced.

'In such circumstances it is almost impossible to believe that this young woman could have taken the risk of making a single visit to the flat on 18 May,' said His Lordship. He suggested that if she had made this single visit it was 'astonishing' that she took nothing with her before completely disappearing again, since her clothes were still in the flat. Nor had she left any trace whatever of her visit, for which there appeared to be no rational explanation.

He pointed out that if it had been Mrs Wilkie at the flat, that meant she had been murdered after 18 May, and there were 'grave difficulties' in the way of accepting this hypothesis.

'The most important is that she was strangled by her husband's tie,' he pointed out. In the face of that, it was difficult – if not impossible – to believe that Helen Wilkie, having deliberately abandoned and cut herself off from her husband, would have continued to carry the tie in her handbag for months. If she had disposed of the tie, how had it come to be used by her murderer?

In addition to all this, the jury would have been required to accept two remarkable coincidences. The first was that if Mrs Wilkie had been murdered after 18 May, her body was buried just off the route she and her husband had taken on 3 February. The other coincidence being that when she was murdered she was, in all probability, wearing the wine-coloured dress she had changed into on 3 February.

Lord Emslie thought there were other 'more direct' indications that Mrs McCabe was probably mistaken in her identification of the woman who had called at her home on 18 May. He said she had not known Helen Wilkie that well and her encounters with her must have been infrequent and fleeting. Other evidence suggested Mrs McCabe may not have been all that observant. She had said a photograph she had been shown of a woman friend of the Wilkies, who had stayed at the flat after Mrs Wilkie had disappeared, could have been Mrs Wilkie. Both Mrs Wilkie and the woman in the photo were hairdressers and had blonde tips and streaks in their hair, which they wore in the same style.

As Lord Emslie coolly dismissed one by one the main planks of the appeal, the parents of the accused man sat with growing anxiety at the rear of the court. Mrs Wilkie, realising that her son's prospects of freedom were slowly ebbing away, brought out a white handkerchief and pressed it to her face to stem a flow of tears.

Jimmy Wilkie himself had remained surprisingly composed throughout. Dressed in a black leather jacket and checked shirt, he sat in the dock chatting amiably with his prison-officer escorts while he waited the appearance of the trio of appeal judges who would decide his fate.

When they finally rejected his plea that he was innocent of the murder of his young wife, he turned to his parents and gently shook his head. Mrs Wilkie broke down, sobbing emotionally. Later, after the two had chatted in an ante-room for ten minutes, they hugged each other in a corridor before he was taken back to prison.

While he served out his sentence, Wilkie and his family continued to protest his innocence. His parents and legal advisers took the case to Justice, the London-based campaigning group led by broadcaster Ludovic Kennedy which had successfully won the release and pardon of Paddy Meehan in a high-profile appeal hearing. However, after considering the Dundee case, the group decided it lacked strength and turned down the plea for assistance.

Jimmy Wilkie completed his life sentence. Soon after his eventual release, he died in a road accident.

4

THE NOT SO ORDINARY
JOHN SMITH

When she first heard it, the sound was almost gentle – a soft sigh that could have been a restless turn in the night or a fleeting gasp for breath. It wasn't loud but its presence in the still house had been just enough to make the young woman stir in her sleep.

It was 5 a.m. and as she lay in the darkness the 21-year-old occupant of the upper floor bedroom drifted uncertainly between slumber and wakefulness. The half-heard noise that had roused her seemed to have come from the bedroom of her mother a short distance away, but silence had once more descended. Drowsily, she dismissed what she thought she had heard as her mother's restlessness or her own dreams. Either way, it was unimportant. As she started to turn on to her side in an attempt to return to sleep, she heard another sound. It was just as soft, but this time it was unmistakable and much closer. Someone was in the room. She knew that beyond doubt. Whoever it was, was breathing quickly, the way they would if they had exerted themselves – or were excited. Then a hand reached out and pulled back the bedclothes.

What confronted her was no longer any kind of dream but the beginning of the worst nightmare a woman could have. Silhouetted in the gloom of the half light was the figure of a powerful man holding a knife. He stepped forward and when he brought the blade up to point threateningly at her she saw that both his hands were covered in blood.

Then he lay down on the bed and told her he had just killed her mother and unless she did what he asked, she would be next. There was no reason to disbelieve him. The knife, like his hands, was blood-soaked and his chilling words explained the unusual sound which had come from the next room, which was now completely silent.

Practically paralysed by fear, the young woman shuddered at what she knew was about to happen. Then through her half closed eyes, she made an astonishing discovery. The agitated man lying beside her was a neighbour of the same age who lived only two doors away in the row of neat terraced houses.

Almost as soon as she realised who he was, her terror intensified. Her recognition meant she would be able to identify him to police – and he would be just as aware of that. He could not simply vanish anonymously into the night. It meant that what was about to occur was likely to have only one ending.

Her torment seemed endless. In the anguish that followed, she was raped repeatedly. Attempted protest was met with the knife again being held menacingly into her face. Resistance brought the repeated threat that she, too, would die as horrifyingly as her mother.

Her ordeal lasted two hours. As daylight filtered into the room, the devastated victim knew the scenario would soon be about to change. She began to plead for her life, begging her captor to spare her. At first her words were desperate, then, as it seemed he was hesitating in his intentions, she somehow found the resolve to be gently persuasive. Everything would be all right if only he would leave quietly and without any further trouble, she assured him. He could depart before the neighbourhood was fully awake and no one would be any the wiser.

The performance of the 21-year-old that April morning in 1983 was remarkable for its courage and, almost unbelievably, it was also successful. The man who had terrified and violated her, nodded slowly, gradually convincing himself of the seeming logic of her plea.

With a final threat that the trembling woman before him

should keep his identity secret, he backed slowly out of the room, departing as silently as he had come.

She lay in the bedroom for long minutes after that. She needed to be sure he had gone and she needed to stop shaking from the horror that was enveloping her. But she knew, too, that she had to go the bedroom next door to find out about her mother, even though she was certain of what awaited her.

The sight that greeted her was something no daughter should have of her mother. Only then did she flee the house and leave the scene of unspeakable horror behind to make her way to the home of a friend to haltingly describe what had taken place.

Things happened rapidly after that. At the arrival of the police she told them her attacker was John Smith and supplied his address. But when they went for him he was not there. Detectives quickly traced him to the home of his sister and found him on a sofa fast asleep after his monstrous night's work.

He did not lie about what he had done. In the car on the way to police headquarters the 21-year-old whose full name was John Cant Smith calmly described how he had broken into the house and had 'stabbed someone.' But he did not explain that he had swung his kitchen knife so often that his helpless 61-year-old victim had had no chance to defend herself. Casually, he admitted that he had gone to his sister's house to wash the blood from his clothes, and, if they wanted it, they'd find the knife in a rubbish bin near her home. Under caution at headquarters, he explained further that on the evening leading up to the atrocities he had had a lot to drink and on the way home had decided to break into his neighbour's house to steal. There had been no intention to kill, no plan to rape, he volunteered.

Although his story was not disputed, there is every reason to believe that he might have been fully aware that there were no men in the house when he forced his way in. The murdered woman, who was described as a 'credit to the community' and faithful church worker who had been in much demand as a singer at local functions, spent most nights alone because her husband was a bakery worker on overnight shifts. Her daughter's boyfriend visited frequently, as he had done that night, but had departed before midnight. Since Smith lived so close to the semi-detached house in the Lochee housing estate, he was in a position to be aware of movements at his neighbour's home.

In light of his early admissions, there was no need for a trial. Two months after his crimes, Smith appeared in the dock at the High Court in Edinburgh and again confessed to what he had done.

Sentencing him, Lord Wheatley looked at Smith with unconcealed distaste and told him:

> In view of what has been said, there is nothing I can say to you, save this: These two atrocious crimes were carried out within a home and people, particularly women, are entitled to expect that in their home they are safe from attacks such as you perpetrated. If women cannot be safe in their own home, then society has reached a sorry state. Therefore, in order to mark the court's great displeasure and anxiety at such offences and to deter others, I propose to fashion my sentences accordingly.

His Lordship said the law prescribed but one penalty for murder – life imprisonment. As far as the rape was concerned, he would impose a separate sentence of seven years' imprisonment, explaining that this would place it on Smith's record, to be taken into account when his possible release was being considered.

Referring again to the life sentence, Lord Wheatley added that he would make a recommendation – something he seldom did – that Smith should serve a period of at least 12 years. He ordered that the two sentences should run concurrently, meaning that the seven years for the rape would be served at the same time as the sentence for murder.

Compared with present-day sentencing protocols, when judges are obliged to suggest a minimum tariff, 12 years might seem a relatively lenient disposal, particularly in the circumstances of a brutal and unprovoked murder followed by the repeated rape of a second victim. But it was not particularly exceptional at the time and brought no public outcry.

However, Lord Wheatley, then Scotland's most senior judge, might have felt differently had he had known how John Cant Smith was to behave in the future. He was not to know, either, that 12 years was nowhere near to the time the murdering rapist would actually spend behind bars.

A little over three years after descending the steps in the dock of the High Court to vanish out of public view and into the penal system, Smith once again burst into prominence. But this time it was not a helpless young woman who was to become his hostage but a prison officer.

Along with two other lifers held with him at Peterhead Prison, Smith took part in a riot in an attempt to air alleged grievances. The trio petrol-bombed a section of the jail's A Hall and seized one of their guards before embarking on an orgy of destruction. By the end of the five-day stand-off they had caused £260,000 of damage and made national headlines before surrendering.

His fellow rioters were every bit as dangerous as himself. One was William Ballantyne, a 27-year-old jailed shortly before Smith for stabbing a man to death in a Glasgow street brawl. The other was one of Scotland's most notorious criminals – 32-year-old Andrew Walker, a former Army corporal who had machine-gunned three soldiers to death in a £19,000 military payroll robbery 18 months earlier, for which he was given a 30-year sentence.

To justify his actions, Smith made an eloquent plea during his trial at the High Court at Peterhead, claiming that he had 'taken desperate measures because of his desperate situation.'

His written plea in mitigation of his actions read:

Can anyone ever understand the horrors of prison life, even by visiting prison? No one can understand this without being part of it, feeling the anxieties, knowing the helplessness, living in desolation.

Prison life does not provide the creative correction and training needed for a man to be able to make a new beginning on the outside. Instead, it is geared to use the men as labour, punish them if necessary and disregard their inner spirits as of no consequence.

Physical and mental brutality does exist in Peterhead. This matter can only be resolved with the introduction of rehabilitation. If the prison authorities insist on treating prisoners like animals, then prisoners will naturally continue to act like animals.

Prisoners (including myself) have been described as incurable psychopaths, subversive and hell-bent on destruction. This can only be described as an excuse rather than a truth. I ask you, have prisoners been given the chance to express themselves in any other way? Certainly not in Peterhead.

However well-expressed, the plea cut little ice with presiding judge Lord Murray. He made no distinction between the trio and sentenced each of them to 10 years, terms he wanted taken into account when their life sentences and eventual release were being considered.

Smith had plenty of time to reflect on prison life and its care of inmates. He was to remain in Peterhead for another 16 years before eventually being freed on licence. Altogether he had served 19 years. Notwithstanding his words to Lord Murray, he claimed that during his incarceration he had 'found God' and reformed his ways. Some police officers and social workers who knew him doubted his conversion and considered his new-found faith to be little more than a ploy to obtain his freedom. Privately, they called him the 'master manipulator'.

It was a description that seemed particularly fitting considering Smith's next brush with the law.

Several months after his release in October 2002, the man with the violent past attended a Saturday night dance in Stonehaven where he befriended a 49-year-old Canadian-born woman. After a few dances, he talked her into allowing him to walk her home. He even persuaded the woman, a bank manager, to invite him into the cottage she shared with her daughter for a cup of coffee. Within a short time, however, and for whatever reason, Smith's new acquaintance became uneasy. Regretting her offer of hospitality, she told him to leave. Reluctantly, he agreed and, after some hesitation, departed.

But a few days later, in the early hours of one morning, he returned to the cottage, which was in darkness.

He moved cautiously, sure he was unobserved. He did not know, however, that his stealthy approach had been detected. The woman's daughter, who had risen from bed for a glass of water, had spotted him walking up the garden path and became instantly apprehensive. Ducking out of sight, she watched, terror-filled, as the handle of the door slowly turned from the outside. Her heart pounded so hard she was certain the uninvited visitor on the other side would hear it. Desperately, she tried to remember if the house had been locked up for the night or if the door would start to open. She closed her eyes and prayed. When she opened them again, the handle had ceased to turn and the sound of footsteps moving round the side of the house told her her God had been listening.

The girl let out the breath she hadn't been aware she'd been holding and after a few moments quietly alerted her mother. Together the pair remained silent but petrified as the man who had killed prowled around the exterior of the house, peering into various windows. Whatever his original intentions, and to the enormous relief of the terrified mother and daughter, Smith appeared to have a change of heart and a few minutes later departed. Once he was out of sight they called the police and a short time later the sinister, unwelcome visitor, was found close by and arrested.

After being taken to the police station in Stonehaven, Smith requested permission to visit the toilet. It was then his earlier intentions became all too evident. Checking the WC immediately after he'd used it, police found a knife and a packet of condoms in the cistern. The discovery raised questions in the minds of the officers but, with nothing else to go on, they dismissed the find as just the actions of an anxious man brought in for a minor offence. Had they been aware of their prisoner's history and the chilling echoes of the last time he had used a knife for a murderous sexual spree in a house where a mother and daughter were alone in the early hours, they might have viewed matters differently. That same knowledge would certainly have unnerved the two women in the cottage far beyond their most fearful imaginings.

Surprisingly, Smith was again treated unexpectedly lightly at his subsequent court appearance. Although on licence from a life sentence, he was jailed for just three months, a term which seems inconceivably lenient considering the marked similarities to the circumstances of his crimes some 20 years previously. One explanation may be that the sheriff dealing with the case was unaware of the ghastly background to the crimes which had led to Smith's long confinement in Peterhead.

If that is the case, the judge's ignorance was nothing to that of the next innocent victim who was to receive the attention of the killer rapist.

Some three years later, on the evening of 3 February 2006, Smith surfaced once more to become the centre of a police hunt – and again it was for terrorising a woman.

A slightly built lady doctor was loading shopping into the passenger side of her vehicle in a supermarket car park near Broughty Ferry when she was suddenly seized from behind by two powerful hands grabbing her round the waist. The attacker pinned her arms to her side and, in the darkness of the isolated area, dragged her round the vehicle. She screamed but the few late night shoppers who heard her, dismissed the incident as a domestic squabble and went about their own business.

Seconds later, her panting assailant had opened the driver's door and bundled her into the seat after placing one hand round her throat and the other over her mouth. He got into the car with her, at first sitting on his helpless victim then ordering her to move over into the passenger seat. Then he ripped the car keys from her hand. Despite her fear, the 41-year-old victim continued to struggle. She attempted to escape by opening her passenger door but was propelled back into her seat by an arm across her throat. When she tried to shout out, the broad-shouldered man with the pale eyes roughly stifled her call for help. 'Don't do that. Stop doing that,' he instructed, the quietness of his words adding to the menace. But even after he had started the engine, the woman found unexpected courage to continue her fight. She managed to pull the keys from the ignition and, fighting off his attempts to pin her back in her seat, succeeded in switching on the car's hazard warning lights and sounding the horn. Other shoppers paused in their haste to get out of the cold of the February evening and looked curiously towards the vehicle. But once more they discounted the disturbance as a minor family row where outside interference might not be appreciated.

Perhaps because of the attention her actions were starting to attract in the car park, or maybe thanks to her surprising pluck, the situation suddenly changed. The aggression slipped away from the man in the driver's seat and he slowly opened his door and began backing out of the vehicle. Then in an urgent, raised voice he pleaded, 'I really need your help. I'm really desperate. I really need your help.'

The woman who had been his prisoner until a moment before but who had somehow taken control of the situation, asked what help he required.

'I really need to get to Lochee,' he said, naming the suburb several miles away at the opposite end of town and where his notoriety had started two decades earlier.

Calmly she replied, 'I can't take you there. You've really scared me. You know I can't take you there.'

Her firm response seemed to be all that was required to drain the last traces of aggression from her captor. Without another word he slid out of the vehicle, pushed the door shut and quietly moved off into the shadows of the car park. The trembling woman in the passenger seat quickly locked all the doors, anxiously watching his departure. It was only after he vanished towards a nearby housing estate that she found sufficient courage to leave the car and re-enter the supermarket to ask staff to call the police.

Despite press appeals and the study of the supermarket

company's CCTV recordings, the identity of the man who had appeared from nowhere to transform a woman's routine shopping expedition into the most frightening experience of her life, remained unknown. The tapes picked up his arrival at the store some 40 minutes before the incident began and he was tracked wandering round the store without attempting to buy anything. He was also pinpointed hanging around outside, apparently watching other shoppers, and then moving towards a cash machine as though to use it. But, however helpful the images were, they were insufficiently clear to establish who the man was.

The breakthrough the police were searching for came when an observant detective reviewed the CCTV footage. Magnification of the images showed distinctive features on the jacket, sufficient to allow the manufacturer to be traced. They in turn advised that it had been part of a batch supplied to a charity second-hand furniture organisation in Dundee.

Within hours of that information being received, the recycling firm were able to tell police that the owner of the jacket was John Cant Smith. They knew him as a released murderer but had been 'motivated by humanity' to give him a chance by taking him on as a volunteer. At first he had been employed part-time, then, latterly, full-time. They were able to tell police, too, that on the day of the abduction, Smith had not turned up for work.

Three weeks after the incident, he was arrested. At first he denied having any part in it, but later, before he was due in court, he confessed to what he had done, saying the offence hadn't been sexually motivated but had been carried out because he had a cocaine habit and owed a dealer £350.

Even after his arrest, Smith's latest female victim remained unaware of his appalling history. It was only after he had faced justice – again in the High Court in Edinburgh – for the ordeal he had subjected her to, that she learned the full extent of his violent past. Perhaps it was as well she was such an innocent or she might never have found the nerve to confront him in the valiant way she did.

As in the previous incidents, when he forced himself upon unsuspecting women, Smith again sought in court to explain away his actions as having much less sinister motives. His defence counsel said that following his release from his 19 years in Peterhead, Smith had lived alone and had obtained employment. However, just as he had admitted to police, he was a drug addict and required extra money. An examination of blood samples taken from Smith and also of his bank account, confirmed these facts. On the day of the attack, the defence QC went on to explain, Smith had little recollection of events but his intention had been to rob someone at a cash machine. When he had been unable to do so, he turned towards his victim and when that plan went wrong, his next thought was to have her drive him to a less busy machine.

Jailing him for five years, Lord Kinclaven remarked that the term would have been seven years except for the fact that he had owned up to his crime at an early stage and also because he had been returned to prison immediately under the terms of the licence releasing him from his original life sentence.

His words were received unemotionally by the man with the ordinary name but extraordinary history of crime. John Smith, who in his relatively short life had murdered, raped, rioted and abducted, was led away silently to return once more to the place he had said left him feeling desolate and hopeless – the place where those behind the towering walls would be bound to act like animals if that was how they thought they were being treated.

5

BILL THE RIPPER

A chill wind swept through Dundee Harbour that late January morning in 1889 when the couple from London hurried down the gangway of the steamer *Cambria*. Neither had been in the city before and they gazed for a few moments at the vast hill dominating the northern skyline – which they would later learn was called the Law – before pulling their collars up and quickly moving on to collect their luggage.

Few of the others going about their business on the dockside that day paid them much attention, except to show a little surprise at how skilfully the diminutive 5-foot 3-inch male handled the large packing box that was discharged along with the rest of their baggage. William Henry Bury wasn't just short of stature, but slightly built and sometimes a shade unsteady on his feet, though that had more to do with the amount of ale he normally consumed than any infirmity. For most of his twenty-nine years he had lived in his native Midlands and the woman who accompanied him was his wife Ellen, four years his senior, whom he had married only nine months before.

Bizarrely, they had met in Kate Spooner's brothel in London where Ellen worked as a skivvy and where Bury had become a frequent visitor after moving south to live in the capital's East End, the previous November.

Their courtship had been brief – a month – before their Easter Monday wedding and it was difficult to understand how Bury had managed to sweep Ellen, slim and delicately featured, so completely off her feet. He was said by those who knew him to be rest-less and quarrelsome, fond of drink and whores and without any kind of obvious future. His father, a fishmonger, had died when Bury was only six months old and a short time later his mother was admitted to a lunatic asylum. A prosperous woman in Wolverhampton took over the family of three orphans but, despite being educated above his class, Bury became a drifter soon after entering his teens. He had some training as a horse butcher and had worked in a locksmith's, but these occupations required a discipline he didn't have and after his move to the East End he eked out a scanty living as a sawdust- and sand-merchant. Most of his customers were publicans and he also tended to quickly become one of theirs.

It was much easier to understand why Bury was attracted to Ellen. She had inherited £300 in shares from an aunt – the equiv-alent of three years' pay for factory workers – and more than one customer at Kate Spooner's had made overtures in her direction. Unaccountably, she had chosen the small, bearded man who had seemed incapable of offering her any kind of future. It was a decision she probably came quickly to regret. Less than a week after the wedding, their first landlady in Bow hurried to their bedroom because of the amount of noise. She walked in to find Bury straddling his wife with the knife he always kept under his pillow in his hand and Ellen shouting that he was in the act of killing her. Another acquaintance of the unlikely couple twice witnessed the petite newly-wed being assaulted by her husband. On the first occasion, Bury punched her full in the face in a pub in Whitechapel. During the next attack, in the street, Ellen was knocked to the ground after suffering a heavy blow to the mouth. The incident ended only when a man stepped in to hold the drunken Bury back.

When he wasn't ill-treating his new wife, the under-sized, under-achieving Bury was rapidly devouring the £300 legacy, first with the purchase of a pony and cart for his sawdust business and later on drink and prostitutes. By the time they arrived in Dundee, little remained. Certainly, there wasn't enough left to fund the purchase of a house or even the rent of fully furnished apartments in the city and when they alighted from the *Cambria* that winter morning, they travelled only a few hundreds yards before finding lodgings at 43 Union Street. Jean Robertson, their landlady, charged them eight shillings per week for the rent of a room but Bury considered this too expensive and, a week later, after unsuccessfully attempting to gain two shillings' reduction, they moved out. The same day, the couple took up occupancy of a two-roomed basement flat at 113 Princes Street, an area overlooking the harbour and on a busy route into the city centre.

Significantly, the closely built tenements were also well served by public houses and, to the delight of their owners, Bury immediately established himself as a big-drinking customer. Ellen, however, appeared only once with him, on the day after they moved into the flat, when she had a glass of port wine in one of the pubs before going home. The little Englishman would sometimes visit the same bar more than once on the same day and was happy to chat to anyone who would listen. He seemed 'a man of means', spoke of selling shares, and said he and his wife had moved north for the sake of Ellen's health – an ironic comment, given the events soon to unfold. He added that they would probably return to London that August.

The couple made an early visit to a shop operated by Mrs Marjory Smith. After buying some domestic utensils, the conversation turned to their previous life in London. When Mrs Smith asked why it was that the capital's famous police force allowed Jack the Ripper to go unchecked, Ellen replied, 'Oh, Jack the Ripper is quiet now.' Bury remained silent.

Bury also became known to Janet Martin, who ran a general provisions store at 125 Princes Street, and around 1 p.m. on Monday, 4 February, the man who seemed to have no interest in finding a job called at the shop and asked for a length of cord. He gave no explanation why he wanted it but accepted the first piece shown, telling Mrs Martin, 'This will do nicely.'

Ellen Bury, the Cockney brothel maid who had inexplicably become infatuated with an alcoholic abuser whom she barely knew and who willingly travelled by ship with him to a land utterly alien to her usual way of life, was never seen alive from that day on. It is likely, however, that she was heard. At around three o'clock the following morning, neighbour David Duncan was awake in his bedroom when he heard three screams of 'desperate distress' coming from the Bury's flat thirty yards away. The terrified shrieks ended as abruptly as they began and he heard no more, though he lay in bed listening intently for the next half-hour. Duncan seems to have been the only one who heard anything. Even his landlady, who shared the same bedroom, slept through the quick, anguished screams.

In the following days Bury was seldom out of the local pubs – his favourite, the Prince Regent Bar, in particular – and none of those he shared a drink with detected anything different about the Englishman who never worked but who always had money for ale. As usual, he was more than willing to buy a drink for anyone he struck up a conversation with, although, as always, he unaccountably declined the same offers in return. Sometimes, he made casual references to Ellen, more than once even taking away a bottle of bitter beer which he said was for her, and no one suspected she wasn't sitting at home nearby as usual.

On Sunday, 10 February, six days after his wife was last seen alive and just twenty-two days after they first had set foot in Dundee, Bury embarked on a course of action that was to guarantee him a notoriety to extend for all of the following century and into the next and see his name echo round the world.

Early that day he called at the home of David Walker, a neighbour who lived round the corner in Crescent Lane, and seemed anxious to talk. They had first met several days earlier in the Prince Regent when Walker, a painter, had been working there. Walker was in bed when Bury called and he tossed a newspaper to his visitor, jokingly saying there might be something in it about Jack the Ripper, whose activities among the whores of Whitechapel had the population gripped in a mixture of fear and fascination in equal measure. Walker added that his new neighbour 'might know something about him'. Bury was unamused and left a short time afterwards. Unexpectedly, he called back an hour later and the pair went for a walk together. As they strolled the roads surrounding the harbour area and viewed the tied-up vessels in the docks, Bury enquired about the times of boats and trains for London, saying he was of a mind to return south to have a drink with his former acquaintances there. He also spoke about the departure times of vessels sailing to Hull and Liverpool.

Shortly before 7 p.m. that evening, Bury went for another walk, but this time with a macabre purpose. Deeply agitated and nervous, he threw on his short black overcoat over his tweed suit, adjusted his felt hat, and – after locking up the flat and swiftly climbing the seventeen stairs from the dingy basement – wound his way down King Street, picking his way between the high tenements by the light of the gas lamps on both sides of the road. As he approached police headquarters in Bell Street, his pace quickened and his heart thumped. He barely lifted his head to see where he was going, for over and over in his head he was rehearsing the extraordinary tale he was about to tell.

By the time he turned into the police offices at the far end of the street, Bury's breathing had become so rapid that he became enveloped in the clouds of expired breath vaporising in front of him that frosty February evening.

Without pausing to regain his composure, he at once asked to speak privately to the senior officer on duty. He was seen by Lieutenant James Parr and in a rush of words told him that Ellen was dead. She had taken her own life a week earlier, he said breathlessly. Now he was frightened he would be arrested as Jack the Ripper. On the previous Monday, he anxiously explained, they had both been drinking heavily and had sunk into a stupor, so much so that he had no recollection of the rest of the night or when they had gone to bed. The next morning, through a drunken haze, he spotted Ellen dead on the floor, apparently brought about by some form of self-strangulation with a rope, which was still round her neck.

Lieutenant Parr, unsure whether he was listening to the ramblings of a demented madman or actually having an extraordinary death reported to him, was further astonished by what came next. Bury, his words tumbling from his mouth, explained that the sight of his dead wife had caused him to be seized by some kind of mad impulse and he had picked up a nearby knife and inexplicably started plunging it into her body. Then, overcome with remorse and in a deep panic that he would be accused of being Jack the Ripper, he had bent up the corpse of his mutilated wife and rammed it into the large packing case he had brought with him from London. In the following days, he said, he had been uncertain what to do next and had wanted to take time to think. He had acted as normally as possible and on more than one occasion had some cronies round for games of dominoes, using the box with Ellen's contorted body inside as the gaming table.

The police lieutenant was stunned by the startling story he had just heard, but, resisting his instincts to dismiss Bury as one of the mentally disturbed citizens who occasionally found their way into police offices, decided not to take any chances. He escorted Bury to a separate room and ordered a constable to remain with him. Then he despatched Lieutenant David Lamb (head of the detective department) and Detective Peter Campbell to the basement at 113 Princes Street, to investigate, taking with them the key Bury had handed over.

Inside, the flat smelled of stale alcohol and something neither officer could easily identify. Lamb went straight to the back room where the three-foot long, three-foot deep, square-shaped box described by Bury dominated the scene. Prising this box open, Lamb recoiled at the ghastly sight before his eyes. Partly covered by a sheet was the near-naked corpse of Ellen Bury, her body twisted awkwardly to fit into her gruesome coffin. Her abdomen had been ripped apart by five or six knife slashes, one particularly long, deep gash exposing the entrails. There were deep red marks on her throat. Beside the mutilated body, which was already in the early stages of decay, were the New Testament, a hymn book, prayer book and other papers, books and some clothing. On the nearby window ledge lay a blood-stained knife with scraps of flesh and hair attached and, on the floor, a length of cord, also with some hairs adhering to it. In the hearth were the remnants of burnt ladies' clothing and the buttons which had adorned it.

The lieutenant swiftly took in the rest of the scene in the sparsely furnished bedroom and noted some empty beer bottles, a whisky flask, and a cigar box containing dominoes. The iron bedstead, bought a week earlier by Bury in the Greenmarket, had its sheets tidily folded back, as though someone had just risen.

A brief search also unearthed a document which read:

January 12, 1889

We, Messrs. Malcolm, Ogilvy & Co. Ltd., Dundee, do hereby agree to take into our employ W. H. and E. N. Bury of No. 3 Spanby Road, London, E. for a period of 7 years. Wages for W.H.B. £2 per week; wages for E. B. £1 per week. To enter duty as soon as Possible. Travelling expenses will Be allowed after one Month from Date of entering employment.

Messrs. Malcolm, Ogilvy & Co.,

Dundee.

W. H. Bury,

Pro. Tem. Ellen Bury.

Witness – William James Hawkins

Lieutenant Lamb left Detective Campbell to stand guard over the grisly death scene and strode quickly from the flat to summon the presence of the police surgeon and the Procurator Fiscal.

From that moment on, William Henry Bury, the insignificant, drunken drifter who had mysteriously decided to set sail from London to settle in a Scottish city he knew nothing of, assumed a worldwide notoriety that has continued to surround him for over a hundred years. Piecing together the strands of the Burys' flight from the Whitechapel area of London, the nature of the unfortunate Ellen's injuries and the references to Jack the Ripper, news agencies quickly made the link to what had happened at 113 Princes Street and the back alleys of the brothel areas of London. The address of the dingy basement floor in an unfashionable part of Dundee was soon to be telegraphed round the world. Within days newspapers as far away as America were proclaiming that Bury and the Ripper were one and the same person, even though he had still to stand trial for the only crime he had been charged with.

In Dundee, news of Bury's arrest, and the possible links with the London maniac who had stalked the back alleys of Whitechapel, spread like wildfire. The day after Bury's breathless admissions at police headquarters, large groups of men, women and children queued outside newsagents to read the third edition of *The Courier* which published at 1 p.m. and gave a full account of what had been found in Princes Street. From then until early evening, when a fall of heavy snow sent them scurrying home, crowds descended on the basement flat to jostle for a position which might give them a glimpse between the crimson curtains over the broken kitchen window into the scene of horror.

Those who got close enough to the winding staircase leading to the flat gasped at what they saw written in chalk on a door at the bottom of the stairs – 'Jack Ripper is at the back of this door' – and on a wall – 'Jack Ripper is in this seller (*sic*)'. Although the writing looked childish, it appeared to have been there for some time.

Meanwhile, other unexpected discoveries had been made at police headquarters after the detention of the flat's occupant. Shortly after arriving in Bell Street on the Sunday evening, Bury had been seen by Constable McKay, the acting bar officer, who instantly recognised him as the man who had twice visited the public benches of the Police Court some days earlier and intently followed proceedings. On each occasion he occupied the same seat at the rear of the courtroom. The first visit had taken place on Monday, 4 February, less than twenty-four hours before Ellen Bury had met her appalling end. The second was two days afterwards, on the Thursday. When interrogated on the matter, Bury frankly admitted his presence, saying he was eager to see how Scottish justice operated.

The police were intrigued by another finding after they arrested Bury for Ellen's murder. When his pockets were searched before he was taken off to the cells, they found a large quantity of jewellery, consisting of several rings, a number of pairs of earrings, a ladies' silver watch, two lockets and chain, and two brooches. In addition were two rings he always wore on the little fingers of each hand and which he told anyone who asked were his 'wedding presents'. Police assumed that at least two of the rings in Bury's possession were Ellen's, since the usual ones she wore on her wedding finger were missing from the corpse.

The eagerly awaited trial took place on 28 March 1889, when Bury pled not guilty and appeared before Lord Young at a sitting of the Dundee Spring Circuit Court. The crowd which packed the court-room was desperate for a sight of the man the world was starting to believe was Jack the Ripper. When at last he stepped into the dock, people leaned forward in anticipation. Gasps of surprise echoed round the courtroom. Strangers seated next to each other on the public benches whispered together in disappointment. Instead of some brooding ogre easily capable of the most unimaginable atrocities, they were faced by a small, dapper man, almost timid in his looks, sitting meekly between two towering police constables. He wore a felt hat and dark, tweed suit and carried a black overcoat neatly folded over one arm. He might have been an elder of their church.

For the next thirteen hours – almost a record sitting for a Dundee court – the spectators on the public benches listened spellbound to every word uttered, sometimes straining to understand the accents of the witnesses who had travelled from London. Bury didn't even give them the satisfaction of shouting out in protest at some of what was said, particularly when witnesses told of his violent assaults on Ellen or how he quickly used up her money. For the entire day, he sat practically expressionless, leaning forward with his right hand at his chin and listening intently to the proceedings.

Among the principal prosecution witnesses was Mrs Margaret Corney, Ellen's sister, who two months earlier had waved the Burys off when the *Cambria* set sail from London. She told the court how reluctant she was to see them depart because she somehow thought she would never see Ellen again – partly because two days before they left, Bury had shown her what he claimed was a letter from a Dundee jute firm offering them employment but with a contract that was for seven years. She explained how she had attempted to persuade her sister, who could not read very well, not to accompany Bury north because the job was for such an extended period. Margaret also identified all the jewellery found in the accuser's pockets as belonging to Ellen, most of it purchased before she met him.

Another key witness for the Crown was Mr David Malcolm, a partner in Malcolm Ogilvy's, who dismissed the job-offer letter as a complete forgery. Asked how Bury would know of the existence in Dundee of his company, Malcolm told the court that a report had appeared in London newspapers about Ogilvy's taking over a new works. There was also a jute company in Whitechapel and it was possible Bury had met up with an employee there, who would likely know of Ogilvy's factory in Dundee. The conclusion was that Bury had forged the letter to help lure Ellen away from London.

Despite the length of the trial, the facts of the case were relatively simple. Mrs Bury was dead and her husband had admitted stabbing the body. But who had carried out the fatal strangulation? The defence case was that Ellen had used a cord to commit suicide, either by hanging herself or by some kind of self-throttling, and that Bury, in a state of panic, had attempted to dispose of her body because he feared being blamed.

Dr (later Sir) Henry Littlejohn and two other medical experts were in no doubt that the marks on Ellen's neck indicated the cord had been tightened from the rear – ruling out self-strangulation.

Two other doctors were brought forward by the defence and they favoured the suicide theory, though they conceded that such an action would be 'most exceptional' and 'almost unprecedented'.

Bury had listened carefully to every word uttered by Dr Littlejohn and when the jury went out at 7 p.m. for supper he too was taken from the courtroom for something to eat. He seemed more upset about what he was given than how the case was going. After remarking that the doctor had been hard on him, he gazed disgustedly at the plate of porridge and milk before him and, after stirring it about for a few moments, protested angrily, 'That is the kind of thing we give to pigs in England.' Then he threw down the spoon, lifted the plate and drank the milk in a single gulp.

When the trial resumed, the public benches were still packed by the eager crowd which had sat there all day, most of them going without any food. Darkness had long since fallen when the all-male jury eventually retired but it did not take them long to return with their verdict. After only twenty-five minutes – just the time it took most of them to enjoy a long-awaited smoke – the foreman, farmer John Ramsay, told the hushed courtroom, 'The jury unanimously find the prisoner guilty as libelled, but strongly recommend him to the mercy of the court.'

The judge, Lord Young, looked startled. 'On what grounds do you recommend him to mercy?'

Ramsay: 'Partly from the conflicting medical evidence.'

Lord Young: 'If you are in doubt about the medical evidence, I must ask you to reconsider your verdict. That is no ground whatever for recommendation to mercy. You must see that. I am afraid I must ask you to reconsider your verdict if you have any doubt as to the guilt of the prisoner. You had better retire again and be sure you are quite satisfied this time.'

As the anxious-looking jurors filed out, Bury was led back down to the cells. For the first time since the proceedings had begun, the prisoner finally started to show some emotion, onlookers noting how his 'hands moved nervously' and 'his features became agitated'.

Downstairs, Bury became even more animated and told the constables, 'It will go well for me. By six o'clock tomorrow morning I'll be packed up and ready to get back to London,' adding by way of further explanation that he would move to a different area from the one where he had become so well known.

Back in the courtroom, many in the crowd shared his view that he would be released, believing the jury would opt for a compromise 'not proven' verdict.

However, after just ten minutes the jurors were back and this time there was no ambiguity. Foreman Ramsay looked straight ahead and said simply, 'We unanimously find the prisoner guilty.' Bury, who had returned to his emotionless self, showed no distress or disappointment at the words and seemed almost indifferent when Lord Young solemnly placed the traditional square of black silk material over his bewigged head and pronounced the death sentence. Bury, he said, would be taken to the prison at Dundee and, between the hours of 8 and 10 a.m. on 24 April, would be hung by the neck until dead – 'And may God have mercy on your soul.'

Still, unmoved by it all, the condemned man did not go immediately back down to the cells but signalled his defence team to come over to the dock, where he earnestly thanked them for all they had done, praising the 'able manner' in which they had conducted his case. When he finally descended the stairs to the cells, Bury appeared to break down briefly. Then, composing himself, he turned to the officers who had sat beside him that long, tense day and shook each of them by the hand, thanking them and saying, 'I will never see you again.'

In the following days, as he awaited the noose, Bury remained the model prisoner he had been since his arrest six weeks earlier, devoting most of his time to writing forty pages of his life story and reading the Bible. Others were more active. His solicitors at once sent a petition to Lord Lothian, the Scottish Secretary, seeking a reprieve on the grounds of the medical evidence and because the jury had taken so little time to reconsider their verdict after being sent back by Lord Young following his rejection of their first decision. For good measure, they threw in the fact that Bury's mother had suffered from insanity. None of it cut any ice in Edinburgh and the plea for clemency was swiftly turned down, a decision that was met with little surprise in Dundee. Police chiefs in the city, who had earlier written to their counterparts in Scotland Yard detailing their suspicions that the man they held in their cells might indeed be the notorious Jack the Ripper the Yard so eagerly sought, penned a second letter, no reply having been received to the first. This time they wrote of the strong feeling in the Dundee community that the Ripper was in their midst. When a response was finally sent by the Metropolitan Police, it was not what was expected in Scotland. The detectives hunting the London maniac, headed by Inspector Frederick Abberline, had enquired into the Dundee allegations but concluded that Bury was not connected to the Whitechapel killings. The curt dismissal of the theory that Jack the Ripper had at last been locked up, even if for an apparently unconnected murder, was surprisingly easily accepted in Dundee, perhaps because it was assumed that the Scotland Yard detective teams were much superior to those on the banks of the River Tay. In all probability, it may have had more to do with the fact that Abberline had a different suspect in mind and seemed blinkered at that time to the possibility that it might be someone else – particularly a person totally unknown to him and who had been arrested by a rival police force.

In the days leading up to his execution, Bury continued to receive regular visits from the Rev. Edward John Gough of St Paul's Episcopal Church in Dundee, whom he had called on shortly after arriving in the city – seemingly in the hope that the clergyman could find him work. He and Ellen had even attended a service in St Paul's within days of arriving in Dundee. Bury had remained in loose contact with Gough and the minister had given evidence on the Englishman's behalf at his trial. On 19 April, just five days before he was due to hang, Bury received another visit from Gough, but this time their conversation extended well beyond their usual religious topics. Haltingly, the man whose time was fast ebbing away told the minister he wanted to confess to the murder of Ellen and then, on the insistence of Gough, he put his account of how he had committed the murder down on paper. The confession was later posted to Scottish Secretary, Lord Lothian.

Bury's final day started unspectacularly. After going to bed the previous evening at ten o'clock, he slept well until being awakened at five in the morning with a cup of tea. For the next hour he sat reading his Bible, then in a calm voice he told the warder in charge, 'This is my last morning on earth. I freely forgive all who have given false evidence against me at my trial, as I hope God will forgive me,' adding that he was resigned to his fate. Later, after a breakfast of tea, toast and poached eggs, he smoked and told the officers who sat with him that he had been grateful for their decent treatment of him.

The minister, Gough, arrived at 7.15 a.m. and the pair spent half an hour in quiet conversation before the execution procession of prison governor, two Dundee bailies, two other ministers and six wardens assembled at the door of the cell. Bury was anxious to go to his maker smartly dressed and had discarded his prison outfit in favour of his own dark trousers, twill shooting coat and shirt with a white linen collar and fashionable blue tie.

The meticulously attired little man with less than an hour left to live would not have believed what was happening outside. In Bell Street and Lochee Road, beside the city-centre prison, the crowds had been assembling from daylight. As 8 a.m. approached, over 5,000 people had gathered, though there would be nothing for them to see since a rough shed had been erected round the scaffold within the prison to prevent the coming spectacle from becoming a peep-show (much to the distress of some would-be entrepreneurs who had hoped to sell vantage points in a high building in Lochee Road).

When Bury came face to face with his executioner, James Berry, the pair shook hands and Bury was asked if he had anything that he wanted to say. He replied that he wanted to thank all the prison staff for their kindness during his incarceration, then, in some-thing of an understatement, he remarked to Berry, 'You have a very disagreeable task to perform.' The hangman replied that it had to be done, but he would ensure that it would be carried out in the least painful way possible. Then he removed Bury's best tie and slipped a white hood over his head to prevent him from getting a sight of the scaffold. During his twelve-yard walk from the condemned cell to the noose, Bury was said to have been the most calm and relaxed person present. His only outward sign that anything unusual was happening to him came when his arms were pinioned to his sides, at which he clenched both fists.

Then, at 8 a.m. precisely, the trapdoor shot open and, with Gough's prayers ringing in his ears, the brutal wife-killer who could seem so mild mannered plunged six feet and six inches to his death. He died instantaneously, his neck snapping and his head falling limp onto his left shoulder.

At that exact moment the clock on the Old Steeple clock a few hundred yards away chimed the hour and the huge crowd fell silent. People only began to stir again when a black flag was run up the prison flagpole, signalling that the execution had taken place. For the following fifteen minutes the prison bell tolled. It was never to be heard in the same manner again, for William Henry Bury, who had first set foot in Dundee only three months earlier, was the last man to hang in Dundee. His remains still lie within the precincts of the new police headquarters that occupy the site, his grave marked with a small stone simply engraved 'W. H. B.'

Could the apparently timid little man who so calmly went to the gallows really have been the same monster who stalked the back streets of London's East End and outwitted Scotland Yard's finest detectives? Might the London Ripper more accurately have been known not as Jack but as Bill?

The passage of so much time means it is unlikely that anyone will ever know for sure and there are now many more suspects than there were mutilated victims of Jack the Ripper. But William

Bury comes high on the list of some Ripperologists – the amateur sleuths around the world who have written millions of words advancing their own particular theory about the maniac who terrorised a city and went on to become a legendary figure, even more fascinating now than he was more than a century ago.

Bury may merely have been what Inspector Abbeline of Scotland Yard dismissed him as: a violent drunkard who married a poorly educated woman for her money then killed her in a rage; a one-off domestic murderer. If, indeed, he had been the same man who had such a pathological and lethal interest in prostitutes, would he not also have confessed to their murders when he knew his last day was nigh, just as he had unburdened himself about Ellen?

Maybe. But there is no escaping that a strong circumstantial case can just as easily be made to indict him. Why, for example, did he so dramatically set sail from London with his belongings to start a new life in a city hundreds of miles away where he had never previously set foot? If there was no particular reason to take him to Dundee, a fair conclusion is that he was fleeing London and wished to put many miles between his past there and his new future. But what was he fleeing from? A string of unsolved murders?

Bury was certainly familiar with the activities of the whores of Whitechapel, the chosen victims of the Ripper, and had even married a woman who had worked as a brothel maid. He was clearly a man of violence, who slept with a knife under his pillow and who savagely ripped his wife apart to such an extent that her bowels protruded. He had, too, trained as a horse butcher. The slight figure could also be calm and methodical, a plotter who could forge a business letter to help induce his wife to abandon her friends and relatives in her native city. While the attack on the unfortunate Ellen was frenzied and brutal, it might not have been as spontaneous as it appeared. Some hours earlier, in complete sobriety, did he not visit the Police Court in Dundee and intently follow proceedings, then a short time later go on to coolly purchase the cord which he used to strangle his victim? The foul deed committed, he behaved perfectly normally for almost a week, even using the impromptu coffin he had fashioned to play dominoes on. When he finally went to the police with his strange story of how his bride of less than a year had met her death, one of the first things he said was that he was afraid he might be mistaken for Jack the Ripper, just as a few hours earlier, during his visits to pub acquaintance David Walker, the Ripper had been a topic of conversation.

Bury may have been religiously devout, attending church within days of settling in the city and spending much of his last days on earth reading the Bible. Yet he did not recoil from packing the mutilated corpse of his wife into a makeshift coffin which also contained the New Testament, and prayer and hymn books. His religious zeal might even have formed an integral part of the split personality he so frequently revealed.

What of all the jewellery he carried in his pockets when he called at police headquarters? It was identified as having belonged to the tragic Ellen Bury, purchased even before she had first met the man who would so horribly end her life. But might some of it, such as the two rings Bury wore on the little fingers of each hand, not have once belonged to the women who had been the victims of Jack the Ripper? In the same way as some of the serial killers who have followed in the century since the London atrocities, did Bury collect his 'trophies' and treasure them?

There can be no disputing the strong similarities in how Ellen and the Whitechapel victims – some, or all, of whom might have been known to her – came to end their days. Just like those who met their fate in the back alleys of the East End, Ellen was first strangled then mutilated with a knife, though the 'surgical' skills might have been better in London. The diminutive man, whose own life ended with a rope round his neck, may have had what he considered a compelling reason for throttling his wife. If Ellen had known or suspected that the man she so quickly became infatuated with was indeed the Ripper, and had colluded with him to flee London for a fresh start hundreds of miles away, might she not also have threatened to expose him after some argument? In that scenario, Bury's premeditation in buying the cord he would use to dispose of her becomes quite reasonable.

Or was there another explanation why he so callously took Ellen's life? Did the occupant of 113 Princes Street, Dundee, suffer from an inherited madness of the kind which had brought about the incarceration of his mother in a lunatic asylum more than twenty years earlier? Or was there a disturbance of his mind induced by venereal disease contracted from a Whitechapel whore, just as many believe was the trigger for Jack the Ripper's outrages?

There is something else. The Ripper had just five certain victims. There were none prior to Bury's stay in London and none after he and his unfortunate wife mysteriously set sail for a new life in Dundee.

6

DEATH IN THE SUBURBS

There was no doubt she was dead. She lay in her night attire on the bedroom floor just behind the door and it was clear she'd been there for some time. Those who saw her wanted to turn away, for there was blood everywhere – in the pool that formed round her stiff body, on her face and on the bed sheets. Even the ceiling was spattered. At first it seemed simple. The elderly lady who had lived alone in the house had been attacked, bludgeoned to death in a violent assault that left her with twelve wounds to the head, two to her hands, and fractured ribs. She had been murdered. And the sixty-strong team of detectives that descended on the peaceful suburb where most of the residents were retired folk living their lives out quietly, thought so too . . . at first. The longer the inquiry went on, however, the more it transpired that all might not be quite as clear-cut as it had seemed.

Mrs Eliza Connelly was aged 74 and had been married three times. After the death of her third husband she had lived by herself in the neat single-person council house at 105 Aberdour Place, a desirable and secluded area in an out-of-the-way corner of Barnhill where the folk were friendly but reserved. There was never any trouble. It was considered a good place to have been allocated a house and hers was one in a row of identical modern cottages, all with small, manageable gardens at the rear. Mrs Connelly had recently been in hospital with a chest complaint, but had recovered well. Sometimes she grew lonely, although she had three sons, a daughter and grandchildren and was regularly visited. She never stopped being house-proud and her apartments were seldom anything but immaculate.

The last time the grey-haired widow was seen alive was at 3 p.m. on the afternoon of Sunday, 12 April 1981. Earlier that day, her eldest son Kenneth had visited. Following his departure, his mother called at the nearby home of a spinster neighbour to use her telephone. There was no reply from the friend she had wanted to speak to and the two women shared a cup of tea and a chat. Then she left. The following day her obliging neighbour knocked on Mrs Connelly's door to inform her she had tried several times to phone the friend but had been unable to make contact. When Mrs Connelly failed to come to the door, the woman placed a note through the letter-box. She noted that the house appeared to be locked up.

The next day, the Tuesday, at around 12.45 p.m., Mrs Connelly's middle son, James, arrived at the house with his wife and daughter to take his mother on one of their regular drives together. This was something he usually did on a Sunday, but had been unable to manage that weekend. When he entered the house, he instinctively knew things were not as they should be. In the living-room a chair, unusually, was hard up against the kitchenette door and the bedroom door was closed, something his mother would not normally have done. He entered the bedroom with growing trepidation but was still unprepared for what he found. The first thing he saw was the blood-soaked carpet and bed-clothes, then, just behind the door, the corpse of the woman he had planned to take on a family car outing.

Detectives were at the scene within an hour – and that was the end, for some time, of the usual uneventful existence of Aberdour Place's silver-haired residents. In the days ahead, police sniffer-dogs scoured the area with their handlers, seeking anything that might have resembled a murder weapon. More than 1,500 people were interviewed but every line of inquiry drew a blank. A post-mortem indicated that the time of death had probably been between seven o'clock on the Sunday evening and ten the following morning. Two youths, carrying bags, had been seen on a pathway close to the home of the 74-year-old widow on the Monday morning and a major appeal was launched to trace them. When they were found they were closely questioned – and eliminated from the inquiry. Other appeals for information met with an unusually poor response, specifically from taxi drivers who had been asked to come forward with details of any fares they may have had in the area over the crucial two-day period.

A few days after the launch of the murder hunt, Mrs Connelly's son James told police he believed up to £100 could have been taken from two of his mother's purses. It reinforced the view of some that the pensioner may have disturbed a sneak thief, who had reacted in panic and battered the life out of her with some kind of object. A plea for assistance was made to members of the underworld in the hope they might have been sufficiently sickened by the fate of the old woman to incriminate one of their own (as had happened following previous attacks on elderly victims). No one responded.

Senior detectives began to feel increasingly uneasy about many aspects of the inquiry. From the start it had seemed a motiveless killing. Nothing, apart from the apparent disappearance of some money, appeared to have been taken or disturbed. There was no evidence of a struggle, no trace of a weapon. Nor had there been any indication of a forced entry or exit. Every surface in the flat was painstakingly examined by forensic teams but there wasn't a single fingerprint which should not have been there. A purse with the dead woman's blood on it was found in a closed bedroom drawer. There were no unexplained prints on that either. Neighbours in the quiet suburb had neither seen nor heard anything to have caused them concern and there was an untypical dearth of witnesses of any kind.

The repeated pleas for information met with virtually no success, the poorest response many experienced murder detectives could recall. If an opportunist thief had, indeed, been responsible, why was there no evidence that drawers or cupboards had been ransacked? Why had nothing but the money been taken and why had some other money and cashable electricity stamps been left? Most crucially, would a casual thief have come armed with a weapon? If he had seized the nearest thing to hand, why was it not still in the room? Nothing that could have caused the kind of injuries inflicted on Mrs Connelly had apparently been removed from the flat. Having committed a spur-of-the-moment murder, would a sneak thief not have been in such a panic that his flight from the scene would have been witnessed, or at least some evidence of his hasty departure from the house left behind? It was also reasonable to ponder whether any house-breaker sufficiently experienced enough to leave not a single fingerprint would have bothered to enter the home of an elderly woman living alone in a council house, since the pickings were unlikely to have been particularly good. Perhaps she knew her killer, for the family thought it unlikely she would open her door to a stranger if she was dressed for bed. But if her attacker were an acquaintance, what possible motive could there have been? Too many questions remained unanswered. Too many pieces of the jigsaw did not fit. Apart from the corpse of the unfortunate Eliza Connelly, it was as though nothing had occurred to disturb the ordered, safe routine of the respectable neighbourhood. Gradually, police began to wonder whether they were investigating an unlikely, but just feasible, tragic accident instead of a murder.

A month after the grim discovery in the house at 105 Aberdour Place, police took the unusual step of submitting a report to the Procurator Fiscal containing every detail of what the exhaustive police enquiries had revealed, including the possibility that the death might have been accidental. Five weeks later, equally unexpectedly, the Fiscal, who acknowledged the intensity of the police investigation, made the surprise announcement that a fatal-accident inquiry into the circumstances would be held. Although such a hearing closely resembled the common English coroner's courts, it was an extremely rare procedure in Scotland.

Even after the fatal-accident inquiry was held, the initial findings were inconclusive. Although not ruling out the original belief that a murder had been committed, police suggested there might also be another explanation for what had occurred. A senior detective, giving evidence at the hearing, described how he had gone to the house shortly after the discovery of the body and had at first believed there had been an accident but had initiated a murder inquiry on the advice of a police surgeon and a forensic expert. He went on to recount how Mrs Connelly's home was in an extremely quiet residential area with a fairly low crime level and how there had not been a sneak-in theft there for ten years. Asked about the discovery of the purse with the victim's blood on it, he replied that he would not have expected a thief who had just committed a serious assault to take money from a purse, then close it and replace it in a drawer, which he also shut. Sneak-thieves went in and out as quickly as possible and would not waste time to see if they were lucky, he told Sheriff Graham Cox: 'They would not close any purse, then replace it in a drawer. They would examine the contents outside and then throw the purse away,' he pointed out.

Much of the hearing took place in Dundee Royal Infirmary, where the dead woman's bedroom had been reconstructed in the Department of Forensic Science. The furniture from the room was positioned to match as closely as possible the layout at Aberdour Place. Even the bloodstained bedding and a blood-soaked hairnet were in the exact spots where they had been found.

The senior detective who had gone to the house within an hour of the discovery of the body proposed that the death could have been the result of an extraordinary set of accidental circumstances. He advanced a theory supporting that view, as follows. Mrs Connelly had been ready to go to bed when she fell – as she had done in the past – between her bed and a wardrobe, striking her forehead on a chair in between. She either lay there for some time before pulling herself on to the bed, or fell back immediately and then lay on the bed, as indicated by the heavy blood-staining on the bedding. From there, the pensioner had attempted to rise but twice struck her head on the wardrobe – accounting for the curious shaped wounds on her head, caused by the doorknobs and a key.

The detective's suggested scenario continued with Mrs Connelly crawling round the floor at the edge of the bed towards the door and, in an attempt to rise, toppling back and striking the back of her head on the open drawer of a chest. Her bloody handprints indicated that she had crawled hand-over-hand round the bed, then held on to a chair. The unusual spread of blood on the walls and ceiling would have arrived there after the first fall, when the injured widow pulled off her hairnet, which had been blood-soaked. The fact that the hairnet was elasticised had caused the blood to spatter the way it had. Supporting his hypothesis in part was evidence from the dead woman's GP that she had suffered from angina for twelve years and had experienced two heart attacks in that time. It was also known that Mrs Connelly had previously been found in the house after falls.

Sheriff Cox suggested that, as an alternative to the detective's conjectures, Mrs Connelly may have sustained her assorted injuries by being thrown about.

'I could not equate the scene in the bedroom with an assault,' responded the officer. 'In these circumstances the woman could not have moved herself from one side of the bedroom to the other. Everything would have been happening in one corner.'

Asked to account for the presence of the blood on the purse in the drawer, he explained that it could have come about after Mrs Connelly had attempted to seek help after her falls. Since she had no telephone in the house, she had gone to the purse to collect her house key before departing to alert a neighbour to her plight – but had been unable to do so.

The police speculation about the events in the house that April day did not meet with any kind of agreement from the forensic scientist who had examined the body of Mrs Connelly. Dr Donald Rushton, bow-tied and peering over the top of glasses positioned on the point of his nose, was customarily categorical in his dismissal of the accident theory, saying it did not equate with the nature and severity of the wounds suffered by the victim.

'On my first visit to the scene I formed the opinion that the deceased had first been assaulted on her bed or at the wardrobe,' he said emphatically. 'Had it been accidental, none of her injuries would have spurted blood to that degree. For them to have been caused by her hairnet it would have had to have been a forcible or frantic removal.' He thought the dead woman could have been assaulted on the bed, then she might have recovered sufficiently to have crawled round it to the place where her body was eventually found. His conclusion was that the majority of her wounds indicated that she had been severely assaulted about the head with a hard object – the sort of which he could not identify – and, in attempting to defend herself, had sustained two injuries to the backs of her hands. Dr Rushton expressed his unhappiness with the idea of the circumstances being explained away as an accident, dismissing the assumptions as implausible and insufficient on medical grounds.

'The injuries were too severe and there were too many of them,' he said. 'There were fifteen separate impacts on the body.' He admitted that a fitter, younger person might have survived the attack.

Nothing was said at the inquiry, however, to provide any kind of explanation for the lack of signs of a disturbance or forced entry or exit. Nor could anyone account for the absence of unidentified fingerprints. One spot of blood had been found outside the bedroom, on the door inside the living-room leading to the hallway, but that did not produce a foreign print either.

The conclusion of the evidence at the inquiry presented the Sheriff with a dilemma. He had two widely differing opinions of what might have happened in the pensioner's flat, each coming from men eminent in their fields but each leaving many questions unanswered. He adjourned the hearing to seek the views of a second medical expert, saying this was the only safe way to deliver a judgement which would be fair to the police, Dr Rushton and Mrs Connelly's family. It was acknowledged, however, that any new evidence would be based on the available written reports, photographs and interviews and not on first-hand experience of the death scene or the body.

Two months later, Professor Arthur Harland of Glasgow University told the resumed fatal-accident inquiry that he supported the opinion of Dr Rushton, saying he believed the twelve injuries to the pensioner's head could only have been sustained by repeated blows 'of quite unusual violence'. He dismissed the idea of the blood trails on the ceiling having been caused by Mrs Connelly removing her hairnet, but admitted they were likely to have arrived there by someone swinging the hairnet – or a weapon.

Sheriff Cox proceeded to find that Mrs Connelly's sad death had been no accident, the 'balance of probabilities' showing that it had resulted from a sustained and violent assault upon her and that she had died around 7.15 p.m. on the evening of Sunday, 12 April.

It was a verdict which met with the approval of Mrs Connelly's family, who had believed from the start that the elderly woman who lived quietly in the pleasant suburb had been murdered by a chance intruder or intruders. Their supposition was that she had been assaulted and forced to hand over money and, after her attackers demanded more cash, she was hit again because they suspected she may have had additional funds secreted away.

Her son Kenneth, who had visited the house that afternoon, told a reporter that after the finding of his mother's body, it was noted that the curtain on the toilet window had been closed, something Mrs Connelly never did because she was too small to reach. That may have been of considerable significance. The window was located next to the front door and visible to anyone passing. Did her killer or killers close the curtain so they could, undisturbed, remove any traces of blood from their person? Or was it because a mystery visitor, who may have been known to the occupant, had stayed long enough to require the use of the bathroom? The drawing of the curtain might even have been the act of a woman, through modesty or because of natural feminine instincts which demanded neatness, a word that in so many ways could have described much – such as the replacement of the blood-stained purse into the drawer – of what went on at 105 Aberdour Place that April evening.

It was one more awkward piece to the jigsaw that, even after an extensive murder inquiry, fatal-accident inquiry and the passage of almost quarter of a century, no one is any closer to piecing together.

7

EIGHTEEN HOURS

Eighteen hours. Not even a day. In a lifetime, a blink of an eye. A fleeting, forgotten moment in time that blurs with a million other hours . . . unless you are one of those unaccountably selected by fate that makes it seem like an eternity. Then you may be left with memories so indelible and so painful they accompany you to the grave.

That was how it was for Charles Smith and his wife Sarah, when a Saturday in May 1971, that started so unexceptionally, turned into a lingering journey through the worst kind of hell. Even when the first fateful component that would change their lives forever entered into the day there was nothing to set it apart.

Late in the afternoon, while the couple were watching an England-Scotland football match on television, a knock on the door of their tenement flat in Broughty Ferry Road interrupted the couple's viewing. The visitor was Charles Shepherd, a 24-year-old acquaintance who lived a mile away and who had called to apologise for an earlier argument. Generously, 33-year-old Mr Smith says to forget about the incident and invites him in. Shepherd is pleased at his reception and, as a gesture of goodwill, announces that he has £4 which he will use to buy drink for the trio. As a further token of his appreciation, he takes Sharon, Mrs Smith's eight-year-old daughter by a previous marriage, and her friend of the same age, to the off-licence with him. They return 15 minutes later, Shepherd having purchased a bottle of wine, a few tins of beer and cigarettes.

After a few drinks, the mood has mellowed further and the visitor makes another friendly offer. If the young girls would like it, he would be happy to take them for runs round the block on the red and white Lambretta scooter he'd arrived on. The eight-year-olds are thrilled at the prospect and Mr and Mrs Smith willingly yield to their excited pleas for permission to make the trips.

Shortly afterwards, Shepherd and his young passengers return to the flat. The girls are animated about their experience and immediately request another spin on the magical scooter. They depart once more and at around 4.45 p.m. Shepherd and Sharon come back without the other youngster, who has gone home for tea. Sharon is even more elated. Shepherd has bought her a bag of butternut sweets. Politely, she offers them to her parents. The mood in the house is jovial, even though the football international has ended with a 3–1 defeat for Scotland.

Half an hour later, with the excitement of her previous journeys on the scooter still the main topic of the little redhead's conversation, Shepherd volunteers to give her one more ride on the Lambretta. The pair set off from the flat once again and as Sharon disappears down the tenement stairs her bubbling laughter rings in her parents' ears.

It is 5.15 p.m. It is also the last time they would hear the joyous sound and the last time they would ever see her alive.

At around 6 p.m. Shepherd returns to the house. He is alone and, in answer to the Smiths' questions about their daughter's whereabouts, he casually explains that he had dropped her off at nearby newsagent's shop where she met up with a chum. He is relaxed and converses freely.

But 34-year-old Mrs Smith is alarmed after noting that his clothing is dishevelled and his shirt is stained with what appears to be blood. Anxiously, she suggests to her husband that the police should be called.

He, too, is apprehensive but in order not to alarm his wife further, conceals his fears and attempts to play down Sharon's non-arrival. Mrs Smith is not appeased and her husband finally accedes to her plea. Eager to be of assistance, Shepherd offers to take Mr Smith round to the nearest police box on the Lambretta. They set off with Mr Smith on the pillion seat his stepdaughter had occupied less than an hour earlier. As events of the next 17 hours start to unfold, that seemingly natural occurrence takes on a surreal aspect.

After he has dropped his passenger off at the police box, Shepherd says he will tour the neighbourhood for Sharon and drives off. Meanwhile, Mr Smith and the officer he's spoken to agree to delay an official search for half an hour to allow the missing girl more time to return home.

Back at the house, Mrs Smith is even more fearful but reluctantly accepts the proposal to defer the launch of the search. When Shepherd shows up at the flat again to say he can find no trace of Sharon, the air of despondency in the house deepens. At exactly 6.30 p.m. Mr Smith returns to the police box to ask for the search to commence.

Bizarrely, almost immediately it becomes a double hunt. As the last known person to have seen Sharon, police are anxious to speak to Shepherd. But he, too, has vanished. A general alert goes out to every officer on duty in the city to look out for him and his red and white Lambretta, registration number 69 BSR.

Two hours after the launch of the search, a constable radios in to headquarters to say he has located the scooter in Robertson Street, less than half a mile from Sharon's home. Detectives hurry to the scene and examine the Lambretta. They lift the saddle and check the toolbox stored underneath. What they discover is as unexpected as it is grim. The first thing they see is an old-fashioned open razor – and it is blood-stained.

The inferences are obvious and efforts to locate Shepherd and little Sharon are intensified. While other officers scour the area, a special plain-clothes team lie in wait near the scooter which has been left in place. Some two hours later, their patience is rewarded when Shepherd arrives and prepares to drive off. He is immediately detained and when detectives note he smells strongly of alcohol the 24-year-old confesses to have been drinking most of the evening. It is the only admission he makes. Held at head-quarters, he is questioned at length but says he has no knowledge of the whereabouts of the pretty child he'd taken for scooter rides that late afternoon.

At midnight, the head of CID, Superintendent William Melville, contacts the media to issue an appeal for the public to report any sightings they may have had of either Sharon or the scooter. One of those who takes his call is a late duty *Sunday Post* reporter who departs at once to interview Mrs Smith. She is distressed but anx-ious to plead for any assistance people can offer to help find her daughter. Then, through her tears, she makes a stunning admis-sion. She says she fears she will never see her little girl alive again and names Shepherd as the person responsible. She even furnishes the astonished young reporter with his address.

Down at police HQ in Bell Street, the man she accuses continues to be unhelpful and protests his innocence, claiming that the last time he saw Sharon was when he dropped her off at the shop close to her home.

The search for the missing child continues through the night and when daylight breaks at 4 a.m. reinforcements arrive to bolster numbers. Police and special constables from Angus and Perth join volunteers from the Territorial Army, Royal Navy Reserve and youth organisations. As Dundee stirs into wakefulness, more and more people join in the hunt for Sharon. Soon, 400 people are checking outhouses and back gardens all over the city. With noth-ing to go on, the search area extends in every direction. It is the biggest hunt ever undertaken in the region. Police dogs are brought in and a helicopter is put on stand-by in the hope that the damp, misty weather lifts. Members of the WRVS and other groups arrive early to provide tea and hot soup for the searchers, many of whom have toiled all night. Their task is made worse when heavy rain starts to fall. Among those in the search parties is a jacketless Mr Smith who is advised by police to return home to await news.

At the same time as the city was being systematically scoured overnight, other police staff prepared special posters and pamphlets bearing Sharon's photograph and details of the Lambretta and the time she was last seen. They are distributed at daybreak to those who have been asleep and unaware of the Saturday-night-Sunday-morning drama being played out. At the same time, loudspeaker vehicles tour Dundee broadcasting appeals for help. Radio news bulletins carry items about the missing girl and others learn of her disappearance when they read the heartbreaking plea of her mother in the *Sunday Post*.

Altogether, it is an unprecedented plea for public assistance – and it pays off. Shortly after 8 a.m., a woman living in Baxter Park Terrace, about quarter of a mile from the Smiths' home, hears a radio appeal which jolts her memory. She recalls seeing a scooter pass her house as she sat at a window the evening before. The more she thinks about it, the more she is convinced that the 'pretty girl with the bonnie red hair' was Sharon. She visualises the scene as the scooter passed by, heading north, and recollects smiling because the little girl's legs were too short for her feet to reach the footrests.

It is enough for the main thrust of the search to be concentrated on the north and east ends of town and the deputy head of CID, Chief Inspector John Bell, then decides to play a hunch. He remembers that as a youth Shepherd had lived close to Linlathen Estate, a large open area between Baldovie and Claypots, and he directs large detachments of the search teams there. It is a rewarding tactic.

While the drenching rain continues unabated, two police officers decide to check a small, disused War Department brick building standing in isolation on the estate. The sight which greets them is so ghastly that they are moved to tears. Sharon lies sprawled on the floor. She is partially clothed and her throat has been viciously slashed.

It is 11.15 a.m. and 18 hours since her excited laughter sounded on the stairs of her home where she said goodbye to her parents for the last time.

Charles Hampton Shepherd continued to deny any knowledge of how eight-year-old Sharon's short life had ended so barbarously. But even as he appeared briefly in court the next morning charged with her murder, evidence was stacking up against him. The citizens of Dundee, who had responded so spontaneously and wholeheartedly in the search for the little girl, reacted just as unstintingly to police appeals about the movements of a Lambretta scooter, registration number 69 BSR.

Outraged at the details of her death, numerous people came forward to incriminate Shepherd by saying they had witnessed Sharon being taken on her final journey. All clearly remembered the slender figure in the green cardigan and with the bright red hair sitting on the pillion seat holding on to the young man driving. The pair had been seen all along the route, almost from the moment they had set off until turning at the crossroads in the direction of the scene of her death.

One male witness was particularly helpful. He had previously been a neighbour of the Smiths and had no difficulty in recognising Sharon. He went further and identified the scooter as belonging positively to Shepherd because it bore the name of the accused man's favourite pop group, The Who, in bold black and gold letters.

Tests on the bloodstains found on the old-fashioned open razor discovered in the toolbag of the scooter establish later that the blood group is the same as Sharon's – a different one from Shepherd's.

Yet, despite the overwhelming case built against him, the 24-year-old continued to persist in claiming his innocence.

It was not until two months later, on 14 July 1971, when he appeared at the High Court in Dundee to stand trial, that he finally confessed to his fiendish behaviour. Dressed garishly in a bright yellow jerkin and brown slacks, and chewing gum throughout his short court appearance, he sullenly admitted raping and murdering the little girl who had excitedly asked to be taken for trips on his scooter.

The judge, Lord Emslie, could barely conceal his disgust for the long-haired killer. Telling him he had pleaded guilty to charges of 'unparalleled savagery', he jailed him for life, adding tersely, 'I won't waste words in heaping on you the condemnation that society feels for you.'

With that judgement ringing in his ears, Charles Hampton Shepherd was led from the dock and out of the public gaze, his long incarceration never to feel as endless as the eighteen hours endured by an anguished family.

8

COLLARED

His name was Andrew Hunter and some who knew him thought him a 'perfect gentleman'. He was a member of the Salvation Army, a caring father and a social worker who dealt with needy and problem children . . .

His name was Andrew Hunter and he was a perverted bisexual and ruthless killer who believed he could outwit the police. Some who knew him thought him an 'evil man of exceptional depravity'. . .

Andrew Hunter was all of those things – and much more, for he had many faces and no one saw them all, not even the trio of women in his life who all met untimely deaths in unusual circumstances.

There was little to set him apart from other young men when he moved to live in Dundee in 1977, except for his apparent devotion to God, for not many 26-year-olds would leave their wives in another city to work in a Salvation Army citadel. It was an arrangement that neither of them found unusual, however: Christine, whom he had married four years earlier, was also a Salvationist and supported him in his efforts to carve a career in social work activities. She was eleven years his senior and something of a mother figure for the young man from Paisley who had led a troubled life before their meeting. He had been abandoned by his father after his mother died when he was just three weeks old, leaving him to be brought up by a caring aunt who welcomed his interest in the Salvation Army. It was in that organisation that he met Christine and they married quietly in the Falkirk Citadel. When he moved to Dundee to take up his new post, he initially lived alone in a flat in the city while she remained at home in Elderslie in Glasgow. They resumed living together after he landed a job as an unqualified social worker attached to children's homes in the city.

The couple had a son and together the family moved into a house in Broadford Terrace, in a fashionable estate in Broughty Ferry. Outwardly, at least, life in suburbia seemed routine and settled for the Hunters. He continued with his work in children's homes across the city and in his off-duty time studied for qualifications which would further his social work career. Then, in October 1984, something happened which was to have a dramatic effect on the lives of numerous other unconnected people. Hunter embarked on an affair with pretty Lynda Cairns, a 27-year-old social worker who lived in the same street, in the house directly opposite. She had been helping him out with his studies and at the time resided with Dr Ian Glover, a 42-year-old college lecturer who had been her lover. That affair had cooled and although they continued to live together in the house they had jointly purchased, they did so as friends with separate rooms. It was Dr Glover who had introduced her to Andrew Hunter.

Lynda had led a life devoted to helping others. As a young girl she had been a Girl Guide leader and as she matured she became a Samaritan in Aberdeen, where she did teacher training. After a spell teaching mentally handicapped children, she moved to London to work with others with mental disabilities. It was only when her father's health deteriorated that she returned to Scotland to be nearer her ailing parents in Glenrothes. In 1980 she took a job as a social worker in Dundee, continuing her voluntary duties as a Samaritan.

This attractive young woman who had spent so much of her life living in different cities, first of all in Singapore and then throughout Britain as the daughter of a regular serviceman in the Royal Air Force, and later as a student in Edinburgh and Aberdeen, was at the stage in her life where she longed for a serious relationship and children. Her neighbour, Hunter, was a married man and not ideal, but Lynda became quickly drawn to his charming ways and their shared interest in social work and others less fortunate than themselves. And he was extremely appreciative of her assistance with his studies.

Soon they were in the midst of a torrid affair, with a varied and adventurous sex life forming a major part of the attraction for both of them. Dr Glover accepted the end of what had become just a platonic friendship with Lynda, but Christine Hunter reacted much less calmly when, at Christmas 1984, her husband confessed to her that he was involved in a passionate affair with the woman across the street who was seventeen years her junior. She pleaded with him to terminate the relationship and Hunter grudgingly agreed. But after a few weeks the association between the two social workers resumed and that summer Lynda moved into a cottage she had bought in Carnoustie. A short time later, Hunter walked out of his home in Broughty Ferry to live with her. And that should have been the end of the story. Up to that stage, the threads of the relationships were fairly unremarkable – man gets married at a young age to an older woman, meets attractive and much younger neighbour in a bungalow estate who has tired of her former lover, and an affair begins, culminating with the two main players moving in together. It was the type of scenario played out time and again in corners of Dundee in the 1980s – unexceptional and of little interest to all but the families involved and the neighbours in the estates peeking out from behind their curtains.

Eleven days before Christmas that same year the residents of Broadford Terrace, who had become used to seeing Andrew Hunter returning to his former home at No. 12 to take his son out, had something much more interesting than usual to observe. Father and son – returning from a visit to the cinema – stood on the doorstep of the modern, semi-detached villa, apparently unable to gain access. Christine's car was in the drive, the lights were on, and music could just be heard coming from the house, so it seemed she was at home. After a few minutes Dr Glover, still living opposite, received a visit from Hunter, who asked to use his phone to call his estranged wife so that she might open the door. The call was made. No one replied. Then Hunter, seemingly becoming more agitated, departed, saying he would borrow a key to the house from another neighbour who kept one in case of emergency – which this was beginning to look like. A few moments later, Hunter used the borrowed key to enter his former home, closely followed by his 11-year-old son.

The modern house was open plan. As he called out Christine's name, Hunter glanced towards the loft area and saw her hanging from a rafter, a TV cable wrapped tightly round her neck. She was long past the stage where she might be revived.

No one knows for certain precisely what happened that winter's day in the once-happy home of the two Salvationists. According to Hunter, Christine had earlier dropped their son off at the children's home where he worked and when Hunter had finished his shift, father and son went off to the cinema. Afterwards they travelled to Carnoustie for tea with Lynda, staying for a few hours before he took the youngster back home to Broughty Ferry. It appeared that in the interval the distraught Christine, unable to come to terms with her husband's betrayal and abandonment of their marriage, had finally succumbed to depression and had taken her own life. This was a credible explanation for the sad end to her existence and no one questioned it, least of all those who had intimate knowledge of the events of the previous ten months. For nearly two years they did not doubt the account of that pre-Christmas tragedy. Then, as other dramas began to unfold, the curtain-twitchers started to whisper their doubts to each other. But that lay ahead. New horrors were soon to consume the life of Andrew Hunter.

For whatever reason, Christine's disturbing death signalled a change in the relationship he had with Lynda. It had never been as close, anyway, as she might have imagined, for while he was seeing her – and at the time he was living apart from his wife – Hunter had also embarked on a second affair. It was with another social worker, a 26-year-old colleague with whom he worked, and their sexual relationship lasted for at least a month. Instead of Christine's demise bringing him closer to Lynda, it seemed to drive a wedge between them. They intermittently lived apart, Hunter moving for spells back into the former family home in Broadford Terrace. Their liaison, always volatile and highly dependent on sex, became marked by increasing acts of violence by Hunter – starting just two days after the discovery of Christine's body hanging in the loft, when he assaulted Lynda in a busy and very public car park. That attack was sparked during an argument when Lynda had apparently remarked that there was no need for Hunter to attend Christine's funeral. On another occasion, in her house in Carnoustie, Hunter struck Lynda in the face with an umbrella. Then, after an incident in his house at Broadford Terrace, Lynda was forced to attend hospital to be examined after Hunter had severely twisted her arm and pushed her out of the house, throwing her handbag after her. The worst assault occurred some seven weeks after Christine's death, resulting in Lynda notifying the police, though no charges were brought against her explosive husband.

It seemed that Hunter blamed Lynda for the death of his wife and he would shout at her, 'It should be you that's dead, not Christine.' Both of them became visitors to hospital at various times, Hunter requiring psychiatric treatment for some four months after confessing to suicidal tendencies, and Lynda being detained for a week, apparently after accidentally taking an overdose of sleeping tablets while depressed over the state of the floundering romance and the postponement of their wedding plans. Yet, despite their differences, the couple could not keep away from each other for long. One night, while they were apart, Hunter telephoned Lynda seventeen times. During another estrangement, he called three times within hours of her arriving back home from a holiday with her sister in Corfu.

For better or worse, they decided to wed and on 1 November 1986, they walked down the aisle in picturesque Barry Church, near their home. They rode in a horse-drawn carriage and Hunter, complete with Bible in hand, wore full Highland regalia. The first night of the honeymoon was spent in a four-poster bed in romantic Fernie Castle, in Fife, followed by a holiday in Israel. It seemed their feuding was finally behind them and for a time the marriage, outwardly at least, was a happy one, Hunter boasting that they made love on a daily basis. It was later to emerge that that side of the partnership was extremely adventurous and unconventional, particularly between a Salvationist and a Samaritan. But those closest to Lynda were happy that her new husband's aggression towards her seemed to have subsided, though some had anxieties he had taken Lynda for his wife more to provide a mother for his son than for any deep desire to share a life with her in the cottage at Carnoustie which had become their home.

Hunter gradually began to tire of the marriage, however, and his extravagant sexual appetite took him once more in unusual directions. He secretly resumed a relationship with a gay lover he had met more than a decade earlier in a Paisley sauna, at the same time forming liaisons with a string of prostitutes and paying them for their varied services. Soon he was spending more time apart from Lynda than with her and some believed his old hostility was starting to reappear in the marriage.

Nine months after their high-profile wedding, the couple received the news that Lynda had been desperate to hear – she was pregnant. The prospect of becoming a mother delighted her. Hunter was less pleased, considering an addition to the family as an obstruction to his ever-more bizarre lifestyle.

On 13 August 1987, Lynda travelled to Glenrothes to break the good news of her condition to her younger sister Sandra, who had been bridesmaid at the wedding. Yet, despite her obvious pleasure of impending motherhood, Lynda was troubled. She revealed that although she and her husband both had the day and night off the following Friday, and despite her frequently feeling sick because of the pregnancy, Hunter had chosen not to spend that forthcoming evening with her, preferring instead to go to a works night out. They agreed that Sandra would keep Lynda company in Carnoustie while Hunter shared the evening with his colleagues. It was, however, a meeting that never took place. Indeed, the sisters never saw each other again.

On the bright, sunny morning of 21 August, Lynda and Andrew Hunter – the two social workers who on occasions could not get enough of each other but who also shared a troubled and stormy past – argued for the last time. Lynda, who had been unwell the previous day, was still off-colour with morning sickness and they rowed about Hunter's determination to attend the night out regardless of her feelings. At 10.15 a.m. they went together to the local health centre and a nearby chemist shop for assistance for Lynda, before returning home. Half an hour later, they drove away from the cottage in Lynda's Vauxhall Cavalier Antibes. With them in the vehicle was Shep, the ailing 14-year-old cross-bred terrier Lynda had bought seven years earlier from the city pound to save it from being put down. There were no witnesses, apart from Shep, to precisely what had happened during the previous thirty minutes in the house, but it seemed that yet another dispute erupted between husband and wife and Lynda said she wanted to go to her parents' home in Glenrothes in Fife, some thirty miles away. Hunter insisted on taking her but, before departing, phoned his social work supervisor to say he would be late to keep an appointment, explaining that his wife required the car and he would be forced to use the bus.

It is unclear when murder first entered Andrew Hunter's mind. It may already have done so. But within an hour of leaving Carnoustie that is the exact act he committed. On a quiet road in Fife, he pulled the white Vauxhall hatchback off the highway, parked in a quiet spot near a wood and turned to face his pregnant and unhappy wife. Then, after another brief angry exchange with her, he reached for the lead of the mongrel terrier lying across the back seat and wound it round both hands – then round the throat of the terrified Lynda. She lost consciousness within seconds and died almost immediately afterwards. Less than two miles from the scene lay Fernie Castle, the smart hotel where months earlier the two had shared such a joyous first night of marriage.

A sudden urgency overtook the wife-killer. If he was to avoid detection, he knew he had to dispose of the body which lay slumped in the seat beside him, and quickly, for anyone might pass without warning. He left the car, hurried to the passenger side, then lifted the body of his dead wife from the vehicle. With the kind of unexpected strength found only in moments of desperate need, Hunter surprised himself at the comparative ease with which he picked the corpse of poor Lynda up into his arms. He walked with her off the rough track where the car lay, then picked his way awkwardly through the forest for thirty metres. At a concealed thicket, he lowered Lynda to the ground at what he hoped would be her last resting place. Then he drove quickly back in the direction of Dundee. A few miles further along the road Hunter stopped the white Vauxhall, removed the collar from around Shep's neck, then put the devoted pet out of the car. As the man who had just committed murder resumed his journey to Dundee, Shep gazed at the back of the disappearing vehicle, as bewildered as it is possible for a dog to be.

What took place the rest of that day demonstrated with absolute clarity that 'cool, calculating killers' do indeed exist. Hunter's actions spoke eloquently of that species. Shortly after noon he walked calmly into Strathmore House residential home to drop off with his supervising social work officer an essay that was required as part of his studies to become qualified. He explained his warm and sweaty appearance as being a result of having walked up from the centre of Dundee after getting off a bus from Carnoustie. A short time later he briefly visited his own place of work at Ann Street children's home, then left after after a few minutes, saying he would spend the rest of his day off in the garden but promising to meet up with his colleagues later that evening at the works night out. Back in the city centre, he withdrew £150 from his building society account before returning to the family home at Carnoustie.

Sometime around 3 p.m. Lynda's sister Sandra arrived at the cottage for the get-together the two young women had arranged a week earlier. Hunter explained that he and Lynda had fallen out and she had departed mid-morning to travel to her parents' home in Glenrothes, taking Shep with her. He thought she might return at any time and coolly suggested that while they wait they should sit in the garden, enjoying the warm August afternoon sunshine. Later, the pair visited the health centre in Carnoustie where Hunter asked if there was a prescription waiting for his wife. Told there wasn't, he declined the offer of an appointment for her with a doctor later in the day, saying he believed she 'had something planned'. Then Hunter took the woman whose sister he had so callously strangled a few hours earlier for a game of putting before they had tea in a nearby hotel. Sandra, a little anxious but confident her sister would ultimately arrive back home, departed at around 7 p.m. when Hunter explained he would be leaving for his night out in about an hour's time.

As arranged previously, a neighbour gave him a lift into town shortly after 8 p.m., dropping him off at the Celtic Club in Hilltown where his social work colleagues had gathered for the farewell party for a workmate. Although his mind must have been in turmoil about the events of the day, Andrew Hunter was a picture of composure for the next two and a half hours, appearing relaxed and affable, even posing with a wide smile on his face while a photograph was taken of him with two female workmates. Few noticed that throughout the evening he drank very little. Shortly before 11 p.m. his obliging neighbour returned to take Hunter home. On the way, the man who had killed spoke easily about his enjoyment in the club but admitted that he felt a little troubled about the row he had with Lynda that morning and her non-arrival home. Back at Carnoustie, Hunter bade his neighbour good night and disappeared into the High Street cottage.

He did not go to bed. Less than an hour later, he furtively slipped out of the house and made his way through the darkness to the spot in town where he had parked the Vauxhall some twelve hours earlier. Then he drove through the night, headed south. No one who glanced at the driver would have known him, then or again, for Hunter by now was wearing a woman's blonde wig. It was not the type of disguise completely unknown to him. Once, at a Hallowe'en fancy dress party at the children's home where he worked, he had turned up dressed as a woman, complete with wig, fish-net stockings and suspender belt. He had been asked to leave.

After an hour the car lumbered to a noisy halt. Moments after crossing the Forth Road Bridge, and while heading for the route to England, a wheel of the Vauxhall punctured on a roundabout. Cursing his ill-fortune, Hunter threw off the wig and hurried to change the wheel. After being given assistance by the driver of a passing van, the anxious killer resumed his flight at ever-greater speed.

His bizarre journey ended some 300 miles away in Manchester, where he abandoned the car in Dale Street. At 7.35 a.m., the female wig long since discarded, he boarded a train to take him back to Scotland. After a change in Glasgow he arrived back in Dundee at midday and went to a city-centre shop, where he bought a pair of trainers as a birthday present for his son, then had a haircut. It wasn't until seven o'clock that night that he finally reported his wife missing. By then he was confident the trail would lead away from him. Besides, he had the perfect alibi. Hadn't he been at a farewell party the night before, not arriving home in a neighbour's car until almost midnight, and the next morning gone shopping in town? The electronically timed and dated receipt for the trainers he'd bought could prove conclusively that he had been in Timpson's shoeshop in Murraygate at precisely 1.06 p.m. Hunter had also been cunning enough to abandon the car on double yellow lines in Manchester so that it would attract a parking ticket. That happened within hours of him hurrying away from it, at 9.10 a.m., and when police went to the vehicle the following day they found it had also been broken into. It all helped to establish the methodical killer's apparent alibi.

It didn't take police long to begin suspecting that there might be reasons for not simply treating the disappearance of the relatively recently married social worker as a missing-person case. There appeared to be no logical reason why she should suddenly vanish off the face of the earth. Even if she had been unhappy in her marriage, there seemed no cause for her not to have maintained contact with her parents, to whom she was devoted; and, being pregnant, she also had much to look forward to. It was beyond explanation why she would apparently drive hundreds of miles from her home to Manchester, then mysteriously go to ground. Hunter was questioned on several occasions and expressed suitable concern, but police noted that he appeared curiously unemotional for a man whose wife had supposedly walked out on him in mysterious circumstances. When they remarked on his seeming coldness, he brushed their questions off, saying it was simply how he was made, that he preferred never to show his emotions.

He was much more hot-blooded in private, however. Within weeks of his murderous act in the Fife countryside he resorted once more to satisfying his insatiable sexual appetite in the company of prostitutes, even taking them back to the cottage in Carnoustie and the marital bed. One of his favourites was a 22-year-old drug addict he had met in his capacity as her social worker. His compassion appeared to extend no further than using her services to fulfil his deviant fantasies.

As Lynda's family and friends became increasingly anxious about her disappearance, Hunter figured ever more prominently in the minds of detectives as the person who could solve the riddle. But in the absence of a body, there was little headway that could be made. Furthermore, it seemed he could satisfactorily account for his movements during the crucial period of his wife's disappearance.

It was to take almost another four months for the breakthrough the frustrated detectives were looking for to arrive. On 9 December the circumstances of the mystery were featured on BBC TV's *Crimewatch* programme, the first time a Scottish case had been included in the broadcasts. It brought a flood of information. Callers told the waiting teams of police officers that on the day Lynda vanished they had seen a car similar to hers near Fernie

Castle being driven by a man and with a woman 'in a distressed state' in the passenger seat. An Edinburgh taxi driver told how at 1.20 a.m. the next day he had seen the white Vauxhall Cavalier at a roundabout near the Forth Road Bridge having a wheel changed by two men. The taxi man had been inexplicably suspicious, to the extent that he had written down the number of the broken-down vehicle. It matched, apart from one digit, the registration number of Lynda's car.

The day after the programme was broadcast, police announced that a dog matching Shep's description had been seen in the St Michael's area shortly after Hunter had released it. It was also disclosed that the dog had been collected as a stray and put down a week after being found. Convinced that the body of the missing woman could be in the woods at St Michael's, police mounted a full-scale search with a team of more than sixty officers. Special 'body dogs' used in the hunt for the notorious Moors Murders victims were brought north to help in the probe. The search continued for three days before being called off. Hunter, secure in the knowledge that the corpse being sought was in a different forest a few miles away, had even joined the search teams. Lynda's broken-hearted parents, devastated at the continuing uncertainty over the whereabouts of their devoted daughter, announced that they would offer a £1,000 reward to anyone who could find her.

Two months later, on 11 February 1988, a man walking his dog in Melville Woods, near the main Dundee–Kirkcaldy road, came upon Lynda's badly decomposed body. The dog lead, which her husband had so efficiently used six months earlier to bring about her death, was still knotted round her neck.

When police called to break the news of the grim find to Hunter, he was in the company of the drug-addict prostitute he had evidently become attached to. Twenty-four hours later, she too was dead – apparently as a result of having taken a drugs over-dose in her multi-storey home in Dundee. A fellow prostitute said it had been a deliberate act: she felt responsible for Lynda's death, having apparently told Hunter many months earlier that if he had been as tired of his wife as he had said during a conversation, he should 'bump her off'.

But this sad and premature demise may not have been brought on by an attack of conscience. Perhaps it had been a simple mis-calculation of the potency of the drugs she had consumed. Perhaps it was neither. Perhaps she had secrets that could have assisted the murder inquiry which had been launched the previous day. Whatever the actual circumstances surrounding the disturbing death of the tragic young prostitute, it beyond doubt marked the untimely demise of a third woman intimately involved with Andrew Hunter. All within a twenty-six-month period and all by unnatural causes.

The unexpected finding of Lynda's remains gave police the final missing piece of the jigsaw they had started to put together. The evidence of the argument in the car and the sighting of the Vauxhall near the Forth Road Bridge started to point even more firmly in the direction of her supposedly distraught husband. His alibi was examined and re-examined. Police retraced the route from the cottage in Carnoustie to the spot where the body had been found and meticulously noted how long the journey took. They matched that with the time Hunter first put in an appearance at work on the day Lynda vanished. Then they drove through the night from Carnoustie to Manchester, taking different routes, and detailing the precise times. Next, they closely questioned British Rail officials about the movement and exact timings of trains between Manchester and Scotland on the vital day. They walked, stopwatches in hand, from Dale Street – where the car had been left – to the railway station and did the same along the route between the different stations in Glasgow where someone travelling to Dundee would have had to change trains. They found it would have been perfectly possible for someone to have made the overnight journey by car then return by early-morning train and be back in Dundee at 12.49 p.m., giving a more than adequate twenty-one minutes to be in Timpson's shoeshop by 1.06 p.m. the same day.

Hunter became aware that the spotlight of suspicion was being pointed even more in his direction. Four days after the discovery of Lynda's body, he spoke exclusively to *The Evening Telegraph*, saying emphatically that he had nothing to hide.

'I am aware of local speculation and since I am her husband and the last person known to see her alive, it is no more than I would expect,' he said coldly. 'I have nothing to hide, from the police or anyone else.' He then discussed at length the couple's movements on the day of Lynda's disappearance and added, 'I cannot feel anger yet about who murdered Lynda. It has not really sunk in.' He even spoke about the circumstances of the apparent suicide of his first wife Christine, describing her death as a 'terrible shock'. Before the interview concluded, he agreed to be photographed – but only after insisting the picture be taken showing the right side of his face, his 'better side'.

Meantime, police continued to gather evidence and issued a second appeal on the *Crimewatch* programme.

On 1 April, seven weeks after the discovery of the body of the missing social worker had been found, and after more than 5,000 people had been interviewed and 1,200 statements taken from witnesses, Hunter was finally arrested.

His trial that summer attracted enormous interest and drew the biggest crowds to the court-house in Dundee for more than thirty-five years. For each of the eleven days the evidence was heard, queues began to form outside from 7 a.m. onwards, three hours before proceedings began. Those too far down the queue to be admitted remained outside on the court-house steps to be first in line for the afternoon session, taking refreshments from flasks and sandwiches they had brought with them. Many of those who had been in court during the forenoon forsook lunch to join immediately the queue to get back in after the court re-opened. Every day more than twenty reporters packed the press benches.

They got their money's worth. The revelations of the large number of witnesses opened a window on the extraordinary relationships that can exist in the lives of apparently ordinary people. Prostitutes shared the witness-box with Salvationists and the daily happenings in the Bell Street court-house played out like episodes from a TV soap opera. The defence presented a picture of a caring and ambitious social worker who had tried to put the unfortunate death of his first wife behind him to build a new life for himself and his son, only to be tragically caught up in the unexplained murder of his new bride. The Crown systematically dismantled that scenario and meticulously assembled a portrait of a cold-blooded and perverted man capable of playing a game of putting and going to tea with the sister of the woman he had callously killed just a short time earlier. Vitally, they demolished the alibi Hunter had so resourcefully created with his 300-mile overnight flight by car to England and cunning purchase of a birthday gift to secure a timed and dated receipt. That helped establish how it would have been possible for him to have committed the murder; but it did nothing to prove he had actually done so.

The prosecution case turned on the evidence of two separate witnesses who came forward to say that on the day Lynda had disappeared they had seen her in her white Vauxhall in Fife accompanied by a man. One said she appeared to be distressed. Both witnesses believed the man behind the wheel to have been Hunter.

In the end, however, the crucial factor was the discovery in the Carnoustie cottage of the dog collar belonging to the luckless Shep. Hunter, who believed he had cleverly covered his tracks, had slipped up. After removing the collar when he abandoned the terrier a few miles from the murder scene, he had taken it home and thrown it behind a basket where it was later found by police. The court heard that Shep was never taken out without it and Lynda was so devoted to her pet and anxious about him becoming lost that she had two address tags on the collar – one for her home in Carnoustie and the other bearing the address of her parents in Fife. Prosecutor Peter Fraser QC, the Solicitor-General, succinctly put it to Hunter in court: 'If the collar was found in your house subsequently, there is only one remaining conclusion to be drawn and that is that you were present with your wife in the car. And if you were present in the car, you are exclusively responsible for your wife's death.'

Hunter, who had seemed to have an answer for everything else put to him, and who spoke confidently all the time he was in the witness-box, for once could find no satisfactory response.

The jury took less than two hours to return a verdict of guilty by a 12–3 majority. When he stood before Lord Brand awaiting sentence, the 37-year-old was as cold-eyed and emotionless as he had been for the entire duration of the trial that had attracted record crowds. His Lordship looked straight back at him and told him, 'You are an evil man of exceptional depravity. The sentence of the court is that you be imprisoned for life.'

Ten months later, Hunter returned to the dock when his appeal against the verdict was heard at the High Court in Edinburgh. The proceedings then were much more brief. The three judges dismissed the appeal without even bothering to call the prosecution to rebut the pleas of Hunter's counsel, Lionel Daiches QC.

One of the judges, Lord Cowie, pointing to the critical evidence of the dog collar being found in the family home, remarked: 'In all other cases we get a possible explanation, but here this dog always wore a collar and the collar was discovered in the house.' The treacherous killer had been as impassive as usual, except for a quick wink he gave to a friend sitting in the public benches. Then he was led away to resume his life sentence.

That was not the finish of his story, however, for the man who came so close to evading justice finally succeeded. On 19 July 1993 – almost six years after ending the life of his pregnant wife – Andrew Hunter, the man of many faces, died of a heart attack in Perth Prison. Some believe he took just as many secrets with him. . .

9

LESSONS

News reporters spend their lives waiting for the phone to ring. They arrive at work most mornings utterly unaware of what the rest of the day will bring. Some of their time is spent on routine assignments from that day's diary – court duty, interviewing visiting personalities, minor crime – but most of all they wait for the call that will alert them to the breaking news story, the big one that will lead the front page. They don't exactly pray for disasters or major loss of life, but if it happens on their shift the most dedicated are first on their feet to start chasing ambulances and fire appliances. Their lives and professional peaks are vicariously shared with those experiencing extreme misfortune or overwhelming joy. It is a strange, parasitical – but intoxicating – existence.

In the newsroom of *The Evening Telegraph* on the morning of Wednesday, 9 June 1965 there was little to become excited about. The international news coming in over the wires announced that President Lyndon Johnson was again being criticised for America's policy on Vietnam. Locally, Lord Provost Maurice McManus was to open an accident-prevention exhibition in the Caird Hall and the John O'Groats pub in Cowgate had been broken into. It wasn't the liveliest of days.

Shortly after 11 a.m. and with the haze of cigarette smoke that always engulfed the room beginning to descend over the large communal desk and its bank of aged, but sturdy, row of Underwood typewriters, the phone rang for the umpteenth time that morning. There was no stampede among the half-dozen reporters on duty to answer it. The earlier calls had been the usual bunch of photo-requests, damp-house complaints and pleas to keep some of that day's court appearances out of the papers. This time, though, the caller had an altogether more interesting tale to tell. In breathless bursts he gave John Marshall, the youngest person in the room and still a trainee, a graphic account of how he had just witnessed the body of a man somersaulting to earth from the top flat of a fifteen-storey block of flats in the Lochee area. The corpse, explained the caller, still lay sprawled on the concrete forecourt of Kilspindie Court, one of the proliferation of multi-blocks put up by the council as a quick but unsatisfactory solution to the city's housing shortage problem. The featureless tower blocks also fulfilled another, unintended purpose – they provided a convenient and virtually foolproof jumping-off point for suicides, most of whom seemed to be young drug addicts.

Marshall began to mentally switch off. Suicides never made the lead story for the front page. But with any luck it might have been an accidental fall by a workman. Either way, it was still better than a road-safety exhibition; so he headed for the door and Lochee, unaware of the extraordinary events that were to follow.

Up at Kilspindie Court, knots of residents and passers-by gathered at the scene. They were watching, but saying little, for they knew no more than what was presented before them – the body of an apparently young man lying face down on a sunlit, tarmac courtyard. He wore a shirt and trousers and was barefoot. Directly above, on the fifteenth floor, was a shattered window which, fellow residents among the onlookers explained, was in the kitchen of the flat. A neighbour, who had been working in his garden, told everyone within earshot that he had heard the sound of breaking glass and looked up to see the man tumble from the window to the ground 140 feet below. John Marshall entered the multi-storey block and unexpectedly found no one barring his way to the lift doors. Seconds later, and accompanied by a police officer who evidently had more on his mind than the young reporter's identity, he found himself walking into the living-room of the flat at 14C.

The scene resembled something he had only ever previously witnessed in the cinema. Lying, strangely serene, on the floor was a woman in her mid 20s wearing a nightdress. A black tie was knotted round her neck and her face and other parts of her body were stained with blood. More blood had formed in pools round about her and instinctively Marshall pulled up his trouser bottoms to avoid it as he pointlessly walked round the corpse of the attractive, but very dead, woman stretched in front of him. In the kitchen, breakfast dishes lay unwashed and on the floor was a basin. Beside it was a kettle, with one end of its electric lead dangling in the water that filled the basin and the other end plugged into a live wall socket. On his way out of the house that was otherwise so ordinary, Marshall noticed for the first time that the living-room walls were splattered with blood. Whatever had happened in the flat, he knew without doubt what was going to lead the front page of *The Evening Telegraph* that day – and probably the next.

By the time the reporter had returned to the forecourt of the multi-block, police had sealed off the entrance and were allowing access only to those who lived there. Groups of reporters from rival newspapers gathered behind the cordon, desperate for details of what had gone on, but Marshall had no intention of enlightening them until he had found a phone box to file his copy back to the newsroom. Only then did he share with the competition what he knew they would anyway read in his words in the early editions.

As the day progressed, the full events of the horror that had played out in flat 14C slowly began to unfold. The dead woman was 26-year-old Mrs Margaret Lundie, an attractive mother of two, estranged from her husband who had gone to live in London. For some time she had been involved in a passionate relationship with Owen 'Chris' McAuley – the man who had somersaulted to his death. They had lived together in McAuley's flat in another part of town until two days earlier, when Mrs Lundie had moved out with her children and into her mother's top-storey multi flat in Kilspindie Court. The dead woman had apparently become unhappy with her partner – who had also separated from his own wife – because he constantly worked nightshift. In addition, she was contemplating a reconciliation with her husband in London, whom she had spoken to by phone on the evening before her death.

On the morning of the day which would change lives forever, McAuley had finished his nightshift and waited patiently for Mrs Lundie's mother to depart for work. Over and over he rehearsed what he was going to say. Then he went to the tower block in a bid to resolve the difficulties with his lover and convince the hairdresser's receptionist to take him back. The discussion became heated and the couple began to argue loudly. Suddenly, in a moment of uncontrollable rage, McAuley took off his tie, wound it round the neck of his struggling mistress and kept pulling tightly until all resistance passed. Only after she slumped to the floor did reason start to return to him and by then it was much too late. The woman he so desperately wanted back in his life now lay lifeless at his feet.

What followed, and what Marshall the young reporter had seen evidence of but had initially been unable to piece together because of its surreal elements, demonstrated just how much McAuley had instantly regretted his actions. He went straight into the kitchen, placed a basin of water on the floor and, after removing his socks and shoes, stood in the basin. Then he placed the lead from an electric kettle in the water and switched the other end on at the wall socket. Unaccountably, the shock didn't kill him. When it became clear he would remain alive, the demented 24-year-old took a large kitchen knife back into the living-room and began slashing at his wrists. He lost so much blood that it was extraordinary he did not succeed in his purpose. Finally, and having run out of options, he staggered back into the kitchen, climbed on top of the sink unit and hurled himself through the window high above the ground. Only then did he achieve the result he so desperately sought.

Owen McAuley was not alone in ending up prostrate on the pavement. When Mr John Orr, the city's Chief Constable, arrived at the scene he surveyed the corpse and promptly passed out – an event which, unhappily for him, was photographed and recorded in the next day's *Daily Express*.

The police chief probably learned something about himself that morning. John Marshall, the young reporter, also learned lessons. He learned the benefits of getting to the scene of an incident as quickly as humanly possible. And he learned that in newspaper offices the reporter who is first to answer the phone is usually the first to fill the front page. Most of all, though, John Marshall learned never to make assumptions.

10

ANYTHING YOU CAN DO . . .

Nobody paid him any attention. He was just a young soldier who seemed to know exactly where he was going as he walked purposefully through the gates of St John's RC secondary school in Dundee one afternoon in 1967. He spoke to no one, for 19-year-old Robert Francis Mone had other things on his mind. He had been a pupil at the school until being expelled a few years earlier and had gone from there to an approved school. Now he was dressed in the uniform of a private in the Gordon Highlanders and carried a long, narrow object wrapped in brown paper. Still, no one gave him more than a second glance or asked what his business was.

It was 2.15 p.m. on 1 November – All Saints' Day, a bizarre irony, given the terrible events that were about to unfold. On the top floor of the school, 26-year-old teacher Nanette Hanson was beginning a needlework lesson with eleven third-year girl pupils when the door burst open and the slightly built soldier ripped the paper away from his package to reveal a shotgun. The girls giggled. It was nothing more than a prank by a stupid show-off wanting attention. Mrs Hanson would soon sort him out.

Almost instantly they knew they could not be more wrong. The intruder, his eyes flashing wildly round the room, began to shout and swear, waving the gun at the girls and ordering the 14- and 15-year-olds, some of them now crying, to barricade the door with their sewing tables . . . and that was the start of an ordeal that was to last for two hours. It was also the opening sequence of a chain of events that was to reverberate for more than a decade, leaving eight people dead and making the name Mone one of the most feared in the whole of Scotland. Additionally, it bestowed on Dundee the unwanted distinction of being the birthplace of a father and son unrivalled for wickedness.

In the needlework room, a new order was being imposed. The sandy-haired youth who had thrust his way into the class was now sitting on the teacher's desk and issuing instructions. He produced ammunition from his pockets and lined it up along the front of the desk. He told the pupils he would blow their heads off and one by one asked the girls their ages. Some were so afraid they could barely respond. Others whispered to each other and one even suggested to a classmate that they seize an iron from another part of the room and attack their captor with it. When Mrs Hanson – just seven months married – told Mone she was aged 26, he mocked – 'You're just a pensioner.' Then he snatched her glasses from her face, threw them to the floor and trampled the glass into the wooden boards with his army boot. When some of the pupils sobbed too loudly, the gun was put to their head and they were advised to keep quiet or he would silence them.

He ordered everyone into a small changing-room attached to the sewing section and began strutting back and forth, his eyes bulging in their sockets. He smirked as he told his hostages that he had come to the school to gain revenge for being expelled. In particular, he sought retribution against one of the Marist Brothers who helped oversee the Roman Catholic education in the school. Mrs Hanson was the calmest person present. She spoke softly to the young man with the gun and gently advised the girls to stop crying because they might use up the limited amount of air in the small ante-room that had now become a prison. She repeatedly tried to reason with their captor, pleading with him to release the girls and to detain just her.

Outside, the sounds of disturbance had attracted the attention of Miss Margaret Christie, head of the domestic science department, who taught in an adjoining classroom. Puzzled by the unexpected noise emanating from what was normally the quietest class in the entire school, she went to investigate and found that the upper glass panel in the door had been screened with dressmaking material. As she stood outside the room with another needlework teacher, some of the cloth was moved away and she could see Mrs Hanson making her way in their direction.

Then a blast of gunfire almost deafened them. Glass in the top half of the door showered over the pair, sending piercing shards into Miss Christie. Ignoring the pain and emerging blood, she fled with her teacher companion back along the corridor to alert the rest of the school to the frightening events taking place on the upper floor.

If any of those being detained inside the room had any doubts about the seriousness of their position, they now knew better. Some of the pupils screamed. Most of them wept.

Within minutes of the shot ringing out, police began converging on the school and the usually peaceful Harefield Road area found itself ringed by blue flashing lights and vehicles from all the emergency services. News of the siege quickly found its way on to radio news bulletins and media teams from across the country raced to the city. Among those hearing of the dramatic events unfolding in their home town were the members of the Dundee Police football team, taking part in a cup-final tie a hundred miles away.

Meanwhile, a state of emergency had been declared at St John's and the other thousand pupils were rapidly evacuated from the cordoned-off building. Three police officers, backed by a team carrying riot shields, made their way to the upper-floor corridor. Detective Superintendent Donald Robertson – the Clark Gable-lookalike head of CID – Detective Chief Inspector William Melville and Sergeant George McLaren hoped to negotiate with Mone, but the moment they approached the vicinity of the shattered door window, they were treated to blasts from the shotgun.

An impasse appeared to have been reached. Officers shouted suggestions that they should enter the room to speak with him.

Each offer was met with the warning that they should keep back or the gun would be turned on the girls. One of the 14-year-old hostages was led to the door and had the gun pointed at her head while Mone called out that she would be the first to die if anyone tried to force an entry.

By now adrenalin was surging through his body and he was becoming increasingly aggressive towards the terrified pupils. Three of the girls were ordered at gun-point from the changing-room – where the heat was almost intolerable – into the main classroom. He kissed one of them and sexually interfered with the other two. He exuded power and, to demonstrate his absolute control, he released one 15-year-old, instructing her to inform the growing number of people gathering on the ground floor that he should be left alone. She hurried downstairs to carry out his order just as plans of the school were being scrutinised to determine if there was a possible route into the classroom.

At the point when police were considering ending the deadlock with tear gas, Mone called out that the only person he would be prepared to speak to was a girl who had lived near him in the houses on the northern edge of the Law, the hill that had been his childhood playground. Her name was Marion Young and they had met four years earlier at a youth club. They had hit it off together and, he explained, she seemed to understand him.

By good fortune, police were able to make quick contact with her and she was rushed under escort to the scene. Then aged 18 and a student nurse, she unhesitatingly volunteered to go into the classroom to negotiate with Mone. Police were reluctant to allow the gunman another hostage and indicated that the negotiations should take place from behind the door. Marion knew this was not what her long-forgotten acquaintance wanted and insisted she go into the room, as this would offer the best chance of the petrified pupils being released. After some hesitation, police agreed. Seventy-five minutes after the siege had begun, Marion found herself face to face with the baby-faced ex-pupil she now hardly recognised.

Mone had eagerly anticipated the meeting. Awaiting her arrival, he filled one of the classroom sinks with water and washed his face and hair. Then he sat singing to himself while police sped Marion across the city. His first words to her weren't exactly the customary greeting of old friends: 'You thought you were being a brave little girl? How did you know I wouldn't blow your head off?' he asked with a small smile.

The young trainee nurse hadn't been taught anything about counselling or how to negotiate with someone so obviously disturbed, but instinctively she seemed to understand how to respond. Referring to him as 'Bobby', the name she had always known him by, she laughingly said she knew he would never do that to her. Then for ten minutes she and Mrs Hanson gradually convinced him that the pupils should be released, particularly since the changing-room had by then become unbearably warm and the children were beginning to suffer from the stifling heat.

Mone, almost disinterestedly, agreed and Mrs Hanson, in a deliberately unhurried manner, went to the little room and led the ten petrified girls towards the door. But she was not to be allowed to leave with them. As the girls prepared to depart, Mone called out to the teacher, 'Not you – you're not going – I want you here.'

At first the relieved pupils walked slowly from the room; then, out in the corridor, they began to run, faster than they had ever done in their lives, some of them slipping and cutting themselves on the shattered glass beneath the room door. Their ordeal was over. The same could not be said for the two women remaining in the room.

Mone's behaviour was becoming increasingly irrational. He produced some sandwiches and gave one to Marion. Then he asked for a cigarette from Mrs Hanson. When he laid the shotgun down for a few moments, the teenage nurse who had infatuated him four years earlier picked it up and casually started to inspect it. Almost immediately she found herself on the floor after Mone launched an attack on her, grabbing the weapon back.

In the corridor, the posse of police officers, many of them now armed, were joined by Mone's grandmother and Guy

Hanson – Nanette's husband, whose job in Dundee had brought both of them to the city from their native Yorkshire.

Things were not going well in the needlework room. Mone acted even more bizarrely and he began aiming the shotgun at different parts of the room, at the same time demanding to know if his hostages thought he was capable of killing anyone.

'Do you think I can do it?' he taunted. To show he meant business, he pulled the trigger of the gun several times, but its faulty mechanism prevented it from discharging.

He pointed the weapon at Mrs Hanson and asked, 'Do you want to be a saint?' Then he squeezed the trigger. Again it failed to go off. Next he aimed at Marion and tried to fire once more. Once more the gun did not respond.

The unintentional game of Russian roulette finally paid off for him when he successfully directed a blast at the room door after he detected a movement outside. Mone was by now enraged at the weapon's poor performance. He had bought it in London on his way home on leave from the Gordon Highlanders' base in Minden, Germany, and had not tested it before purchase. If he had done, he would have found that the firing mechanism was erratic, with no pattern to its successful operation.

But Robert Mone had come to kill that All Saints' Day and he would have gone on pulling on the trigger for as long as it took to achieve his purpose. In the event, it required just one more squeeze.

Anxious that a police sniper might be waiting for a sight of him, he instructed Mrs Hanson to close the only curtain in the room that remained open. As she reached up to do so, he fired without warning at her back from a distance of just seven feet. For a moment the gentle, softly spoken teacher remained motionless. Then, as Mone prepared to send off a second round, she dropped slowly before him. Her exuberant assailant looked on, marvelling at the grace with which she sank to the floor.

The gallant teacher was not dead. Horrified at what had taken place, Marion Young rushed to her aid and used her nursing training to establish that a faint pulse was present. Mone seemed indifferent to what was going on. He laughed dementedly and sang. He had fulfilled that afternoon's purpose and now he didn't care what came next. Dismissively, he told Marion she could do what she wanted when she pleaded with him to allow Mrs Hanson to be taken to hospital. When ambulance men arrived at the classroom a short time later, Mone allowed them to enter without any conditions. They were accompanied by two of the St John's teachers, Brother Bede and Brother John, who came in, praying, behind a shotgun shield.

By this time the soldier hostage-taker had apparently lost all interest in his situation. He continued to laugh without reason and appeared not to notice as Mrs Hanson was taken from the room on a stretcher, accompanied by Marion.

Minutes afterwards, when police burst into the room, he was still sitting quietly, alternately singing and laughing, the shotgun at his feet. He offered no resistance when he was handcuffed and led away.

Two hours after it had started, the siege of St John's was over. In total, eight shots had been fired that afternoon when the innocence of youth vanished for so many.

All eleven of the schoolgirl pupils who had formed the needlework class were taken to Dundee Royal Infirmary for examination, a few of them being treated for cuts sustained after falling into the broken glass as they ran to freedom. Most of them were still there when they learned that Mrs Hanson had died from her injuries in another part of the same hospital without having regained consciousness. It was many months later before they found out that their brave teacher had been in the early stages of pregnancy with her first child.

On 23 January 1968, Robert Francis Mone, the laughing teenage killer, appeared at the High Court in Dundee. The hearing lasted only eighteen minutes. Medical evidence was led that the 19-year-old was insane and suffered from schizophrenia 'which had developed insidiously over approximately two years'.

When Lord Thomson ordered him to be detained without limit of time in the State Mental Hospital at Carstairs, Mone looked up at him, smiled once more and muttered, 'Good for you.'

The extraordinary bravery of the two young women who secured the release of the pupils was justly marked when they were honoured by the Queen. Marion Young was awarded the George Medal, and Nanette Hanson, posthumously, the Albert Medal. Two months after going to Buckingham Palace to receive her medal, Marion was married in the city. Her groom was also a soldier and, like Mone, he too had served in Germany.

Every 1 November in St John's High School, a special Mass is said for Nanette, a police superintendent's daughter who was described at her funeral by Brother Bede as 'a heroine, a martyr, who died for these children.' He did not remind anyone that the day she met God also happened to be All Saints' Day . . .

The lives of everyone involved in the siege of the sewing class changed forever that November afternoon which had started so innocently. For some, it left wounds that will never heal, but others succeeded in locking away the memories securely enough to allow them to go on gradually to resume a near-normal existence. They put the name Mone into the recesses of their minds and started to go for weeks, even months, without ever thinking about him.

Just over nine years later, everything changed. On the evening of 30 November 1976, a siren belatedly sounded in the darkness at the State Mental Hospital, Carstairs, to announce an escape that was unprecedented in its savagery. Three people had been axed and stabbed to death in a bloody killing spree that began in the hospital's social club and ended seventy miles away after a police car chase.

At the centre of the débâcle was Robert Mone and his friend and fellow inmate whom he idolised, Thomas McCulloch – a bisexual who had been sent to the institution after the attempted murder of two people in a double-shooting in 1970. McCulloch, armed with two guns, had shot a hotel chef in the face after complaining he hadn't been given enough butter on a roll. He then shot the hotel manageress in the shoulder.

The escape had been six months in the planning and was masterminded by Mone with almost military precision. Between them the two cold psychopaths had spent weeks fashioning a deadly arsenal of weapons, somehow managing to conceal them within the west wing of the institution. This arsenal included two wire garrottes, an axe, several knives and a sword. In addition, they had constructed a rope-ladder and had stolen false beards and moustaches from the hospital drama group. They also possessed forged identity cards, nurse's hats, £25 in cash and a torch.

The timing of the breakout had been worked out with the same meticulous detail as the rest of the plan. It would happen after the drama group finished reading extracts from John Steinbeck's book *Of Mice and Men*. When the escape was launched McCulloch, a one-time painter and decorator, strapped on a home-made belt that carried three knives and the axe. Mone had knives concealed in his shirt and trousers and believed the sight of them would be enough to frighten anyone who got in his way. He was convinced the escape would succeed without the need for bloodshed. He clearly knew nothing of the evil which lurked within his 26-year-old companion.

Entering a safe-cupboard where Neil MacLellan, their supervising nursing officer, was speaking to another patient, Ian Simpson, the pair unleashed their attack. Mone threw paintstripper into the face of Simpson (a double-killer who had been sent to Carstairs fourteen years earlier after being found insane and unfit to plead to his crimes). Mone had intended that the liquid would be enough to overcome any resistance and that the victims would be locked in the cupboard, allowing the rest of the escape to proceed unhindered. But Simpson and MacLellan put up an unexpectedly powerful fight and the carefully prepared plan almost foundered in the first minutes. While Mone grappled with Simpson from the front, McCulloch attacked him from behind with the axe. Blood spurted over Mone.

Then McCulloch turned his attentions to the nursing officer who was desperately trying to overcome the effects of the paintstripper sprayed into his eyes. McCulloch pulled out one of his knives and slashed repeatedly at the nursing officer, finally sitting astride him and swinging the cleaver. As he continued his murderous attack, McCulloch shouted at Mone to find the keys to lock their victims in the cupboard. While he was doing so, he saw Simpson stir and reach out for one of the knives that lay discarded on the floor. Mone lifted up a pitchfork that had been left lying against the office wall and returned to the fray, thrusting the twin forks into the already seriously wounded Simpson, who collapsed, all resistance ebbing away.

Then the architect of the scrupulously prepared escape moved on to the next phase of his plan, cutting the wires of the internal and external phones. As the partners in murder prepared to don their makeshift nurse's caps and false beards and moustaches to begin the journey to the perimeter fence, McCulloch called out that he was returning to the cupboard to seize the keys to the drama-room doors, which surprised Mone since the doors were already open.

The little Dundonian did not understand the man he had idolised for four years as well as he thought. McCulloch was by now less interested in locking doors than satisfying his bloodlust. Inside the cupboard, he flashed his axe again and again, reigning blows on the heads of the helpless Simpson and MacLellan, stopping only when it was clear he had at last ended their lives. Like a matador, he claimed his prize, slicing off both of Simpson's ears.

By the time the escapees had scaled the barbed-wire fence using the rope-ladder they had so painstakingly fashioned, it was 6.30 p.m. Another half-hour was to elapse before the corpses would be found in the social club.

In the meantime, Mone was successfully executing another crucial chapter of his precisely planned escape programme. He lay down on one of the main roads within the greater hospital precincts, carefully positioning himself to look like an accident victim. McCulloch, by this time wearing his nurse's hat and false beard and moustache, stood at the roadside and waved his torch to signal to the first car that come along to stop. After being informed that there had been an 'accident', the driver, Robert McCallum, left his vehicle to give assistance.

The steps he took through the darkness towards Mone, who was preparing to spring to life, might have been the last he would ever have taken but for a chance twist in the unfolding events. A passing police car on routine patrol unexpectedly arrived on the scene and pulled to a halt, its two constables alighting to offer aid.

Moments later the second bloodbath of the day was being enacted. The defenceless officers could do little to protect themselves as the escapees launched an attack. Mone by now had possession of a woodcutter's axe and McCulloch swung his cleaver with practised ease. Both of them carried knives in their other hands.

Of the victims, PC John Gillies survived but PC George Taylor was not so lucky. Although he managed to stagger away from the bloody scene, he later died from his horrific injuries.

Robert McCallum, who had fled in his car while the first exchanges were taken place, alerted a gatekeeper to the horrific drama being played out in the shadows a short distance away. While the shocked gatekeeper urgently telephoned the police, the two crazed escapees raced from the scene in the stolen police panda car, McCulloch at the wheel and frantic to put as much distance as possible between themselves and the hospital. Mone tried to operate the police radio to find out how much the authorities knew of their whereabouts, but was unsuccessful. Ten miles along the road, they hit a patch of ice and skidded off the road, the car ploughing into an embankment and being rendered immobile. Mone's head shattered the windscreen and he fell unconscious for a few moments. He came round to hear McCulloch shouting to two men travelling the same road in a van who had witnessed the crash and who had stopped to give assistance.

'Help me with the prisoner,' McCulloch called.

As they came over, both were set upon, one being struck on the head by McCulloch, the other being stabbed seven times by Mone. Then the two dazed and bleeding Samaritans were dragged into the back of their own van, which McCulloch had commandeered to continue the flight to freedom.

Once more the poor driving skills of the bloodthirsty killer let him down. After successfully getting clear of the area, McCulloch later drove into a field because he thought he saw the lights of a police roadblock ahead. The vehicle became bogged down and the pair ran off into the darkness, leaving their two captives in the rear of the van alive. Mone and McCulloch disappeared in the direction of lights they saw shining from a farmhouse. On the way, they were forced to wade into a stream. McCulloch crossed without difficulty, but Mone lost his footing and became stranded and called out to his fellow-killer to help. McCulloch looked back from the bank, pondering whether to leave the little Dundonian where he was, then stretched out the shaft of the axe for Mone to grasp and be pulled clear.

It was fortunate that the farmer who opened the door to their insistent knocking did not know the full history of the two desperate men who had come calling, for it is difficult to imagine a more terrifying scenario. Facing him were two mud and blood-spattered psychopathic killers on the run from the high-security state mental hospital for the criminally insane: they were armed with an axe and knives; in their young lives they had, between them, shot three people; and earlier that evening they had hacked to death three others. In the same bloody orgy that night, three others had been injured by the weapons the visitors now brandished.

As they forced their way into the isolated farmhouse, Mone and McCulloch pulled the phone from the wall. The farmer's four children ran terrified down the hall into the arms of their mother. Fortunately, the escapees showed no inclination to linger. They wanted only the family car, parked outside, to continue their frantic journey, for they were still within twenty-five miles of the scene of horror that was just beginning to be fully pieced together at Carstairs. Inexplicably, it took the hospital managers forty minutes to set off the escape siren after the corpse of Nursing Officer Neil MacLellan had first been discovered.

It was to be almost another two hours before one of the most dramatic nights ever played out in Scotland came to an end. The breakout duo sped away from the farm and headed south for England. By now police all over Lanarkshire and the Borders had been alerted to the atrocities at Carstairs and the stolen Austin was sighted by officers on the A74. A high-speed chase reaching 90 m.p.h. followed and police vehicles pursued the car all the way to the border and beyond. Finally, just north of Carlisle, a police car packed with armed officers rammed the getaway vehicle, but the desperate duo were still not finished. They attempted to hijack another car and Mone, still holding on to his knife, was dragged, struggling from the passenger seat, by a police officer who grasped the blade in his hand and held it firmly. McCulloch was captured by other officers as he threatened the car driver with his axe. Their bloody flight to freedom had at last come to an end.

When the pair were searched, McCulloch was found to be carrying a faked identity card bearing his photograph and purporting to show him as an inspector of the Apprentice Scheme of the Building Industry of Scotland. Mone possessed an identity card in the name of 'Thomas Hunt'. His photograph depicted him wearing a false moustache and dark glasses, with his hair combed back.

The three Cumbrian police officers who captured the killers were each awarded the Queen's Gallantry Medal.

Three months later, when they appeared in the High Court, McCulloch admitted killing Nursing Officer Neil MacLellan, fellow patient Ian Simpson and PC George Taylor. Mone admitted murdering the policeman. Lord Dunpark, saying the pair had been involved in the 'most deliberately brutal murders he had dealt with', ordered that they spend the rest of their natural lives in prison.

It was not to be the last time the name Mone was to terrorise a community, however. . .

Almost two years later, at the very start of 1979, Detective Chief Inspector David Fotheringham sifted through the daily missing-persons reports which were routinely passed from the uniformed section of Dundee police to the CID. Usually they reported nothing more sinister than a runaway teenager or an assaulted wife who had walked out on her husband. More often than not they were returned to the beat officer for action, when time permitted.

That morning, something told the experienced detective that the report detailing the disappearance of 78-year-old Miss Agnes Waugh from her home in Kinghorne Road required closer examination, and with some urgency. The elderly woman had not been seen for a few days, since the afternoon of 29 December, and the circumstances following her departure from her usual routine raised suspicions. She lived in Gray Memorial House, a block of flats on the side of the Law, known locally as 'No-man's Land' because the letting regulations stipulated that the houses could be rented only to females. Other occupants had become alarmed when they found the door of her flat open and the gas fire in the living-room on, with no sign of Miss Waugh. Checks at the hospitals were negative. There was also snow on the ground and she was unlikely to have wandered far.

Detective Chief Inspector Fotheringham launched a major hunt, sending uniformed and plain-clothes officers into the area and instructing that every other flat in the block should be entered, even if it meant breaking down the doors of any which were locked.

That proved unnecessary. There was only one house, on the ground floor, where no one appeared to be at home. On the afternoon of 4 January, a detective went to the rear of the house and forced open the living-room window and pulled aside the curtains. At the far end of the room, and barely visible in the fading light, a lifeless hand and arm dangled from a bed recess.

When the startled officer and a colleague burst their way in they found a scene more macabre than anything they would ever witness in the worst kind of horror film. On the bed was the body of a woman in her twenties with a stocking and an electric flex knotted round her neck. In armchairs at either side of the fireplace, facing each other, were the corpses of two women in their seventies, both with stockings tied tightly round their necks and knotted several times. Each of the women were bound to their chairs at their wrists and ankles by polythene bags. All three women had been severely beaten about the face.

The two elderly women were quickly identified as Mrs Jane Simpson (70), the occupant of the flat, and the missing Miss Waugh, whose flat was at the other end of the ground-floor corridor. Just as the initial efforts were being made to determine who the third victim was, an agitated man appeared on the scene, concerned about his bride of less than two weeks whom he had reported missing after she vanished on 29 December – exactly a week after the wedding and the first time she had gone out without him since their marriage. She had departed to visit the bank and to shop, though he suspected she may also have gone drinking. He had learned of the discovery of the corpses and, knowing his wife had frequented the Hilltown area on previous drinking binges, he feared the worse. His name was John Millar and a short time later he identified the third body as his 29-year-old wife Catherine.

Forensic experts confirmed that the women had been dead for several days, probably since 29 December, when both Miss Waugh and Mrs Millar had last been seen. The post-mortem revealed that the oldest woman had an unusual injury on her right cheek. Among the bruises, probably inflicted by punches, was a wound that was consistent with her attacker having worn a prominent ring. It was to prove a vital – and extremely ironic – piece of evidence.

In the following days the city found itself in the midst of one of the largest murder hunts ever launched. Anyone with connections to the women were being questioned and every public house and betting shop in the area was visited by the detective teams.

Among those interviewed was the nephew of Miss Waugh – Robert Christopher 'Sony' Mone – the 52-year-old father of the St John's and Carstairs killer. He was a small-time housebreaker and thug who had graduated from petty offences to serious assaults and prison sentences of up to five years, a detested figure in his neighbourhood, easily moved to violence after drink and indifferent to whether he struck men or women. Small and slight, like his son, he longed to be a big-shot among the Dundee criminal fraternity. He swaggered about town with his thumbs stuck into the cutaway pockets on his trousers and dyed his long straggly grey hair brown, wearing it in an obvious comb-over style in a failed attempt to look younger. He loved tattoos and had them on his arms, legs and torso. Across his chest he carried the initials 'IHS' – representing In His Service, a reference to the Devil. His prize exhibit, however, was the 'TNT' emblazoned on his penis.

Sony Mone also had much greater claim to what he saw as fame. He revelled in the notoriety of being the father of the man who had terrorised a Dundee school and had then burst his way out of a high-security mental hospital leaving a trail of butchered victims. Night after night, in city pubs, he would ramble on about his affection for the son he referred to as 'the Carstairs Killer' and spoke longingly of his desire to be with him in prison.

Significantly, when members of the murder squad visited the Vennel public house in Hilltown, just round the corner from the scene of the triple-slaughter, they learned that on the day of the murders Mone had been a customer, and a troublesome one. He had become intoxicated and had started to shout and swear, threatening violence to anyone who complained. Throughout it all, he boasted he would become more famous than his son . . .

When he was questioned about his movements on 29 December, Mone readily admitted that he had been in the murder apartment, having gone there with someone he referred to as 'Billy Rebel' but whose actual name was Stewart Hutton. The two had met up in a pub and had gone to the house with a carry-out because

Hutton knew Mrs Simpson as a drinking acquaintance. Mone added that Catherine Millar was another drinking companion of Mrs Simpson. The booze session, he said, had gone on to mid-afternoon when the carry-out had been consumed, after which he departed to get fresh supplies.

The 22-year-old Hutton told an identical story – except that it was he who had gone for the alcohol and that at no time had Miss Waugh been in the flat. The younger man explained he had a 'strange feeling' about the atmosphere in the house and did not want to return. Instead, he had spent the money he had been given for the drink in a betting shop, at one point collecting £8 when he picked a winner. Checks at the betting shop later revealed that Hutton had spoken the truth. He was also satisfactorily alibi-ed for the remainder of the day.

Police were now convinced that Mone was the man they had been hunting. He had placed himself in the flat at the crucial time, was known to be violent towards women and, probably most important of all, had boasted he would be more famous than his double-killer son. The theory was that he had first beaten and strangled Mrs Millar and Mrs Simpson, then went along the corridor to bring his aunt to the scene so that she could become his third victim – one more than his crazed son had achieved. He would thus be more famous. The hypothesis, though probably accurate, lacked just one essential ingredient for a conviction – evidence.

Throughout the days following the grim discovery of the bodies, Mone was questioned at length on several occasions. He never admitted to the murders. But nor did he deny them. With typical swagger, he indicated he knew more than he was saying, hinting that he would disclose precisely what at some future discussion. During one session with Detective Inspector William Hart, he said he no longer cared for the 'jungle outside' and talked of being with 'someone he loved' in prison.

'All I live for is to be in there with him,' he said. 'If I was there, I would see he gets everything that's going – pills, booze, anything, the lot.'

Every time he was interviewed, police looked to see if he wore a ring with a prominent face. He didn't. Then they had a major breakthrough. Other enquiries revealed that Mone did indeed have such a ring, a silver band with a large jade stone, which had great sentimental significance. It had previously belonged to Robert Junior who had gifted it to his father because he was prohibited from wearing it in Perth Prison after being transferred there from Carstairs. All they had to do was find it and try to match it with the wound on the cheek of Miss Waugh. A special search warrant, detailing the description of the ring and its importance to the case, was issued and Detective Inspector Hart began the hunt to recover it. He searched Mone's and his sister's house and even travelled to Glasgow, where Mone's estranged wife lived, to check her home. All attempts to find the ring drew a blank, however.

While the murder squad urgently strove to build a case, their suspect took a trip out of town, going to Perth Prison to visit the son with whom he had become so obsessed. The events in 'No-man's Land' on the evening of 29 December doubtless figured prominently in their conversation.

Meanwhile, conversations between the police, the Procurator Fiscal in Dundee and Crown Counsel in Edinburgh in mid-January arrived at the mutually agreed conclusion that investigations by that stage had established a case 'of sorts', but a borderline one. Then, on the morning of 18 January, two weeks after the discovery of the strangled and beaten bodies of the three women, Detective Chief Inspector Fotheringham received the call he had been waiting for. Although the evidence was thin, Crown prosecutors felt the public interest was so great that an attempt to convict the prime suspect had to be made. A warrant was issued for the arrest of Sony Mone. Almost unbelievably, when the chief inspector arrested him later that day in the street near his home in Glen Prosen Terrace, Mone was wearing the ring police had devoted so much time searching for.

The silver-and-jade keepsake that had been passed from killer son to father formed the linchpin of the trial. The day before the arrest, forensic scientists had removed a triangle-shaped piece of skin from the cheek of Miss Waugh which bore the unusual wound and made a cast and resin model. They did the same after receiving the ring.

Five months later, at the High Court in Dundee, the jury heard how the model of the cheek displayed a wedge-shaped puncture with four small abrasions below and a tiny oval depression alongside – marks which corresponded to the pattern and shape of the ring. More crucially, the ring bore traces of blood group A – the same grouping as Miss Waugh and Mrs Millar.

One of the trial witnesses was the accused man's daughter, Rose Ann, who, through her tears, told the court that her father had loaned her the ring the previous year but had asked for it back after a short time. 'My dad said it was useful in a fight,' she said.

The jury decided Mone's guilt after seventy-five minutes. Passing a life sentence, Lord Robertson told him, 'You have been convicted of what I can only describe as a terrible crime. In view of the enormity of the crime, I shall make a recommendation to the Secretary of State that you serve a minimum of fifteen years.'

Mone listened without a flicker of emotion, looked at the judge, and responded, 'Would you mind back-dating it?' Then, with typical aggression, he struggled with the police constable taking him down to the cells, dug him in the ribs and shouted, 'Get your hands off.'

Three and a half years later, in Aberdeen's Craiginches Prison, Sony Mone was stabbed to death by a fellow inmate wielding two knives. He had been loathed inside prison as much as outside and preyed on the youngest inmates to satisfy his perverted sexual appetite. He intimidated them with his physical fitness and showed off by hanging by his feet from a beam ten feet above concrete with his arms folded. His killer described him as 'probably the most obnoxious person in the country'. No one was particularly surprised at Robert 'Sony' Mone's violent end. Even fewer cared.

In August 1989, Stewart 'Billy Rebel' Hutton, who had been with Mone in the murder flat ten years earlier, also met a violent death when he was killed in the street in London, a Dutchman being charged with the incident.

A few years earlier, in 1981, the name of Mone had again been linked with trouble. Rose Ann Mone, sister of a double-killer and daughter of a triple-murderer, appeared in court, aged 17, charged with attempted murder after attacking another girl with a knife and bottle. The charge was reduced to severe assault and she was sent to a young offenders' institution for three years.

Robert Mone Junior, whose fateful visit to his old school that November afternoon in 1967 sparked off a chain of events that left eight people dead, has the profile of the classic psychopath. With above average intelligence, he was abandoned by his mother at the age of two, then terrorised by his bullying father. When he was twelve, a local man – a family friend in his 50s – raped him and, along with other males, continued to abuse him for two years. He under-achieved and by the time he was expelled from St John's Secondary School at the age of 14, he was well on his way to developing the schizophrenia that was to dictate his life. A teacher described having him as a pupil as being similar to sharing the room with a live hand grenade.

The teenager who was to go on to become one of his home town's most notorious killers moved to London as a 15-year-old where he was reunited with his mother, who had by this time remarried. They did not bond in the way Mone had hoped and he soon moved into a flat of his own, embarking on a lifestyle of heavy drinking and homosexual affairs. At one stage, he entered into a relationship with a man in his 50s, living with him for a time in an apartment in Kensington. On another occasion, Mone claimed to have been drugged and forced to participate in a pornographic film with several men. His excessive drinking led to bouts of clinical depression, causing him to attempt suicide with a drugs overdose. Eventually, he tired of the London scene and joined the army.

When he returned home on leave from his unit in Minden, Germany, in November 1967, he knew he was on the brink of a gross act which would cost a life, either his own or that of someone else. He had no clear idea of what would happen but was aware he wanted to put himself into a position of power. He also knew within himself that he would never return to the army. When passing through London he bought a shotgun and ammunition, then in Dundee he booked into a hotel where he kept the gun, though for some of the time he lived at his grandmother's. During his leave he drank excessively and became depressed. He argued with his father one night at a club and uplifted the gun with the intention of shooting him and only his grandmother stopped him from pulling the trigger. He even tried to commit suicide again by taking an overdose of sleeping pills.

On the wretched day he returned to St John's, he had been AWOL for one day. When he awoke that morning he knew there would be a siege, but did not know why. He was also aware in the back of his mind that someone was going to die but had no idea who.

In an unauthorised prison interview with the *Daily Record*, Mone says Mrs Hanson's needlework class was chosen at random.

> I can remember seeing her looking at me and being shocked. She was so calm. She spoke to me about my life and asked me about the Army and talked to me about various things.
>
> I wasn't frightening her and soon I was beginning to feel that she was disarming me. That made me feel worse.

Mone recounted how entering the room with the gun had made him feel powerful for the first time in his life but Mrs Hanson had taken that from him by being gentle, strong and decent.

> She was a beautiful person but I had made up my mind and things were getting to the stage that if I didn't do something I would have failed again.

He said that when it came to the shooting he couldn't even look her in the face and asked her to close the curtain because her back would be turned.

During his time in custody, Mone developed academically, going on to pass A-level exams and studying for a law degree. But he continued to resent authority. In the early years of his incarceration he took part in a roof-top demonstration. Later, he sued the Scottish Secretary for compensation after some of his property was damaged in a prison riot. On another occasion, he sought to take a case to the European Commission on Human Rights in Strasbourg because he had been kept in his cell for practically 24 hours a day, for 10 months, turning him into a 'state-induced junkie' because of the sleeping tablets he was prescribed. In 1995, he had six months added to his sentence for attacking a fellow inmate with boiling water. Seven years later, he used Human Rights legislation to have his minimum term of imprisonment fixed at 25 years. At the same time, he adopted the name James Smith as part of his preparation for his hoped-for release. Today, he writes poetry and studies philosophy. Part of his work duties have included transcribing books into braille.

In 2006, the Parole Board indicated he should begin the process of training for possible freedom. A year later, he was photographed on a day trip out of Perth Prison to Crieff. Other outings followed to venues such as the Scottish Parliament and the Burrell Collection in Glasgow.

Throughout the period of his long detention, Mone – or James Smith as he may now like to think of himself – has had a number of sexual relationships with fellow prisoners. In a letter to one who was 30 years his junior, he even confessed to having seduced an inmate in the chapel of Shotts Prison. He also wrote of his dream of moving to England after his release where his notoriety would not precede him, hopefully finding work in an office.

At the same time as Mone was making his plans, the man who butchered his way out of the state hospital with him in the Carstairs bloodbath was also en route to training for freedom. Thomas McCulloch, his one-time gay lover, had appealed to the

European Court of Human Rights at the same time as his co-escapee and had his minimum sentence fixed at 30 years.

Despite having been described by Lord Dunpark as an incurable psychopath, and having had a longer minimum tariff imposed, McCulloch fared better in his quest for freedom. In 2007, he was permitted day release from Greenock Prison to work as a road sweeper. Then, in early 2009, he was moved out of secure accommodation and transferred to the open prison Noranside, near Forfar. Later the same year, after almost 40 years behind bars, he was housed temporarily in a flat provided for prisoners training for eventual release in his native Dumbarton. Recalling the experience of spending his first night free from the presence of guards and locked doors, McCulloch related how he had not gone to bed but had sat at a window in the flat gazing in wonderment out into the street. Ironically, the house was located in Risk Street and when local residents learned the identity of their new neighbour they protested. He was transferred to another flat in the town but hounded out of there by other angry householders and was returned to Noranside.

Bizarrely, during his subsequent spell in the open prison, the man who used an axe to hack three people to death in the bloody rampage at Carstairs was allowed out of the jail to take a course at an Aberdeenshire nature reserve on how to chop down trees. He was even presented with a certificate for his achievements in honing his skills, the photograph of the presentation proudly appearing in the prison magazine *The Gallery*.

When Noranside was closed down, McCulloch was transferred to the open prison at Castle Huntly near Dundee. He continued to enjoy outings, frequently going shopping and sight-seeing in the city and surrounding area.

On one of more than 100 excursions, he made the acquaintance of a 48-year-old, twice-divorced Dundee grandmother who had approached him in the belief he was actually his fellow Carstairs escapee Robert Mone. The pair began a relationship and shared time on numerous other outings and in a flat in Dundee. They were even photographed outside a jeweller's shop after she bought him a ring for his wedding finger. At the end of 2012, McCulloch made a sixth request to the Parole Board for permanent release and finally received the answer he longed for. He was told that after 43 years locked up he would be permitted back into the community under licence. Five months later, amid a barrage of Press publicity, he was driven out of the jail and into Dundee, apparently to move into the flat of his lady friend. Ironically, McCulloch's new accommodation was situated only a mile or two from the school where Mone had begun his own criminal career with a gun. Aged 65, wearing a smart suit, collar and tie, trilby, and sporting a neatly-trimmed goatee beard, the small figure with the genial countenance bore no resemblance to the image most people might have of a man who once in his life had shot two people over a row about a sandwich and later broke his way out of an institution for the criminally insane, killing three people with an axe in the process.

All this must have been received with a mixture of envy and resentment by the St John's school killer. While McCulloch enjoyed his new life back in the community, Mone remained detained in a secure prison despite having been eligible for parole five years before McCulloch. In setting McCulloch's fixed term at 30 years before consideration for parole, and Mone's at 25 years, the European Court of Human Rights had clearly taken into account that the former had been convicted of the murder of the three people killed in the Carstairs bloodbath compared to Mone's one, the police officer. The one-time soldier's conduct in prison and the perceived risk he might be to the public have obviously been major factors in his continuing detention.

During his time inside, he has been held in virtually all of Scotland's closed penal establishments. When McCulloch was driven out of Castle Huntly to freedom, Mone was confined at Glenochil Prison, where he was a privileged 'passman', trusted to move throughout the jail cleaning offices and toilets and earning £13 a week, much to the displeasure of some more poorly paid inmates.

At the time of writing (2013), Mone remains one of Britain's longest serving prisoners, having spent almost 46 years in custody. He has told others sharing his various institutions that he yearns for an existence where no-one knows him. In addition to his earlier hopes of moving to freedom in England, he has expressed an interest in settling in a quiet location such as Oban. He also continues to be permitted trips out of prison. A recent outing was to the National Museum of Scotland.

Reflecting on the St John's siege and his feelings towards his father, Mone once said, 'I wished I had killed him. If I had, seven lives would have been saved. The three he killed, the three at Carstairs, plus Nanette Hanson.'

He did not seem to consider that the same result might have been achieved had he not made such a poor job of trying to take his own life in the days before he so fatefully re-visited his former school that grey All Saints Day.

11

THE BODY IN THE BAGS

It was the practice of Sergeant Ronald Fyffe to exercise his dogs up to five times a day. As the man in charge of Tayside Police's dog section, he led by example and his Alsatians, Dirk and Tyke, weren't just the fittest in the force but also the most highly trained. And they had the most interesting canine playground in the city – the wooded slopes of the Law, the proud landmark that watches over Dundee and its citizens, which was just a short walk from the policeman's home.

When the animals came to make their most spectacular discovery, however, Sergeant Fyffe wasn't with them. That day, the second last of 1992, he was on other duties and the morning exercise stint had fallen to his young daughter who was only too glad to help fill in her Christmas school holidays by walking the dogs – they were as much family pets as an important working unit of the local constabulary. When they bounded away over the frost-covered grass, their panting breath vaporising in the chill December air, Dirk and Tyke did not deviate in the route they took. They went at once to three plastic bags which lay dumped behind a low pile of logs on the lower slopes just behind the allotments in Law Crescent, a long way from the war memorial at the top of the hill and a convenient place for disposing of unwanted rubbish.

The Alsatians knew exactly where the bags were, for they had rummaged among them on the two previous days before called away by Sergeant Fyffe and his librarian wife Pamela. Their daughter did not follow her parents' example and the animals quickly tore apart one of the bags. It did not contain the household debris her parents had imagined. Instead, a human arm with hand attached dropped out.

Any child returning home from walking the family pets to tell her mother they have found part of a body is unlikely at first to be taken too seriously. Mrs Fyffe had no such inhibitions. Her daughter was ashen-faced and anxious and the words that tumbled from her mouth contained no trace of humour. Mrs Fyffe also recalled that the dogs had been reluctant to leave that part of the Law the previous evening. She immediately called the police. They arrived in strength a short time later and the two other bags were split open to reveal the upper portion of a human torso in one and the lower section, along with an upper arm, in the other.

It is no understatement to say the grisly find was met with some consternation. The absence of a head was obviously going to make identification of the body portions difficult and New Year leave for the detectives in Central Division was about to be cancelled. They were confronted with a unique dilemma – they were not only looking for a murderer but also a victim. Putting a name to the partial corpse would clearly make the hunt for the killer easier and pathologists and forensic scientists worked round the clock to establish some sort of description which could be issued to the public, along with a plea for their assistance in determining who he was.

Late the following day they released a number of details, including the fact that the dead man had at one time undergone surgery to his stomach and had suffered a fracture to four ribs. Marks on the left wrist also indicated that a thick bracelet of some kind had regularly been worn there. He had 'well-maintained' hands with fairly long, well-manicured fingernails, and was also suntanned. He was thought to be aged between 30 and 50 and about 5 feet 10 inches tall. By this time police also knew that the victim was probably homosexual because of evidence of recent anal intercourse. Another line of enquiry revealed that the plastic bags came from a batch which had been supplied to Spar shops in

Dundee, and one such shop was in Hilltown, close to where the body parts had been found.

While these details were being released to the public, an army of police officers embarked on a search for the remaining body parts. One of the most intensive hunts was conducted at the Baldovie incinerator, where the domestic refuse of Dundonians is cremated. More than 100 tons of rotting garbage was sifted through without result.

The newspaper and broadcast appeals to the public brought much greater success. Within four days police had taken calls from ninety people concerned that the Law victim may be their absent friend or relative. One of the worried callers was James Dunbar, an art teacher from Carnoustie, who was anxious about his 52-year-old half-brother: Gordon Dunbar had been due to travel to Carnoustie to join the family for a meal on Christmas Day but had never arrived. When James contacted his brother's landlord at the Anchor guest house in Victoria Road in Dundee, he was informed that Gordon had not been seen for about a week. Other information, including confirmation that his brother was homosexual, and had once had four ribs broken after being mugged, as well as having undergone abdominal surgery to locate an ulcer, prompted police to make an immediate swoop on the first-floor bedroom Gordon Dunbar had occupied in the guest house. Fingerprints and DNA tests taken from material in the room matched the body parts.

The first part of the riddle was solved. They had the victim. Now the hunt for his murderer could be launched in earnest.

The profile they built up of the man whose life had ended so grotesquely did not yield any immediate clues to the identity of the person who had disposed of his body. Dunbar had been born in the Belgian Congo, the son of missionary parents, but had returned to Scotland to live at the age of eleven. He was brought up by an aunt in Montrose and had studied architecture in Dundee. Going on to work for the city Corporation for several years, he played a major role in the design of Ardler Community Centre, among other projects. Later, after receiving an inheritance from his aunt, he moved to France to work with the War Graves Commission. Then he purchased a café in Arras which was popular with members of the gay community. But the business failed and his long-term relationship with a French male partner also disintegrated.

He returned, disappointed and distraught, to Dundee, eventually moving into the Anchor guest house, which was largely a hostel for the homeless and unemployed. There, fellow guests regarded him as colourful in appearance but otherwise quiet and friendly. He was also responsible, troubled no one and appeared to be recovering slowly from the trauma of his experiences in France. He made no secret of being gay and, according to the guest house owner, was a model tenant who always paid his rent on time. He liked jewellery and wore an earring but his favourite piece was a 9-carat gold bracelet made from his grandfather's watch chain. There was nothing in his lifestyle to suggest that he would meet a gruesome and untimely demise, or that he knew anyone capable of bringing that about.

The last time he had been seen was on Christmas Eve, when he had set off from the guest house in the forenoon wearing his distinctive long overcoat for a visit to the city centre. He later met some of the other Anchor residents for a festive drink in the Club Bar in Union Street, leaving at around 6.30 p.m. to call at the Caledonian Bar a few yards further up the street. After fifteen minutes, he departed, apparently alone. It was the last confirmed sighting of Gordon Dunbar.

A search of his bedroom produced only one thing of major interest. A bank account showed that he had deposited £60 that morning, but that at 9.22 that evening he had apparently withdrawn £150 from an autoteller in Commercial Street. Police were puzzled. Why would anyone go to the trouble of making a payment at a bank on one of its busiest days of the year, only to withdraw more than twice the amount later the same day?

Whilst detectives built a picture of Dunbar's last known movements, other officers routinely checked local and national crime files for people with previous convictions for offences of extreme violence, particularly any with a connection to Dundee.

Among others, the computer at the Scottish Crime Records office delivered the name of Alastair William Thompson, a 43-year-old lifer out on licence. Almost twenty-five years earlier, as an 18-year-old in Edinburgh, he had achieved national notoriety after murdering his grandmother in a sustained, frenzied attack when he stabbed her sixteen times with a carving knife then smashed her skull twice with a hammer. Much of the sixteen years of the life sentence he had served before being released was carried out at Perth Prison. After being freed he married a social worker he met while in prison and they settled in Perth. The marriage did not last long, however, and Thompson moved to England. Significantly, he eventually returned north, to live in Dundee, and had become res-ident-caretaker of the home in Haldane Terrace in Kirkton which was used by the Scottish Association for the Care and Resettlement of Offenders (SACRO) to provide accommodation for ex-prisoners.

It was useful information but there was no indication of any link with the unfortunate Gordon Dunbar. The caretaker figured on the catalogue of suspects but did not head the list. On 8 January, two days after the official identification of the body parts unearthed by the exercising Alsatians, police received a phone call which instantly gave impetus to the inquiry. The caller disclosed that a man named Alastair Thompson had spent the New Year holiday weekend in Perth and had spoken at length and in considerable detail about the Law murder in Dundee. Police rushed the twenty miles up the dual carriageway to Perth, where they traced some of those Thompson had spoken to. They also took possession of an antique gold chain which he had given to a female acquaintance on Hogmanay. It matched, identically, the description of the one said to have always been worn by Gordon Dunbar on his left wrist.

That evening, a squad of detectives staked out Thompson's house in Haldane Terrace and when he arrived home they pounced and led him away, amidst his protestations, for questioning. While that was taking place at headquarters in Bell Street, teams of police and forensic scientists combed the suspect's bedroom. Among the intriguing discoveries were clothing and two holdall bags and a pair of shoes, all heavily blood-soaked. In addition they found an electricity bill bearing the address, '9L Butterburn Court' – one of the city's tallest blocks of multi-storey flats, built on the edge of the Law and overlooking the precise spot where the body parts had been dumped in the plastic bags. A set of keys, none of which fitted any of the locks at the Haldane Terrace address, was also found in Thompson's room along with, intriguingly, a scrap of paper bearing four numbers. When the name of the person who was listed as the tenant of the Butterburn council flat was routinely checked with criminal records, it brought a startling result – the occupant was a 'lifer' out on licence after years inside for a murder.

With mounting anticipation, the officers headed at once to the multi-block dominating the Hilltown landscape, taking the keys for flat 9L with them. When they effortlessly inserted them in the lock and the door swung open, the sound of thudding heartbeats was almost audible.

They knew at once they had come to the right place. Inside were several plastic bags similar to the ones found on the hill. There was also a half-torn label which fitted with a label portion found among the severed limbs in the bags. A roll of tape, similar to the type used to seal the Law bags, also lay in the flat. Most chilling – and sickening – of all, they walked into a blood-splattered bathroom where body tissue clung to parts of a wall. More tissue almost blocked the traps of the drainage system and on the floor lay a blood-stained hacksaw blade. Never could a murder scene have spoken more eloquently of what had taken place there.

It was quickly established that the tenant of the flat, despite initial suspicions, had played no part in the depraved activities that had taken place. He had departed for London two months earlier and had passed the keys to Alastair Thompson, the man who nearly quarter of a century earlier had been convicted of hacking his grandmother to death. It was never established how Thompson had come to know the tenant of the multi-storey flat, but it seemed likely they had become acquainted in prison or at the SACRO hostel for former inmates.

Within hours of the repugnant discovery being made, Thompson once again found himself charged with the most serious crime in the statute book, this one even more monstrous than the first.

Murder squad officers set about constructing a scenario of the macabre events of that Christmas Eve in 1992. They concluded that the pair had somehow met up in mid-evening after Gordon Dunbar had visited a grocer's shop to purchase Camembert cheese, garlic granules and powdered soup, all of which were later found in Thompson's bedroom. The two men had gone to 9L Butterburn Court.

When the bisexual Thompson had taken Dunbar to the flat that night the atmosphere had at first been convivial and festive and homosexual activity had taken place. But during the course of the encounter, the mood turned from romance to robbery when Thompson threatened his companion with a knife and demanded his bank card and personal identification number – the same four digits as the ones, apparently meaningless, which had been on the discarded scrap of paper found in Haldane Terrace. After parting with the card and number, the terrified victim was stabbed to death through the heart. Thompson, wearing Gordon Dunbar's long overcoat to conceal the blood stains on his own clothing, then made his way down town to the bank autoteller in Commercial Street, where he withdrew £150 in ten-pound notes.

While others in Dundee made preparations to attend Watch-night services in churches across the city, the man who that Christmas Eve had murdered and robbed was on a mounting high that could not be further from the seasonal ethos of goodwill towards men. He returned with his victim's groceries to Kirkton, still wearing the overcoat which he explained away to other hostel residents as being an early Christmas present from a woman friend, and waving the wad of crisp banknotes which he said were winnings from the horses.

Thompson washed, changed clothes, then headed back to Butterburn Court to view his handiwork. That night he brought Christmas in at Arthur's Night Club in St Andrew's Lane. No one who saw him there could have remotely imagined what he had been engaged in a few hours earlier. He danced and laughed, wished other revellers a Merry Christmas and bought drinks for two women he struck up a conversation with. At 2.30 a.m., he and another male left the club with the ladies, going to the home of one of them where Thompson remained, the life and soul of the party, until departing at 5 a.m. Few females could have unwittingly spent Christmas morning in such deadly company.

Whatever else may have been said about Alastair Thompson, he was not a stupid or unintelligent man. Although he had been detained in approved schools, borstal or prison for almost all of his life between the ages of twelve and thirty-five, he had benefited from a good education, gaining Higher passes in modern studies and geography and engaging in a detailed study of political development of the USSR. Reflecting many years later on his troubled childhood at home, he disclosed that the happiest period of his life had been when he was held in Loaningdale Approved School, remaining there longer than he need have done because he volunteered to do so. During his life sentence in Perth Prison he joined the Salvation Army for a brief period and then, after his release on licence and within a year of moving to Dundee, he landed a job at the large NCR factory in the city. Personable and persuasive, he could articulate his thoughts clearly on paper as well as vocally and he was elected by 97 per cent of the workforce as shop steward of his section.

His obvious intelligence made it all the more strange that he seemed to do nothing to conceal the tracks of his iniquitous activities on Christmas Eve. Indeed, he appeared to leave a trail that would inevitably lead to him. In addition to the damning pieces of evidence he left behind, he spoke freely to acquaintances about some of what had taken place. On Christmas Day he borrowed a hacksaw from a friend, explaining that he wanted to cut up some kitchen pipes. The next day he complained that the blade had broken and he was given the loan of a second one. This time, he bizarrely revealed that the true purpose of his request was to enable him to dispose of a body, which he had volunteered to do for two 'hit men' from Glasgow who had killed a man. Pressed, he explained that he had made a night-time journey to Dudhope Park, about a mile from the Butterburn Court multi, where he had left some of the body. The head had been placed in a refuse skip in Kirkton, he said, close to where he lived and at that point the remainder of the body was still in a bath of salt and detergent.

Recalling the conversation, the incredulous friend was later to say, 'I took it all as a joke. He said he was going to have get rid of the rest of the body and said it would take three or four trips with it being heavy.

'He said the Law hill would be a better place because he wouldn't have so far to carry them.'

Thompson even put the name of Gordon Dunbar to the remains of the corpse he was so anxious to dispose of. Later, he asked the same man if he had an open coal-fire in his house so he might burn a bank card. These were hardly the words of a man taking every precaution to ensure that his dastardly deed would go undetected.

It isn't known just how many people ultimately came to suspect Alastair Thompson for the murder which attracted headlines across Britain. Police certainly received a number of calls offering information. One anonymous tip-off said some of the missing body parts could, indeed, be found at Dudhope Park. After officers hurried to the scene, they came upon a number of bags among shrubbery on an access road leading to the car park. These bags contained a lower leg, feet – one in a woman's stocking – and the remaining arm.

Thompson stood trial at the High Court in Edinburgh and the ghastly nature of the case guaranteed a rapt audience among those who packed the public benches and the thousands throughout the country who followed every word of the newspaper reports.

It was not, however, a case which contained many complications as far as the evidence was concerned. Although he exercised his right not to go into the witness-box, Thompson's admission to some of his friends – who were called by the Crown – made it clear his position was that he had dismembered and disposed of the body, but that he had not been the person who had carried out the killing. The possessions he had of the victim – the long coat, bracelet and a key-fob – had been found by himself. In the circumstances, it was probably the best defence he could muster. There was an abundance of evidence linking him with the sad figure of Gordon Dunbar and even more which pointed to him having cut up the body in the bathroom of 9L Butterburn Court. His incredible story that he had simply been assisting two 'heavies' from Glasgow, in return for them being prepared to assault a brother he despised, did not exercise the minds of the jury overly long. Although the trial had lasted for nine days, they took only seventy minutes to return with their verdict. As they filed back into court, each juror was treated to a penetrating stare from the dark, deep-set eyes of the grey-haired, bearded man in the dock. None of them returned his gaze. Juries which unanimously convict seldom look at the man they are about to despatch to prison; this jury was no exception.

Lord Weir did not suffer the same inhibitions. He fixed the slightly built man who stood defiantly before him with an unwavering look and almost spat the words:

> The jury have convicted you of nauseating and barbaric crimes. The sentence is imprisonment for life.
>
> In view of the fact you have previously been convicted of murder and in view of the wicked nature of these crimes, it is my duty to recommend to the Secretary of State that you should not be released on licence until at least twenty years have elapsed.

After Thompson was removed from the dock, the judge turned to face the jury. With sympathy replacing the venom he had directed at the accused man, His Lordship told them softly, 'I would not have wished your task on my worst enemy. You have had to listen to distasteful and horrendous evidence and have stuck to your task manfully. Your part in this sordid affair is now at an end.'

It was not the finish of the story, however, as far as the man who had been incarcerated for his second life sentence was concerned. Three months after ending up once more in Perth Prison, Thompson revealed to an acquaintance where he had taken some of the other body parts, even drawing on a biscuit wrapper a map pinpointing the location under a disused rail bridge in Strathmartine Road, near Kirkton. They were discovered precisely where he had indicated. But despite a massive citywide search, the head of his victim was never found, though it was suspected it may have been deposited in a rubbish skip near the killer's home in Haldane Terrace.

Nearly two years later, Thompson was back in the dock in Edinburgh, this time to hear the Court of Criminal Appeal turn down his plea that he had been the victim of a miscarriage of justice. He was well used to protesting his innocence. Four days after beginning his second life term, Thompson had penned an eloquent, perfectly punctuated, 3,000-word letter to the *Courier* newspaper – which went unpublished – the thrust of which was that he had not killed his grandmother. He also gave a detailed, and in places, moving account of his largely institutionalised life.

Turning to the murder of Gordon Dunbar, the butcher of Butterburn Court concluded:

> The jury reached a verdict and though I could argue that it was the wrong one I cannot but accept it and in accepting it I accept that I am likely to die in prison. There is nothing else that can be done to me than that and it is a punishment I would not wish on my worst enemy.

During his second life term, Thompson apparently 'found God' and he pursued his new interest with zeal, occasionally causing other inmates to complain about his 'bible-bashing' activities. In

2002 he designed a Celtic cross t-shirt which was worn by school-children during the Pope's visit to Scotland. The double-killer even dreamed of becoming a Church of Scotland minister after his hoped-for release.

That did not materialise. In December 2010, having served more than seventeen years of his minimum 20-year term, Alastair Thompson's earlier prediction came to pass. He died, aged 61, in Perth Prison. Most of his life from the age of twelve had been spent in one form of custody or another.

12

BABES IN THE HOUSE

When the curtain of rage that had descended over her at last lifted, the child-killer smoothed her dress and walked from the room, not even looking back as she gently closed the bedroom door behind her. The injuries she had inflicted were violent, sustained and quite deliberate. Pretty Helen Laird had been hit, repeatedly bitten and strangled. She was found in bed in her home in Blacklock Crescent, part of the Linlathen timber-house estate on Dundee's north-eastern perimeter, at 1.20 in the morning and to this day no one knows why she had to die. She was only just three and the birthday presents she had received four days earlier still lay in the room beside her.

The person who caused the little child to suffer was also in the house, sleeping on a couch, and she couldn't explain either what little Helen had done to bring on such a ferocious attack. Whatever it was, the unaccountable fury that detonated inside her that September night in 1972 thrust upon Annette McGowan the kind of infamy that usually exists only in the dark pages of horror stories. At thirteen years of age, Annette that day became the youngest killer her native city had ever known; indeed, she was, and remains, among the most tender-aged females to have taken a life anywhere in Britain. If this notoriety conjures up images of a juvenile monster, evil beyond words and capable of the worst kind of unspeakable atrocities, that would be a mistake.

For in reality Annette was the second victim in this wretched encounter when death came calling. By any definition, she deserved much of the sympathy that came her way. Some even thought she

Gordon Johnston, the gun shop manager who was axed to death to aid kidnap and mail van robbery plots.

His 'Monday Morning' killers, Ryan Monks and Paul Mill.

GOW'S

Barbour

Detectives gather outside the scene of the bloody murder.

Elizabeth McCabe and Carol Lannen, the Templeton Woods sisters-in-death whose killer or killers have never been traced. A photofit of the Carol Lannen suspect (above right) who bears a striking resemblance to depraved social worker Andrew Hunter (below), jailed for the murder of his wife Lynda Hunter (right). Hunter insisted on showing his 'good' side when he posed for the picture.

© PRESS ASSOCIATION

Record crowds gather at the courthouse for Hunter's trial.

© DC THOMSON & CO LTD

The chilling stare of double killer Alastair Thompson (top left) on his way to start his second life sentence. His victim Gordon Dunbar (above), whose head was never found.

Police search for body parts. In the background is the multi-storey block where Thompson, the 'Butcher of Butterburn Court', killed and cut up his victim.

The block of flats where Robertson concealed Margaret's body under the kitchen floorboards.

Margaret Robertson, the second bride to die at the hands of her husband Peter.

Sister Raphael, a teacher at the school.

Robert Mone Junior, pictured in his army uniform three weeks before he walked into his old school with a rifle and began shooting.

Marion Young, the teenage heroine who entered the siege classroom to negotiate with Mone and who was later presented with the George Medal by the Queen.

Nanette Hanson, the pregnant teacher who died after being shot in the back by Mone and who was posthumously awarded the Albert Medal for her bravery.

Some of the St John's pupils on their way to hospital after running to freedom.

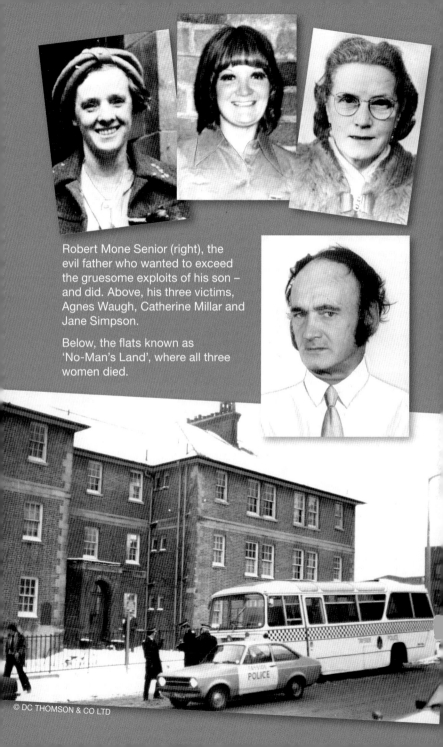

Robert Mone Senior (right), the evil father who wanted to exceed the gruesome exploits of his son – and did. Above, his three victims, Agnes Waugh, Catherine Millar and Jane Simpson.

Below, the flats known as 'No-Man's Land', where all three women died.

Michael Wilkinson (right), the Jekyll and Hyde child-killer who strangled his young victim while his daughter watched.

A happy picture of James and Helen Wilkie taken shortly before she went missing.

The remote spot in the country where a chance in a million led to the discovery of Helen's remains four years after she disappeared.

© RON GAZZARD

© DC THOMSON & CO LTD

Charles Shepherd, the 'friendly' neighbour who lured his eight-year-old victim to her death by taking her for trips on his scooter. And the small outhouse on the outskirts of the city where her body was found thanks to a detective's hunch.

© DC THOMSON & CO LTD

Police mug-shots (right) of 'Confessional Killer' Henry Gallagher, whose murderous spree spread to two countries. The house (below) where his trail of slaughter began.

669409 GALLAGHER. H.

© DC THOMSON & CO LTD

Convicted and cuffed. The 'not so ordinary' John Smith (left) – killer, rapist, prison rioter and abductor – is led away for his latest stretch. 'Little Boy Blue' Robbie McIntosh (above), the fifteen-year-old killer who stabbed his victim twenty-nine times, leaves court to begin a sentence set at a minimum of fifteen years.

Angus Elliot, the martial arts expert who used a Commando knife to end the life of Irene Martin, the policewoman he hoped to marry, and the block of flats he set alight in an attempt to cover his tracks.

should not have been alone when she came to sit in the dock of the High Court to answer for her actions.

The events that took her there were straightforward enough. The mothers of the two girls were friends, living in neighbouring estates with unhappy marriages behind them. Between them they had ten children – Annette was one of seven to her 37-year-old mother, Mary McGowan, and Helen was the youngest of three daughters to 32-year-old Sheila Laird. The two women who bore these offspring were like many others of their generation – young mothers in post-war Dundee, a city struggling to come to terms with high unemployment and doing its best to house much of its population in new, but soulless, housing developments far from the city centre. Broken marriages abounded and the women left with the children sought an outlet from their boredom and enforced poverty with nights out at bingo parlours, or on drinking binges. The age had passed when women did not enter a public house without the company of a man and, like the bingo palaces, lounge bars with live music were flourishing in the city. That Saturday night the mothers of the two children went to visit one of them, The Blair, halfway down Princes Street and on the bus route from Linlathen into town. Thirteen-year-old Annette, not for the first time, was called upon to babysit for the Laird children – Helen (3), Susan (5) and Elizabeth (7).

The mothers departed in mid-evening and, in their terms, the night turned out to be a resounding success. They met two men and went off with them to a party in another part of town. At 1.20 the following morning, the pair finally returned to Blacklock Crescent. When they entered the house, Annette, who had been sleeping on a settee in the living-room of the flat, woke up. Mrs Laird went to check on her three daughters but could not find Helen in either of the two bedrooms. The two older children, who shared a bed, were roused and when Elizabeth was asked where her youngest sister was, she pointed to the bottom of the bed and answered, 'There. She's there.' Anxiously pulling back the blankets, the mother saw the still, cold figure of Helen huddled in a corner at the base of the bed. She knew instantly that she was not sleeping.

'Helen's dead,' she shouted over and over. By this time Mrs McGowan was in the room and she desperately lifted the little girl into her arms and tried as best as she knew how to administer the kiss of life. It brought no reaction from the child who had long stopped breathing.

Later that day, Annette was charged with her murder.

Eleven weeks on, and with Christmas just a week away, Annette McGowan sat nervously in the dock of the High Court in Dundee as the whole bewildering panoply of a trial in the most solemn court in the land was played out before her. She wore a dark coat and bright, multi-coloured dress and tightly clutched the hand of the policewoman seated beside her.

The question of who had killed little Helen was never really an issue. A dental expert told the jury that he 'did not entertain the slightest doubt' that the many bite marks had been inflicted by the 13-year-old babysitter. What required to be determined was the level of guilt that should attach to the child perpetrator of the manual strangulation that had brought on the death. Was it culpable homicide, as had ultimately been libelled, or should the charge be reduced to assault because of the special circumstances surrounding the case?

There were plenty of those. Psychiatrists explained to the court that Annette suffered from a mental disorder linked with epilepsy and also an unusual genetic eye condition which was known to be associated with other defects. She was of diminished responsibility. Mr R. D. MacKay, the prosecuting advocate depute, told the jurors they faced a task more difficult than the one usually confronting juries, because they could not allow the facts to be clouded by sympathy and emotion.

'You may feel sympathy for the accused, her unhappy background, her physical disabilities,' he said. 'On the other hand, you may feel a certain horror and shock that an attractive little girl should die in this way.' However, he urged them to put their feelings aside and accept their responsibility of looking only at the facts.

Mr Charles McArthur, QC, defending, described the case as 'particularly tragic' and asked the jury to find Annette guilty of assault only. He pleaded: 'It is extremely tragic and very distressing for you and for me to find myself responsible for the little girl of thirteen sitting in the dock.' He agreed that the case depended on the facts, but said sympathy could not be put out of mind. Then, as though reading the minds of many of those who sat in the High Court that pre-Christmas day, he struck out, saying:

> Perhaps one is a little less sympathetic to those who are responsible for their small children being looked after. I find it very distressing little children should be left to be looked after by a young girl to a very late hour. That may just be part of the whole tragic set-up.

When the jury returned after an absence of only seventeen minutes to find her guilty of culpable homicide, Annette started to cry quietly in the dock and turned to cuddle closer to her policewoman escort, gripping her hand even more tightly. Her mother, seated in the public benches, sobbed loudly and was assisted from the courtroom by friends.

Most of the court time was taken up in discussion about where the tearful 13-year-old could be held to serve her sentence. Mental health experts said the State Mental Hospital at Carstairs was the only place in Scotland suitable for Annette, though it was not ideal, and there was no room there for her. One consultant in child psychiatry explained that Annette required long-term, consistent care in 'graduation security'. He thought the security would be at the beginning rather than the end of her period in detention and that ideally the prognosis would be satisfactory enough to allow her 'eventual return to responsibility'. 'Regretfully, I know of nowhere in Scotland which can provide this treatment,' he said with some resignation.

Another consultant psychiatrist opined, 'I think it is necessary for the girl's own safety, and possibly the safety of others, that she be in conditions of security before one should begin a plan. That would mean she would be long enough in one place to develop satisfactory relationships, at least with adults and perhaps with people of her own age.'

Lord Keith on the bench, who had listened intently to the medical experts, continued the case to allow more time for a suitable place of detention to be found. He looked gently at the weeping Annette and told her that no one could avoid feeling very distressed about the nature of the case or a great deal of sympathy with her about the circumstances, problems and sad events that brought her to the court, or the fact she was there at all. Three weeks later, at the High Court in Edinburgh, at the resumption of the hearing, His Lordship was informed that little real progress had been made and there was no place in Scotland which was suitable from the point of view of security and the kind of assistance Annette required. Ultimately, it was decided that the tiny figure who sat in court with a bright red ribbon in her hair should be accommodated in a new special care unit for disturbed adolescents forming part of Balgay Approved School in Dundee.

Lord Keith ordered that she be detained for ten years. But he told her that while the order he had made specified that period of time, it did not necessarily mean she would be held for that duration. The Scottish Secretary, he said, had the discretion to allow her release on licence when he thought fit.

Annette McGowan disappeared from public view that day, 5 January 1973, and what ultimately became of her is not commonly known. She vanished beneath the cloak of anonymity given to offending juveniles and there is nothing to suggest she ever appeared in a court again. Nor is it publicly known for how long she was detained. That is not surprising. What is remarkable, given the deep interest in more contemporary times of the activities of children who kill, is that the case of Annette McGowan did not attract more attention than it did in her home town when the unusual and disturbing events were played out. A quarter of a century later, there are few in local police or legal circles who are aware she even existed.

13

THE CARRY-OUT KILLER

The approach of Christmas 1970 seemed to signal a change in fortunes in the troubled life of Leah Bramley. Twice married and with three young children, she had moved away from Yorkshire five weeks earlier to seek a new start in Dundee, leaving her miner husband Bernard back in Castleford.

The move hadn't begun well. After spending a few days residing with her sister, the 33-year-old took up the tenancy of a small flat in Springhill. But it was too cramped to accommodate the whole family and the three children – the products of her first marriage – had to be split up. The oldest girl, aged fourteen, remained with her, but her 9-year-old daughter and 7-year-old son were sent to live temporarily in a Salvation Army hostel in Lochee. Then things suddenly took a turn for the better. Out of the blue and to Leah's surprised delight, she was given the keys to a brand new council flat in Dundee's developing Whitfield housing estate. She moved at once into the first-floor maisonette at 389 Ormiston Crescent and wrote excitedly to her husband with the news, telling him how he could help her get established when he came north for a Christmas visit. 'Dundee has been lucky to me at last,' she enthused.

A few days later, as the fairy lights twinkled in the recently occupied houses in the new estate, the small, attractive blonde was found dead in the flat she had been so proud to occupy.

She was slumped in a rocking chair, an imitation fur coat over the shoulders of her green jumper, and her lower body was naked with a broom-handle protruding from her intimate parts. Although there were signs of manual strangulation and three superficial cut injuries to her neck, these did not appear to be the main cause of her death. That had come after a series of severe sexual assaults by the broom-handle and a drinking glass, which were both found nearby, heavily bloodstained. Among other items scattered near the body, and the large pool of blood which had formed under the chair, was an empty McEwen's Export can and a tin-opener. A number of pieces of burnt paper were also on the floor beside the corpse.

Detective Superintendent William Melville, the head of Dundee CID, whose distinguished career was to see him successfully solve more than forty homicides in the city, described the killing as 'one of the worst sadistic murders I have ever seen'.

Murder squad detectives made two significant discoveries. There was not a fingerprint to be found in the room, not even of the victim, with every surface seemingly having been wiped by a damp cloth; and there was no evidence of a break-in, suggesting that Leah had known her killer.

Although the body of the petite blonde had been found at 5.30 p.m., the city's senior police surgeon said he believed she had died many hours before – probably in the early hours of that day. His post-mortem indicated that the light cuts on her neck could have been made by a tin-opener and that the violent injuries to her private parts had been carried out while she was still alive, but that she had probably been rendered unconscious a short time before the intimate assault by blows to the chin, combined with a form of strangulation. If she had not been insensible, she would have screamed out because of the intolerable pain caused by the massive internal injuries.

Enquiries quickly established that at about 7 p.m. on the previous night Leah had gone with a woman friend to the Heather Bell bar in William Street, where she consumed more than half a dozen lagers. As the mood became merrier, she had asked the guitarist who entertained in the pub to play a particular song. He obliged, then she asked him to join her for a drink.

Witnesses told police that Leah had become 'very friendly' with the singer and had proceeded to invite him to a party, requesting that he bring some drink along in the form of a carry-out. Others described how a little later that night, just after closing time, Leah had knocked on the door of the pub to ask for the musician, who had stayed behind for an after-hours drink. After apparently expressing some annoyance at being disturbed, the musician, who used the stage name Ron Gibson, bought a dozen cans of export and twenty cigarettes and left. He was last seen driving off with Leah in his two-tone red and grey Ford Zodiac.

Eighteen hours after the presumed time of the murder, the guitar player – who in reality was Alexander Stuart, a 25-year-old married man who also lived in the Whitfield estate – was invited to police headquarters to make a statement. He was a character with a complex life. As well as using assumed names to dodge the taxman when he sang round the city's pubs, he worked as a hairdresser and also as a part-time taxi driver with Handy Taxis (one of the leading companies in town). Stuart related how the woman who had earlier asked him to sing had requested that he drive her to her sister's home in Mid Craigie, which he did. When they arrived, the sister was walking in the street and Leah had left the car to briefly speak to her, before returning to ask him to drive her home to Ormiston Crescent. Halfway there, however, in Pitkerro Road, she wanted him to stop the car. He did so and she got out. He had not seen her since.

Stuart went on to explain to detectives how he had subsequently gone taxi-ing and had driven round various estates on the northern edge of the city but hadn't landed a single fare. He had even tried several times to phone the taxi company headquarters seeking work, but the phone had been constantly engaged. Eventually, he had gone home to Whitfield and called at a neighbour's house, where he knew his wife had been spending part of the evening with a couple who were friends. He had taken his carry-out of twelve cans of McEwan's Export with him, he said.

The neighbours corroborated the latter part of his story, telling how he had arrived at the door shortly before 1 a.m. and had then spent some time with them, drinking and singing and playing his guitar. There had been nothing unusual about his behaviour or anything in his demeanour to suggest he had undergone some kind of terrible experience, they said. He had spoken about sex, which was a usual part of his conversation when in their company, and had, equally typically, taunted his wife about his supposed sexual conquests.

At 3.30 on the morning of 14 December, less than twelve hours after the body of Leah Bramley was so dramatically found sprawled and bloodstained in the flat she had been so thrilled to move into, Alexander Stuart, the singing hairdresser was charged with her murder. He replied simply, 'I dropped her off in Mid Craigie.'

Several weeks later, while the accused man was held in Perth Prison awaiting trial, his solicitor, John Clarke, received a remarkable handwritten letter at his office in Victoria Chambers in Dundee. It read:

I gather you are Stuart's lawyer. I want to confess the Whitfield murder to clear my mind and free an innocent man. On Saturday, 12/12/70, I picked up a woman at the bottom of Pitkerro Road at about 11.35–11.40 p.m. She asked me to take her to Ormiston Crescent.

In the car she was at my privates. We went to her house and we had intercourse. After it she laughed at me and said she was on her 'periods'. I went berserk and I choked her. I then took her tights and strangled her. I cut her on the neck with a can-opener and a knife.

The confessor then described how he had further sexually assaulted his female companion with a broom-handle, beer can and a tumbler.

The letter went on:

I robbed her of £1 18 shillings and 3 pence. I am guilty of this murder and getting away with it. No fingerprints. I know Stuart was in her house because he dropped something with his name on it. I tried to start a fire but her blood put it out. The CID will confirm everything I have told you.

I don't think I will have any bother sleeping now I have got this off my conscience. I am going to write to the papers and let them know.

Signed, Taxi Man.

The letter, apparently written on the torn-out fly-page of a book, was a bombshell. Police and the Crown prosecutors knew that if the jury in the forthcoming trial took it at face value Stuart would be exonerated and would walk free. The letter contained information which at that stage had never been made public and the writer had either killed her himself, or was closely connected to the person who had.

Detectives went at once to Perth Prison and launched rigorous investigations, interviewing prison officers and inmates in an effort to trace the source of the letter. They made a series of startling discoveries. A mutilated copy of *The Sunday Post* had been found in Stuart's cell and a series of words had been cut from it. Checks revealed that many of the missing words were identical to some of those contained in the letter of confession and it seemed that whoever had so painstakingly extracted them from the paper may have initially intended to use them to form a letter. They thought this plan might have been abandoned because some of the words in the confession were not the sort usually to be found in a newspaper like *The Sunday Post*.

The police team examined every one of the four hundred or so books in the library of 'C' Hall in the prison, the wing where Stuart was held. They found one, *The Kingdom of Melchior*, with a ripped-out fly-page which apparently corresponded to the tears on the letter of confession.

Most crucially of all, however, was a third discovery. When forensic experts subjected an untried prisoner's letter form pad, which had been issued to Stuart, to special lighting, a series of indentations were found, apparently pressed there by someone who had used the pad as a rest to write on. The indentations formed the words 'Taxi Man', '12 Victoria' and 'Dundee'. A more detailed examination revealed phrases and sentences which matched exactly most of those in the letter of confession.

When he stood trial at the High Court in Dundee the following February, Stuart gave the jury a different story to the one he had told police. Instead of continuing to deny that he had gone to Leah Bramley's home in Ormiston Crescent, he admitted he had accompanied her to the flat but had become disgusted when she exposed herself.

'I would not wear it,' he told the jurors. 'I lifted my beer and walked out of the house. When I got to the door she shouted she was sorry and said, 'Will you take me back to my sister's?' 'He went on to recount that he had driven her around for some time while she kept changing her desired destination and that he had finally become frustrated by her and had dropped her off in the Mid Craigie area.

Questioned closely about the supposed letter of confession, Stuart declared that he had been angry when it had turned up because it had a detrimental effect. 'I had a good case until this letter came,' he protested. 'It was done to do me down and is making my case worse.' He said he believed that someone 'had it in' for him.

He then proceeded to give a detailed account of how the cut-up *Sunday Post* finished up in his cell and how he believed the indentations had come to appear on his writing pad. The newspaper had been his, he admitted, but he had passed it on to other prisoners after he had finished reading it. Later, when he was throwing out old newspapers, he saw two papers in a dust-bin in 'C' Hall and had removed them to read, unaware that one of them was actually the *Sunday Post* which he had disposed of.

He had a similar tale to tell about the writing pad. Because he had been bored sitting in his cell for practically twenty-four hours a day, he had asked for the pad so that he could make up crosswords. After drawing about half a dozen lines on the back of the pad, it had ripped and the next morning he threw it out with a pile of other rubbish when cleaning out the cell. The next time he saw it, it came through the observation hatch in his door, folded up and accompanied by a note repeating much of what was in the letter of confession that had been sent to his solicitor.

Stuart went on to relate how he had also received two other notes through the door of his cell. He read one of them out to the jury. It stated:

Don't think I'm a nut. I know you are innocent. It's me who done that bitch in. I thought you would get lifted for it. I'll explain how later. But I'll do what I can to clear you. But if you tell the screws I'll clam up.

Pressed by the prosecution, he denied writing the notes himself.

The jury could hardly be blamed for being sceptical about the 'evidence' which had been intended to absolve the accused, but any lingering doubts they might have entertained about his innocence completely evaporated in the face of scientific revelations which the Crown admitted formed the linchpin of their case

Police had recovered each of the twelve cans of McEwen's Export that Stuart had taken away with him when he and Leah Bramley had gone off together from the Heather Bell. One can, bloodstained, had been removed from her home and the eleven others, empty and bearing the identical batch number to the one taken from the murder scene, had been gathered from the refuse bin of Stuart's neighbour where he had gone for a drink and sing-song later the same night.

On one of these tins was a minute trace of blood. Tests revealed that the blood grouping was OMN – the same as Leah's, but also the same as the accused and all of those who had been in the neighbour's house that evening.

The bloodstain initially appeared, therefore, to prove nothing. However, realising the vital significance of the trace of blood,

Dr Donald Rushton – the senior Dundee police surgeon, who had been the principal forensic witness for the prosecution – was determined to establish if the OMN grouping could be further refined, perhaps eliminating some of those in that broad category of people whose blood was of that type. He knew of a sophisticated test, developed in England and never previously used in a Scottish criminal case, and instructed that the sample from the beer can, and others from all the people involved in the case, be sent to London for detailed examination at the Metropolitan Police Forensic Science Laboratory. He went south himself and stood by as the meticulous analysis was carried out.

The results were better than anyone could have hoped for. The blood on the Export can was found to be of the rare OMN AK2/1 group, found in less than 2 per cent of the population. Vitally, it was identical to Mrs Bramley's grouping and was the only sample from those of the others tested which matched.

It meant with near certainty that the brutally murdered Leah Bramley had come by her terrible injuries *before* Stuart had left the house taking his unopened eleven cans of export with him.

The 25-year-old father of two sat nervously in the dock biting his lip after the jury retired. But it did not take long for him to learn his fate. Half an hour later, the jurors returned with a unanimous verdict of guilty.

The man of many parts, who thought he could outwit the police by wiping every fingerprint from the murder scene and then penning a letter of confession from a bogus killer, had been too clever by half. Instead of deflecting his guilt, the letter merely served to implicate him and he had not been as thorough with the cleaning cloth as he had believed. In his bid to remove clues, he had taken away the carry-out cans of beer but had failed to wipe them first. It was just his bad luck that the woman who had admired his singing had also belonged to a rare blood group.

Lord Emslie told Stuart:

You have been found by the jury to be guilty of the crime of murder. I shall waste no time attempting to explain to you the horror of the crime of which you have been convicted. I content myself in passing sentence against you as prescribed by law. You will go to prison for life.

14

TO LOVE, HONOUR
AND . . . KILL

Margaret Maich classically represented women who reach a particular age and find themselves at one of life's crossroads. She was in her early forties, divorced, with her family grown up and living away from home. The future was depressingly predictable – the gradual onset of old age, probably accompanied by increasing infirmity and, worst of all, loneliness. Although she enjoyed her job in the bakery department of the Tesco supermarket in Dundee's bustling Wellgate Centre, it didn't provide the kind of income ever likely to offer the comfortable financial security she wanted during the twilight years that beckoned. Though she may not have been actively searching for a companion, there was the smouldering hope, never publicly expressed, that her path might one day cross with that of some suitable man.

When it happened, it wasn't quite what she had so keenly anticipated in her quiet moments alone. On a warm day in July 1975 she encountered Peter Robertson, three years older than herself and a presentable figure approaching six feet in height, slim and with a fashionable black moustache. He wasn't the tall, dark stranger of her dreams, however. In fact, she had known him since their teenage days and he had gone on to marry her best friend, Sandra. He had also gone on to kill her and serve nine years of a life sentence for the homicide.

Margaret had never entirely approved of her lifelong chum's association with Robertson. He was something of a ne'er-do-well who had drifted in and out of prison, usually for offences associated with violence, and it was after yet another term in jail that he and Sandra moved to Lincoln to begin a new life. Little changed for the Robertsons in England. He continued to drink heavily and the worst sessions usually culminated in acts of violence against Sandra. After fifteen years of marriage, and with five children, the pair divorced in 1964. One or other of them might have been expected to find their way back to Dundee, but both remained in Lincoln. And unaccountably, given the circumstances of their assault-ridden relationship, they continued to meet – and continued to row noisily.

Almost two years after their divorce, on the evening of 1 July 1966, Robertson paid his ex-wife yet another drunken visit and there was the inevitable argument. It degenerated, as always, into an attack on Sandra. To defend herself, she picked up a poker and struck out at him. He reacted, just as predictably, by meeting violence with even greater violence, grabbing her wrist with one hand and her throat with the other. She attempted to ward him off by kneeing him in the groin; he lashed out at her again, then twisted her arm up her back. Then Sandra suddenly gave up the struggle, dropping the poker and sinking limp to the floor. Her ex-husband gazed down at her motionless body and in an alcoholic stupor lifted her and carried her with difficulty to an upstairs bedroom where he laid her on a bed. She did not sleep then – or ever again – for the drunken bully had finally killed the woman who had borne his five children.

Four months later, at Lincolnshire Assizes, Robertson was found guilty of murder – later reduced to manslaughter – and jailed for life. Before being sent down, he was asked by Mr Justice Moccatta if he had anything to say.

'I didn't mean to kill my wife,' was the short response.

These were virtually the identical words he used to Margaret on bumping into her in Dundee nine years later when he returned to the city immediately after his release from prison on licence. He described the killing as a 'once-in-a-lifetime, terrible mistake' and the gentle, thoughtful – but lonely – woman believed him. Five months later they married.

For three years it seemed as though Margaret's confidence in her new husband's frank admissions were justified. Their relationship was stable and apparently untroubled – 'almost perfect' was how a relative described it – and Robertson, who had found work as a labourer in a jute mill, was attentive and considerate, rarely drinking to excess. Friends and relatives, who, unsurprisingly, had been anxious for Margaret, were relieved that their fears appeared to be groundless. Then the couple changed houses – moving from the outskirts of the city to a ground-floor flat much closer to the centre of town, at 3 Moncur Crescent – and Robertson, almost overnight, changed too. He resumed his old drinking habits and began dividing his time between the local pubs and betting shops. His prolonged absences from their new flat, which Margaret proudly kept immaculate, led to quarrels – as did the accompanying shortage of money. Neighbours became aware of the frequent rows, but none could speak of any acts of violence going on in the spotless ground floor-flat on the busy bus route into town.

At 10.45 a.m. on 2 July 1981, a neighbour and Margaret exchanged the time of day. Then the well-liked woman, who never drank and who asked little from life except a comfortable home and secure future, suddenly vanished. The same neighbour heard noises coming from the Robertsons' prim flat around ten o'clock the following morning – not the rowing they had become accustomed to, but banging sounds. It was not something the woman thought much about and life went on as normal in the peaceful block of flats beside Dens Park, home of Dundee Football Club.

The humdrum routine of the close only altered when Peter Robertson explained Margaret's absence from the neighbourhood by saying she had decided without warning to go off with an unidentified workmate on a short holiday to England. He gave no additional details and the surprised other occupants of the flats discussed how they found their friend's sudden departure curious, the kind of impulsive act they would not have expected of her. Margaret hadn't made mention of the surprise trip south to anybody – not even to a particularly close neighbour, a lady with a heart condition, whom Margaret, in her kindly way, visited on a regular basis to keep a concerned eye on.

The unease shared by many of the Moncur Crescent residents deepened when one neighbour spread the news that Margaret had discussed travelling to Bristol in the weeks ahead to visit a married daughter there. It seemed 'unlikely', she suggested, that Margaret would make two trips to England so close together. Apart from the expense, getting the time off from the Tesco bakery department would have been difficult.

A few days after the disappearance of the well-liked woman in their midst, one of the neighbours received an unexpected Saturday-morning visit from Peter Robertson. He broke the startling news that after Margaret returned from her holiday they would be moving to a new house away from Moncur Crescent. When the neighbour expressed surprise at this turn of events, Robertson soothingly reassured her that his wife would not forget her fellow residents in the block and would make regular visits to them.

Much of the disquiet that was being felt evaporated eleven days after Margaret had last been seen: postcards, signed 'Margaret', arrived through the letterboxes of two friends in the area. They were postmarked 'Lincoln' and told how she was enjoying her short break. No one seemed aware that in the lead-up to the delivery of the cards, Peter Robertson, by now unemployed, had also mysteriously vanished from the scene, or that he had formerly lived in the Lincoln area. No one appreciated, either, that a few days after his wife had last been seen he had called at the Tesco store to explain that Margaret had suddenly taken ill with shingles and was unlikely to return to work for two or three weeks. He produced a note signed in her name authorising him to collect her outstanding wages of £37, which was readily given to him.

It wasn't the only money that was to come his way during the strange absence of the home-loving woman he had wed so soon after release from his life sentence in prison. On 18 July – sixteen days after Margaret had apparently departed for her unannounced holiday in England, Robertson arrived at the offices of Leeds Permanent Building Society in Reform Street, Dundee. He was accompanied by an unidentified woman whom he introduced to staff as his wife Margaret, explaining that they had come to close her account and withdraw the £2,913 it contained. In fact, the nervous female by his side who barely spoke was the girlfriend of an acquaintance whose assistance Robertson had sought. Robertson had told him that Margaret was in England and they had urgent need of her life-savings, but to save her from returning north, and because he knew the building society rules would prevent them from paying the cash to anyone but the pass-book holder, it would be of great assistance if the man's woman friend would briefly pose as Margaret to enable him to collect the cash. As an inducement, Robertson promised each of them 10 per cent of what he received, adding that Margaret herself knew of the arrangement and agreed to the payment.

Inside the offices of the Leeds Permanent, things did not go quite as well as Robertson had hoped they would. A member of staff explained that company policy prohibited them from giving out more than £300 in cash and that the remainder would be paid by cheque. The anxious couple reluctantly agreed to accept the payment on that basis, then immediately encountered another unexpected problem. The clerk dealing with the transaction looked closely at the signature of the 'Margaret Robertson' before him and left without explanation to consult the office manager. He had spotted that the writing differed slightly from the specimen kept in the office and his uneasy instincts about the couple deepened his suspicions. The manager noted the discrepancies between the signatures but also pointed out similarities – which was hardly surprising, since the impostor had spent much of the previous night copying it – and authorised the payment.

After quickly leaving the office with the £300 in cash and cheque, the extremely relieved Robertson hurriedly handed over the promised payment to the woman and her boyfriend who had waited down the street, then vanished into the throngs of people who packed the pavements round the nearby bus stops.

Shortly before midnight the following day, and only forty minutes into his Sunday-evening shift, PC David Murdoch answered the phone in police headquarters in the city's Bell Street to take the most unforgettable call of his entire career. A male, who refused to give his name, spoke crisply but urgently and refused to be interrupted by the attempts of PC Murdoch to ask routine questions. The caller cut him short, telling him he had something important to say and would not repeat it: 'If you go to the house at 3 Moncur Crescent, occupied by Robertson, you will find the body of Margaret Robertson under the kitchen floorboards.' Then the man on the other end of the line told how police would be able to gain access to the flat by using keys which were concealed under the first rose bush in the front garden. The call ended shortly afterwards with the request that police should notify the dead woman's sister about what had happened.

Two uniformed officers hurried to the scene. One of them, PC Angus Low, retrieved the keys from the precise location described in the phone call, then used them to make his way into the darkened house. With some trepidation, he put on the lights and, after noting the house's spotless condition, looked quickly into the bedrooms before proceeding into the kitchen. At the far end of the room he detected the outline of a hatch under linoleum, partly covered by a table and chairs. Taking a screwdriver from a nearby cupboard, the constable prised open the hatch, switched on his torch and, with quickening heartbeat, lowered himself slowly into the opening before him.

Doing his best to ignore the cold air and strange smell that rushed to greet him, he squeezed his way into the five-foot-deep foundations which contained an assortment of boxes and tins of paint. The probing beam of his torch flashed round the

10-foot-by-6-foot compartment, but revealed nothing out of the ordinary. Then, in a second sweep, the light exposed a rough hole in the brick wall at the far end of the basement pit and, protruding from it but barely visible, was what at first appeared to be a heap of clothing. When he moved nearer, he saw the bundle was covered by a sheet of transparent polythene and held together with a rough rope. It was only when he was inches away that the constable realised he had found the body he had searched for but hadn't really expected to find. In his haste to report this gruesome discovery, he kicked over a tin of paint and unknowingly left a trail of white footprints through the house as he hurried from the makeshift crypt to report back to headquarters.

Detectives and forensic scientists were roused from their beds and within the hour the once-anonymous council flat was the focus of intense activity. Other occupants of the block, awakened by the arrival of the procession of vehicles and the excited chatter, knew, without asking, that their missing neighbour had been traced.

Detective Inspector Ernie Brown, who was to lead the hunt for her killer, started the inquiry with a fairly full hand. Although the body had lain in the cellar for some three weeks, the ventilation in the dingy foundations had preserved the corpse in an unusually fine condition and positive identification was quickly established with the aid of a photograph album found in another part of the house. An early post-mortem also revealed that the cause of death was strangulation. In addition, it seemed a reasonable inference that the man who had placed the call alerting PC Murdoch to the existence of the body, was also the killer. His identity didn't present many problems either. The call he had made had been routinely recorded and extracts were played to folk who knew the sound of Peter Robertson's voice. They all said without hesitation that the mystery caller was indeed the husband of Margaret Robertson. Another police check revealed that the man they were now desperately hunting had killed before, almost fifteen years earlier to the day, when wife number one had perished at his hands.

It didn't take long for his likely whereabouts to be determined. Later in the day, as news of the gruesome find was made public and detectives began visiting Robertson's known haunts, another call came into police HQ, this time from a fellow officer in Skegness who was making enquiries into a probable suicide in the English seaside resort. The constable explained that at 9.20 that morning, a female lifeguard had found a pile of men's clothing on the beach at Skegness, arranged neatly at the side of the lifeguard's hut. In the pocket of a jacket was a membership card for Dundee Football Club, a union card and a bill from the nearby Godiva Hotel – all of them bearing the name Peter Robertson. When police had gone to the hotel they searched the single room Robertson had occupied and discovered a letter propped on a bedside table. It read: 'I have told the Dundee police what has been haunting me these past day (*sic*). Between nagging women and these daft horses, life's just a wank anyway.' It was signed 'Peter Robertson'.

On the face of it, it seemed a reasonably logical, if tragic, conclusion to the macabre events that had unfolded nearly three weeks earlier in the neat council flat hundreds of miles away in Dundee. Facing a second life sentence for the slaying of another woman who had married him, and unable to contemplate that prospect, Robertson had unburdened himself in an anonymous phone call to the police, telling where he had disposed of the body. Then, having spent all of the money he had withdrawn from Margaret's building society account and facing almost certain arrest, he had taken the route of numerous other killers: the ending of his own life. The tidily arranged clothing – everything from his suit down to his pants and socks – left on the beach along with the identification documents in the jacket pockets, and the brief note of explanation in the guest house room, neatly fitted the pattern of many suicide victims.

But for Detective Inspector Ernie Brown in Dundee, it was just too convenient. All the instincts and cynicism that police officers possess, acquired from years of dealing with manipulative criminals, told him that the real victims might be the police themselves if they believed what was so tidily being presented to them. His counterparts in Skegness felt the same, but for different reasons. Coastguard officers, familiar with every trick of the tide on that stretch of coast, knew with reasonable certainty that a body which had gone into the water there would inevitably resurface in the same area twenty-four hours later. A continuous search showed that that had never happened.

Teams of officers in Scotland and England embarked on a round of visits to all of Peter Robertson's known haunts in Dundee, Skegness and Lincoln. Scores of pubs, betting shops and lodging houses were scoured for the double-wife-killer. All enquiries drew a blank. It began to look as though the imagined fugitive may indeed have ended his days under the waves.

Then, nearly three weeks later, matters took an incredible and almost unbelievable turn. Police in Dundee received a visit from the woman who the previous month had gone with Robertson to the Leeds Permanent Building Society to masquerade as his wife. She had a remarkable story to relate. A short time earlier, she said, she had gone to the lounge of the Ellenbank Bar in Alexander Street with a female friend and, after just a few minutes, she had become startlingly aware of two men seated at a nearby table. One of them, she became convinced, was Peter Robertson, although he no longer had a moustache and his hair was styled differently. The longer she looked, the more certain she was that she was facing the man being hunted in two countries. Any lingering doubts that she may have had then evaporated when he approached her table and started to make advances. Certain now of his identity, and conscious that his easy conversation was probably an attempt to determine whether he had been recognised, the woman fought her instincts to flee from the bar. Instead, she waited ten minutes, left quietly –and headed at once for the nearest police station to tell her extraordinary story.

Four officers rushed to the Ellenbank Bar and found Robertson standing casually at the bar. His demeanour changed instantly on seeing the policemen and, after a few moments spent regaining his composure, he admitted who he was and said he knew why they were there.

He told the officers, 'She was nagging, nagging, nagging. It was me that done it. I ken what it was all aboot.'

It many ways it was an unexpected admission, given the cunning he had shown in his elaborate attempt to convince police that he had committed suicide. Yet it was no more surprising than the fact that he had inexplicably returned to Dundee to resume visiting the pubs in his old neighbourhood only three weeks after so cleverly placing his clothing on the shore at Skegness. Police may not have believed he had taken his own life, but if he had quietly moved to a distant part of the country and maintained a low profile, they might never have known for sure.

Later, when formally interviewed by detectives at police headquarters, Robertson again readily confessed to the murder. He also spoke at length about the circumstances leading up to the moment when he throttled the woman who for five years had lived with the uncomfortable knowledge that he had killed his previous wife. He blamed Margaret for the increasing arguments they had about that brutal act and how it had caused the slow disintegration of their own relationship. It did not seem to occur to him that her distress was probably due more to his excessive drinking and gambling.

He remained just as unremorseful on the day of his trial on 8 September 1981, saying he wished to plead guilty and telling the presiding judge, Lord Allanbridge, that he did not want a defence counsel. When His Lordship asked him if he wanted to say anything before sentence was passed, he replied, 'I knew Margaret since we were teenagers. She knew my first wife. It was just like holding a gun to my head all the time.

'I tried to get away from her, but I could not. That is why I came back to Dundee. Taking the money was a stupid way of trying to get away from it.'

His Lordship told him there was only one sentence that could be imposed. For the second time, Peter Robertson – who had killed the two women he had promised to love, honour and cherish – was given a life sentence.

15

SUFFER THE LITTLE CHILDREN – HAZEL

As the bus pulled up at her stop, 12-year-old Hazel Phin moved to the exit, turned, and raised a small hand to wave farewell to a schoolmate. A moment later, she was on the pavement and setting out to walk the remaining few hundreds yards to her home. When the bus passed, she smiled and waved again to the boy pulling faces at her from the window. And that was the last time Hazel was spotted alive by anyone who knew her.

It was another 28 hours before she was seen again and by that time she was long dead. Her school blazer and neat navy blue skirt had been removed, along with the rest of her clothes, and her slight body had been buried under a heap of soot, ash and other debris in a cellar below some houses. There was little doubt as to how she had died. An old rope was pulled tight round her throat and her hands and feet were also trussed up.

Hazel had been a pupil at St John's RC School in Dundee where ten months earlier, on All Saints Day 1967, a class of girls had been held at gunpoint before their teacher was shot and killed *(see* Anything You Can Do).

By an odd twist of fate, the man who pulled the trigger that day would go on to become a confidant of the perverted paedophile who had cruelly robbed Hazel of her life. During the long years they spent together in the State Hospital at Carstairs, the secure institution in central Scotland for the criminally unbalanced, the two warped killers from the same town had plenty of time to discuss their depraved acts.

When Hazel failed to arrive at her home in Craigmount Avenue that late September afternoon in 1968, her parents scoured the immediate area without a single trace of their daughter being found. By 7 p.m., and still with no clue as to her whereabouts, the police were alerted and shortly afterwards a full-scale hunt was launched, headed by Chief Constable John Little, who only the day before had arrived from Glasgow to take command of his new force. The 70-strong team of police with tracker dogs first searched nearby parks and after darkness fell they concentrated on buildings and condemned properties. Loudspeaker appeals were broadcast and missing girl posters rushed out. But 24 hours after they had begun, they were still no nearer to tracing Hazel Phin, the little girl with the big eyes and wide smile.

Then a switchboard operator at police headquarters took a call from a man with an urgent message to pass on. He said he was an acquaintance of Karl Anderson Tonner, a 23-year-old, who a short time earlier had admitted casually to him that the girl half the city was looking for was in the cellar beside Tonner's house in Lorne Street. Detectives hurried to the scene, just a short distance from where Hazel had alighted from the bus, immediately discovered her body and arrested Tonner. In his possession they found the schoolgirl's watch and the remainder of the sweets she had purchased after setting out from St John's to make her way home. Tonner told them dark-haired Hazel had been taking a short cut through the back area of his home, where he tinkered with motorcycles, when he spotted her and decided to seize her and force her into the cellar.

'I was going to have intercourse,' he calmly explained. 'When I got there I did not feel like it, so I killed her with the rope and covered her up.' He was so detached he might have been describing a late change of mind about what to have for tea.

When the time came for Tonner to appear in court to answer for his actions, two psychiatrists said he was sane and fit to plead but suffered from a personality disorder, which manifested itself in sexual abnormality. This mental disorder seriously diminished his responsibility for his behaviour and, because of his continuing dangerous and violent criminal predisposition, he required treatment under strict security. As a result of the medical advice, the Crown accepted his guilty plea of culpable homicide. The presiding judge, Lord Grant, ordered that the emotionless Tonner should be taken to Carstairs and detained without limit of time.

In most instances when this is the disposal of the court, little more is heard of the person who has been incarcerated under the Mental Health Act and accordingly afforded the privacy and rights of a hospital patient. Karl Anderson Tonner was not among them. Some 30 years after being confined behind the high-wire fences of the soulless compounds of the State Hospital, and long after Robert Mone, his home town compatriot, had burst his way out in his infamous murderous spree, he exploded back into the headlines. Barely credible though it seemed to ordinary members of the public, the psychopathic killer had devoted much of his hospital leisure time responding to women's lonely hearts advertisements. He had built up an astonishing list of contacts, corresponding with females from as far afield as Japan, the USA and Norway, as well as scores in the United Kingdom. The paedophile had even persuaded more than 100 mothers to send him photographs of their children, some of them as young as 3, and their pictures covered the walls of his room in the institution. A former staff member at Carstairs revealed that Tonner had narrowed down the hundreds of letters he received in order to pinpoint the women he believed to be most vulnerable, provided they also had children. In his letters to the lonely ladies he did not at first reveal that he was detained in Carstairs, merely giving the name of the street of the hospital. Staff opened a parcel he sent out to one of his new acquaintances to discover he had despatched hundreds of business cards he'd run off in the hospital print shop offering a pen-pal service.

After corresponding with one woman for 6 years, she moved from her home in England to Dundee to be nearer to him and his mother in the city. Initially he had told her he was a printer at the hospital, later 'confessing' to being a patient who had been hospi-talised because of 'nervous problems'. They became engaged but the relationship quickly ended after the woman discovered the true nature of his detention and the background to his crime. She was particularly repelled because over the years of their contact she had sent Tonner numerous photographs of her children and grandchildren aged between 18 months and 6 years.

Others among his list of female penfriends were similarly shocked to learn of his activities decades earlier. One, the mother of a 15-year-old daughter, who had corresponded with him for 17 years and also sent snaps of her child, only found out about his murderous past from a newspaper investigating Tonner's letter-writing pastime. Prior to that, he had even begun bombarding her with phone calls, pleading with her to pay him a visit.

As part of his deception, the killer dropped his surname, refer-ring to himself only as Karl Anderson. A year after his horrified fiancée broke off their engagement, he had lined up another pen-pal to wed. A 58-year-old London mother, who was disabled, had been wooed by a constant stream of affectionate letters, followed by nightly phone calls when the killer expressed his love for her. She, too, was unaware of the precise reason he was in Carstairs and, charmed by his advances, agreed to marry him in hospital. It was only in the weeks leading up to the nuptials, and after the Carstairs authorities had persuaded Tonner to inform her of his crime, that she learned the full story of his sordid past and broke off the engagement. At the height of their romantic attachment, and still ignorant of what, exactly, had sent him to the State Hospital, she had even petitioned the Queen and Prime Minister Tony Blair, calling for his freedom.

Thirty-two years after being locked up, Tonner embarked on an audacious bid to secure his release. A fellow inmate at Carstairs, Noel Ruddle, known as the Kalashnikov Killer, had won his free-dom after exploiting a loophole in the law, successfully arguing that since his personality disorder could not be cured, he should be released. Within weeks of Ruddle being paroled, Tonner and two other Carstairs patients – one also a paedophile killer, the other a man who had stabbed a young mother to death and who also attempted the abduction of an eight-year-old girl – lodged appeals of their own on the same grounds, demanding that they, too, be set free.

Aware that the ground-breaking case could open the floodgates for a rush of similar appeals, the Scottish Parliament hurried through legislation to plug the loophole. The case ultimately went as far as the judicial committee of the Privy Council in London, the highest appeal court in the United Kingdom, where the five judges rejected the freedom pleas of the three killers.

Six years later, on 31 January 2007, Karl Anderson Tonner, then aged 61 and whose weight had soared to 20 stones because of lack of exercise and his hospital drugs regime, failed to turn up for an appointment within Carstairs. Staff went to his room and found him dead from a heart attack.

His funeral was one of the briefest on record. In a 10-minute ceremony, he was buried in an unmarked grave near the hospital. Only three council gravediggers and four hospital staff were present to watch his outsize coffin being lowered into the ground. No one attended from Dundee, where almost 40 years earlier he had nonchalantly admitted to taking the life of a little girl making her way home from school.

16

SUFFER THE LITTLE
CHILDREN – PAULINE

Sometimes the act that one person commits against another is so appalling it is almost beyond comprehension. When they learn of it, normal people are bewildered and repulsed in equal measure. They cannot take in what has occurred or understand the extent of another human being's ability to remove themselves so far from civilised conduct.

Michael Wilkinson's capacity for wickedness was all the more surprising because it followed soon after a display of self-sacrifice that was so heart-warming people praised him in the newspapers.

His story began in the autumn of 1971. Then aged 24, his marriage had broken up after he discovered his wife committing adultery with another man. He had assaulted both of them and they moved from Dundee to England, leaving him with three young children to care for. Soon after, the youngest, a boy, was taken to hospital to be operated on for a serious liver complaint. The two-year-old seemed to make a good recovery but one evening at home, without warning, he suffered a relapse. A short time later, he died in his father's arms.

No one gets over that kind of experience, but six months later Michael Wilkinson thought he'd found a way that offered an unusual sort of solace. He read of a 12-year-old girl in Cambridge who was critically ill and required a kidney to stay alive. The appeal appeared to touch Wilkinson deeply and he immediately volunteered to donate one of his own.

'I cannot sit by and do nothing while a little girl lies helpless. I know what the death of a child is all about . . .' he told reporters. In the event, his organ was unsuitable for transplanting and the offer could not be taken up. His selfless gesture gained national headlines and his altruism was applauded in his home town and far beyond. Less than three years later, however, his words were to take on a chilling significance.

On the afternoon of 17 June 1974, six-year-old Pauline McIver failed to return home from school, prompting her worried parents to attempt to trace her movements. Their enquiries took them to a tenement flat in Gourdie Place, in Dundee's Dryburgh estate, the home of one of her daughter's young friends. Mrs McIver spoke to Michael Wilkinson, the child's father, who at once said Pauline had accompanied his own daughter back from school and that the two little girls had played together in the flat. He helpfully explained that he'd sent Pauline home around 4.30 p.m. Mrs McIver, a 26-year-old nurse and the mother of two other young children, hurried back downstairs to pass the news on to her husband who had waited in the family car. The couple departed at once, anxious to continue their search. But by late evening, and having made no progress, Mr McIver, this time accompanied by his brother, returned to Gourdie Place to question Wilkinson once more. The man whose own son had died tragically a few months earlier, expressed concern at the lack of developments but repeated that Pauline had only played for a short time in the house before setting off for home.

At 10.45 p.m., with the late summer light finally fading, and chastising herself for not having done so sooner, Mrs McIver finally alerted the police. A full-scale search was quickly launched and brought almost immediate results. Shortly after midnight, a police sergeant searching in the back yard behind Wilkinson's block of flats, came upon Pauline's body. She lay beside two discarded sinks in a bin recess with practically no attempt having been made to conceal her body. Police were later to say her injuries indicated that she'd been assaulted 'to an unnatural degree'.

Wilkinson was taken to police headquarters for questioning and over the course of the next 90 minutes made three statements. The first two denied any knowledge of Pauline's death and amounted to little more than what he'd told her parents. Then, as he was about to end his explanation of events for the third time, his demeanour changed. He began to sweat profusely, his brow, upper lip and hands all becoming moist.

'Now let me think,' he told Detective Sergeant David McNicoll, wringing his hands nervously. 'I will have to tell someone anyway. Wait a minute. I can't remember it all but it was me that done it.'

When Wilkinson came to stand trial at the High Court in Dundee three months later, two other alleged offences had appeared on the indictment along with the murder charge, narrating how he had punched Pauline on the face and body with his fists and indecently assaulted her before strangling her to death. Allegedly, in the months prior to the killing of Pauline, he had used indecent practices towards two 12-year-old girls in his home and then, on another occasion, with girls aged 13 and 14.

Wilkinson never disputed in court that he had taken Pauline's life but submitted a plea that he was insane at the time and therefore not responsible for his actions; a defence the Crown rejected.

A prime witness in the case was the accused man's daughter, the playmate of Pauline, whose evidence was particularly harrowing. Describing the events of the fateful afternoon, she provided the jury of eight men and seven women with a traumatic account of what had taken place, her simple words illustrating the depths of her father's depravity.

Questioned by Advocate Depute J.G. Milligan for the prosecution, she quietly explained what had occurred.

'Pauline came home with me that day after school,' she said. 'We were playing in my room. My daddy was in the living-room and he gave me some money to buy sweets.

'Pauline said she would stay with my daddy and I went to get some sweets for both of us.'

The young witness went on to tell how, when she returned

home, she found her father and Pauline playing cards. He then took her friend into a bedroom and a short time later she heard screams. It sounded as though Pauline was calling out to go home, she recalled. When her father came out of the room he explained that he'd 'put his hand across Pauline's mouth.'

Asked to describe what she saw, the youngster said Pauline was lying on the bedroom floor.

Mr Milligan asked: 'Was she awake or did she seem to be sleeping?'

'She seemed to be dead,' the little girl told the court.

The young witness recounted how her father then instructed her to fetch her skipping rope.

'He put it round Pauline's neck and pulled it tight,' she said, adding that she also saw him punching Pauline on the head.

The girl's evidence continued: 'Daddy got a big case and put Pauline in it. He took her down to the backs and I stayed in the house. He came back and began to wash the blood from the suitcase. He had taken off her pants and socks. He put them in a bucket and put something in the bucket. He seemed to be cleaning it.'

Mr Milligan: 'Did your father say anything more to you?'

'Yes. If you tell anybody, I'll do the same to you,' was the response.

It is difficult to imagine any other words which could be more despicable coming from a father to his young daughter and some in the courtroom were visibly stunned at their utterance. Yet, for all its vileness, the threat appeared to have done little to alter the natural feelings of affection most children have for a parent.

Continuing to describe the circumstances of Pauline's death, the schoolgirl told how Wilkinson had instructed her to go over the house with an air freshener and to tell anyone who asked that Pauline had gone home of her own accord. Occasionally, throughout her evidence, she looked towards her father in the dock and smiled.

Cross-examined by defence advocate Mr Edgar Prais, she was asked where her mother was.

'Mummy has been in England since I was five,' she replied. Questioned further, she explained that her father had been looking after her and that she still loved him.

Wilkinson displayed little emotion during the trial. It was only when the prosecution later referred to the threat to 'do the same' to his daughter that he became agitated to any extent, calling out several times: 'Keep my daughter out of this.'

Dr Hector Fowlie, a psychiatrist, told the court that at first, on the balance of probabilities, he had believed that Wilkinson would have been insane at the time he had killed Pauline but he had altered his opinion after hearing the evidence of the accused's daughter. If her account was true, Wilkinson would have been sane but suffering from a degree of diminished responsibility, he said. The doctor went on to explain that in an interview Wilkinson had said he could not recollect killing Pauline but had spoken of 'coming out of a blackout and finding himself kneeling over her body in a bedroom.' He had then admitted to pushing the body under a bed, then later, to washing her socks and pants and body after seeing blood on them. Wilkinson had also confessed to placing Pauline's corpse in a bin recess before returning to the house to watch television. Afterwards, he'd gone to a bar and consumed three pints of beer.

During their interview, Wilkinson had further admitted to lying to Pauline's parents and the police about her whereabouts, saying: 'By that time I was frantic because I thought I had killed her, though I didn't know how.'

Dr Fowlie also advised the court that he had treated Wilkinson in psychiatric units at various times some two years earlier because of a personality disorder associated with epilepsy. After his first marriage broke up, Wilkinson had married an 18-year-old girl but that had lasted only about a month because of frequent arguments about her going out with other men.

The jury unanimously rejected the accused's plea of being insane at the time of the killing and convicted him of culpable homicide on the grounds of his diminished responsibility. Lord

Leechman sent him to the state mental hospital at Carstairs, ordering that he be detained without limit of time. The jury also convicted Wilkinson of the indecency offences against the two 12-year-old girls but, on the instructions of the bench, he was found not guilty of the charges relating to the 13- and 14-year-old girls.

Wilkinson's impassive state had returned by the time the verdicts were announced. After being sentenced he said nothing, simply turning away from the jury to stride quickly across the dock and down to the cells.

However, like others before him from Dundee whose monstrous crimes had taken them to the high security hospital in central Scotland, it was far from the last the public was to hear about the paedophile killer with the Jekyll and Hyde personality.

More than two decades after being removed from society to be held at Carstairs, he was back in court, not as a result of any other offence but to argue for his freedom. Some months earlier a fellow inmate at the hospital, Alexander Reid, had successfully won a ruling for his release after being detained for 30 years for stabbing a woman to death. Reid had argued that he should be discharged from the institution because he was not receiving treatment which could alleviate or prevent a deterioration in his condition, his personality disorder being untreatable. Although Reid continued to be held pending the result of an appeal by the then Scottish Secretary, Donald Dewar, it provided Wilkinson with the legal precedent to launch proceedings of his own.

The Dundee child killer, then aged 50, claimed there were no grounds to prolong his confinement because sexual deviancy, such as paedophilia, was not a mental disorder covered by the Mental Health Scotland Act, the law under which he was being held.

The case and its possible consequences for others held under similar court orders, prompted considerable interest in Scotland and beyond, once again gaining Wilkinson national headlines. The prospect of Wilkinson's release was said to have alarmed staff at Carstairs, one declaring publicly that he was a 'dangerous psychopath' and 'a typical child killer who was a model patient never causing problems but never discussing his crime or expressing remorse'.

Five psychiatrists were consulted by the courts, three of whom said Wilkinson was suffering from a mental disorder, and two that he was not. No one disputed that he was a paedophile, nor that there was a risk he could once again offend against children. Ultimately, it was ruled by a bench of Appeal Court judges that Wilkinson should not be freed, on the basis that he was not being held solely because of his paedophilia but because of his psychopathic condition. Reid's earlier successful plea for discharge from Carstairs was eventually overturned by appeal judges in the House of Lords, the highest court in the land.

Wilkinson was present at all the hearings when his case was being argued and the high profile nature of his attempt to return to society meant few with an interest in his abhorrent attack on Pauline McIver were unaware of when he would be brought out of the mental institution to attend court. A close male relative of Pauline had followed the various proceedings with considerable interest and when Wilkinson was taken to the Court of Session in 1997 for his case to be heard by Lord Marnoch, the man was seated in the public benches. When the court rose for lunch, and as the child killer was being escorted out, the opportunity to relieve almost quarter of a century of pent-up anger proved too great to resist. The man sprang from his seat, attacking Wilkinson and knocking him to the floor. Legally, the action constituted an assault. Morally, there were few who disagreed with it.

17

ARSENIC AND OLD MAIZE

For most of his forty years, Thomas Leith led a life that was remarkable only for its ordinariness. He lived in a house that was 150 yards from the shop where he ran his small draper's business and where he worked long hours every day. Sometimes, he would not even return home, preferring to sleep in the tiny attic bedroom over the shop. It was one of the few changes in an otherwise unvarying routine.

When the time came for him to die, it was also within a few hundred yards of where he'd spent his entire existence. But that day there was nothing mundane about the events that surrounded him. He died spectacularly and before an audience of between 15,000-20,000, all of whom had travelled across the city specially to witness his passing. No one knew for sure if he deserved to die or if he really was the evil poisoner they said. It was even possible that he was the victim of someone altogether more wicked.

What can be said with some certainty is that if Thomas Leith had been born a century or so later, his story would have spread far beyond the boundaries of Dundee, doubtless attracting the interest of filmmakers and being argued over in the legal circles across the land.

His life began uneventfully enough. A child of the early 1800s, he was brought up in poverty after his father died at a young age, leaving his mother destitute. She had to beg for food and frequently went from door to door seeking scraps, carrying the infant Thomas on her back. He somehow survived such a troubled upbringing, learned his craft as a tailor and, thanks to an industrious and frugal nature, managed to scrape together enough money as a hawker to eventually buy his own drapery shop at the city's busy West Port. He married at the age of twenty, his wife Ann being the same age and the daughter of a respectable working family in the area. A year later, their first child was born and named after him. In the years that followed, Thomas and Ann went on to have eleven other children but six of them fell victim to the poor health that blighted Dundee at that time and subsequently died.

Such tragedies, like the inexhaustible production rate of many childbearing women in Dundee, were not untypical and the Leiths at first enjoyed what appeared to be a settled and comparatively loving relationship before a gradual deterioration set in. The decline became more marked towards the end of 1845, when a young woman, Isabella Kennedy, went to work in the family shop. It was to be an event that would prove pivotal in the traumatic demise of both the Leiths.

The newcomer and her employer became lovers, inevitably leading to an acceleration in the breakdown of Thomas and Ann's marriage. He became distant towards the woman who had borne him a dozen children and began verbally abusing her and keeping her short of money. It was also said that he had taken to striking her. Unsurprisingly, Ann suspected that her ill-treatment may have been due to a liaison between her husband and the girl who had taken up employment in his shop. She did not know, however, that Isabella had given birth to Thomas' child. Or apparently not.

By the early part of 1847, Leith had become so dissatisfied with the marriage that he sought the assistance of the family minister, the Rev. James Johnstone, in arranging a formal separation, saying they had become incompatible and could no longer live happily together. The clergyman, who had known the couple for eleven years, remonstrated with Leith and, when he spoke to Ann, learned that she was opposed to any kind of break-up. She admitted, however, that she feared that one day she might have to make up her mind and sacrifice her feelings as a mother and leave her children as well as her husband.

No decision was necessary because that March matters took an unexpected and dramatic turn. By this time Leith was spending more and more nights in the garret of the shop and having his meals delivered to him by his children. One evening, after drinking tea prepared by Ann and taken to the shop in a flagon by one of their daughters, he suddenly became ill, calling out in pain and vomiting. A doctor was called and subsequent investigations indicated that the tea had almost certainly contained poison, probably arsenic. Despite implying that it had been placed in the drink by his wife, Leith played the incident down, saying he did not want any fuss because they had a large family to consider. He refused, however, to have any more meals at, or from, home, preparing his own instead.

The Rev. Johnstone, by now stepping into the role of detective as well as marriage counsellor, learned of the incident and took it upon himself, as 'his duty', to question Ann on the matter, asking her outright if she had attempted to poison her husband and pleading with her to tell the truth. She denied any involvement and explained that she had taken her own tea from the same pot before dispatching the flagon to her husband. Questioning the Leiths separately about the presence of arsenic in the house both admitted that a quantity was kept for the eradication of vermin.

Following his apparent narrow escape, Thomas stepped up his efforts to effect a legal separation from his wife. By way of financial settlement he offered to pay her three shillings and six pence per week if she left without the children or eighteen shillings and ten pence if she remained in the family home with them, part of that sum being the rent of the house. Ann responded that she would not contemplate leaving the children, saying she would seek legal advice before coming to any conclusions.

That was another decision that did not require to be made. Some three weeks later, poison again entered the lives of the Leiths, but this time with far more devastating results. On the morning of 21 April Ann prepared a breakfast of porridge for herself and her children. A short time after consuming it, all fell ill. Shortly before 11am, on another mission to negotiate a separation settlement between the couple, the Rev. Johnstone called at the house and found the entire family in varying degrees of distress. By far the worst was Ann, who was kneeling on the kitchen bed in pain. She explained that all of them had been very sick since their meal, adding that she believed they had been poisoned. The minister departed almost at once, hurrying the 150 yards down the street to her husband's shop to alert him to the dramatic situation. On hearing the news, Thomas replied, 'They have tried to poison me but it failed and now they have done it to themselves.' He returned with the Rev. Johnstone to the house and, after asking his ailing wife what had happened, departed on the cleric's instructions to summon a doctor.

During his absence, the minister came to the conclusion that Ann would not survive her ordeal and moved into investigator mode. He questioned her in detail about the sequence of events that morning and she explained that she had only a small quantity of oatmeal in the house and had used it to make porridge for her children, which she poured into basins. She then used some old barleymeal that had been in the house for about a month to make porridge for herself, also using a little of it to eke out the children's breakfast. She informed the preacher that she had not used the barleymeal previously because she thought there was sand in it. After identifying the bag containing the remainder of the barleymeal, which the Rev. Johnstone said he would take away for examination, Ann told him she believed the children were less ill than her because they had eaten only a small amount of the barleymeal batch of porridge, compared to it consisting of her entire meal.

More convinced than ever that Ann was about to expire, he solemnly addressed her and, with more than a little insensitivity, beseeched her, 'Now, Annie, I am going home and you are going to eternity, for you must soon die. I urge on you most affectionately, if you know anything of this matter, not to go to death with a lie on your lips.' Ann, who had been lying on her face, seemed unperturbed by his lack of finesse and turned to him, smiled and said, 'My dear father. I have told you all I know.' He continued on his melodramatic way, 'I have received your dying testimony. Farewell for ever.' It was the last words they were to exchange.

By this time, Thomas had returned to the house, explaining that he had gone to three different locations but had been unable to find a doctor. He urged the Rev. Johnstone to help, placing his hand on his shoulder and imploring, 'I cannot tell you how much I would be obliged to you if you will go for a doctor.' The minister immediately departed for Tay Street where he knew a Dr Crighton was based, returning a short time later with him. Ann's condition had worsened and, as the doctor tried to check her pulse, she started to retch once more. A short time after having her stomach pumped, she died. It was 1pm and, just as Ann's condition had deteriorated with the passage of time, so the children's had improved.

Events moved swiftly after that. Later in the day Thomas was taken into police custody and during the short journey from his home to police headquarters he was followed by a crowd of several thousand, all shouting and denouncing him for the alleged poisoning. At the same time as he was being incarcerated, the contents of Ann's stomach, as well as the bag containing the suspect barleymeal, were being conveyed to three different doctors, all of whom ultimately confirmed that her death had indeed been due to arsenic poisoning, which was also found among the maize.

A little over four months later, when he was described as 'decently attired in black, looking pale and care-worn', Thomas stood in the dock of the High Court before a panel of three judges to plead not guilty in a 'wavering, tremulous voice', to the murder of Ann. The trial lasted all day and after fourteen hours of evidence and speeches, ended almost on the stroke of midnight.

It was remarkable for two reasons. By present day standards, it appears to have been woefully short of anything resembling strong evidence, the main witness being the multi-role Rev. Johnstone. Even the circumstantial case was not particularly persuasive, with the Crown seemingly dependent on little more than suspicion for a conviction. The jury's verdict was similarly unsatisfactory. After considering the 'evidence' for more than an hour-and-a-half, they returned a verdict of guilty by a majority but unanimously recommended mercy. The foreman explained that they disapproved of punishment by death and otherwise they would have brought in a verdict of not proven, effectively setting Leith free.

Lord Cockburn responded by pointing out that Leith had been convicted of the 'dreadful crime' with which he had been charged and 'it was a murder which seemed to comprehend in it all the aggravation of which that offence was capable.' It was distressing that the Court could exercise no discretion in awarding the punishment, he said, because the penalty for murder was fixed by law. And that being the case, even if he thought—which he certainly did not—that murder was a crime which a capital punishment ought not to be affixed, it would make no difference on what the court had to do. Accordingly, Leith would be executed in Dundee in twenty days' time.

Although he enjoyed considerable eminence, Lord Cockburn was not renowned for his leniency. He once told another convicted murderer that he 'would be none the waur [worse] of a good hanging' before sending him to the gallows. Nor did he have a particularly high opinion of Dundee, describing it as a 'sink of atrocity' and 'for many years, the most blackguard place in Scotland.' In the circumstances, it is perhaps not so surprising that the hapless Leith found himself bound for the condemned cell. Equally, if his Lordship or defence counsel had made clear to the jury before they considered their verdict, that the court had no ability to exercise discretion then he would almost certainly have been acquitted.

Leith received the verdict and death sentence with great composure, but before being led away, he was addressed at length from the bench. The Lord Justice-Clerk told him he had been convicted 'upon very clear evidence' and he should not harbour any hopes that the execution would not be carried out. He should, however, use the time leading up to the event making repentance of his life and to 'seek for mercy and pardon through the merits of the Redeemer.' Whether or not Leith accepted the advice is unclear but he was said to have been 'much engaged in devotional exercises' during his time on death row. Since he ceaselessly continued at every opportunity to profess 'with much firmness' his innocence, it may be that any mercy or pardon he asked for was on behalf of his accusers rather than himself.

The day before he was due on the scaffold, word arrived that the execution was to be delayed for fourteen days so the authorities might consider a 'much-signed' petition calling for clemency. It naturally lifted his spirits and would have given him hope that his prayers had finally been answered. It was short-lived relief, however. Several days later the Scottish Secretary, Sir George Grey, rejected the petition, saying he regarded the case as 'so entirely free from doubt' that he could not intervene.

The condemned man never stopped declaring his innocence. He told anyone who would listen that he had 'no hand whatever, art or part, knowledge of, or design' in his wife's death. 'I have no more hand in my wife's death than in making the sun shine in the heavens,' he would say with some eloquence. He remained remarkably buoyant during most of his time awaiting execution but on 4 October, the day before sentence was due to carried out, he fell into depression. It was only a temporary lapse, however. That evening his spirits rose spectacularly, which he ascribed to the 'goodness of God' who was ensuring he would display composure and firmness when he went to the gallows. At one point, Leith suddenly clasped his hands, turned his face and eyes upwards and 'exclaimed in an energetic tone "Oh what happiness! I shall meet with my Redeemer in heaven tomorrow."'

His last visitors, at 6pm, were one of his sisters and his children, to whom he continued to insist that he was innocent of the murder. His eldest son—namesake Thomas—urged him to confess if he had killed his mother but Leith remained adamant that he had no involvement in her death. They parted with both of them in floods of tears and unable to speak.

After going to bed at midnight, the more subdued Leith unsurprisingly had a mainly sleepless night. The next morning the Provost and magistrates, who were to observe the execution, entered the prison at 7.45am and found him in prayer. Three clergymen arrived soon after and joined him in more prayers and singing of the 130th Psalm.

Despite the fate that awaited him, Leith was practically the most composed of all those who assembled to join him in the walk to the scaffold. After being introduced to the hangman and having his arms pinned, he turned to the Prison Governor, telling him 'God bless you for your kindness to me, and I hope we will meet again in heaven.' Walking unaided and declining the assistance of two guards, he climbed on to the scaffold on the front wall of the prison at precisely 8am.

His appearance was met with a roar from the assembled audience who had to come watch the hanging. They had started to gather around midnight and by the morning had swelled to a crowd of between 15,000-20,000—more than a quarter of the then population of Dundee. Newspaper reports the next day described them thus: 'The spectators were almost exclusively confined to the lower ranks of society, a considerable proportion being female.'

Leith made the most of his last moments on earth. By the time all the assorted officials and doctors and guards had joined him on the scaffold, the execution party numbered a dozen. As the central figure, Leith almost seemed to enjoy his role in the spotlight. He made a low bow to the crowd and invited one of the ministers to pray with him. Prior to the adjustment of the rope, the executioner had difficulty locating one of the fasteners. Leith, unperturbed, coolly directed him to where to find it.

He then addressed the vast crowd: 'Man is unjust but God is just and I am going to a place where there is no injustice said or done,' he pronounced. 'I leave the world speaking the truth as I am going in a very few minutes to appear before the Judge of all and I declare that I have had no more hand in taking away the life of my wife than any in this large assemblage.

'Our unhappy differences may, perhaps, have been the cause of her death but I solemnly declare that I have been innocent of the crime as charged by men and had truth been stated instead of falsehood, I would not have been here this day. I commit all to God. I am now about to appear before his bar and mercy-seat, and I forgive all who spoke against me. I forgive all they have done me and hope God will forgive them, as I hope for forgiveness at his hands.'

More prayers followed and one of the clergymen asked for the final time if he was guilty or not guilty. With more than a little drama, Leith placed a hand on his breast and declared: 'with utmost sincerity "I am not guilty."' A white cap was placed over his eyes. In the final moments, the small dignified figure repeated over and over again 'Oh Jesus now. Save me by the blood.' He was still reciting it when the trapdoor snapped open, suddenly silencing him, as well as momentarily doing the same to the rapt spectators. His body was cut down an hour later and the remainder of the prurient finally drifted away.

Leith continued to protest his innocence even from the grave. He had written a very long letter to his children, by then aged between three and nineteen, to be given to them after his death. In it he again insisted he was blameless and asked them to be guided by the 'valuable counsel' of their aunt, his sister Janet, who had taken on the role of their guardian. He warned them about which books to read and urged them to let the bible be their chief study.

Thomas Leith may well have been the evil poisoner he was branded, fully deserving of the fate that befell him. His marriage, after all, had disintegrated after he took a younger lover who gave birth to his child, leaving him with a troublesome wife. Ann's death, had it been accepted as being from natural causes, would have resolved his problems. Pretending that she had tried to poison him by lacing his tea with arsenic could have been an inventive touch to deflect suspicion. It was the kind of love triangle scenario all too familiar in generations before and since.

And yet, too many of the supposed strands of the devious murder plot did not fit all that conveniently. All the evidence indicated that whatever the difference between himself and Ann, Leith continued to be on good terms with his children, whom he treated well and generously. More than one of them spoke in court about their happy relationship with him and of his affection for them. Would such a father place poison in food knowing his beloved children might consume it along with his intended victim? And how could he know for sure that Ann would not have reversed the breakfast procedure and had the oatmeal herself while dishing up the arsenic-laced barleymeal to the children?

Consider the other alternatives. Having been a loving wife who bore her husband twelve children, Ann would surely have been distraught, if not demented, to find her marriage breaking up because of her husband's association with a younger woman. At the very least, she faced a difficult life. At worst, she might even have to accept the unthinkable—a lonely, impoverished existence without her children. In that position, wouldn't many women have contemplated suicide with the added bonus, if she was clever enough, that her cheating husband would be blamed? Troubled minds can frequently be the most creative and ensuring that her children would consume some of the poison, but not enough to kill them, might have been the kind of refinement well within the capabilities of a desperate, betrayed wife.

Is it even possible that the killer was neither of the Leiths but the 'other woman', who wanted rid of her rival and cared little for her children? Or, unlikely as it might seem, could the whole business have been no more than a tragic accident? It would not have been the first, nor last, time that poison, openly bought for domestic purposes, had been left in the wrong container with disastrous results. Thomas Leith, who was either cruelly depraved or seriously wronged, never attempted to do anything but protest his innocence. Either way, he apparently went to meet his maker with a forgiving and happy heart. And that was just as curious as everything else about the case.

18

FORGIVE ME, FATHER

The opening scenes are like sequences from a film – a bunch of boisterous students are taking advantage of an unusually warm spring evening to kick a ball about on a stretch of grass near their halls of residence. The ball bounces into the back garden of a house and rolls slowly down a flight of steps into an open basement area. One of the students shouts mockingly over his shoulder at his friend's lack of kicking skill and takes the steps two at a time to recover the ball. He picks it up and is about to throw it back into play, when he notices a broken pane of glass in a conservatory attached to the house. He peers inquisitively through the window and, staring back at him but seeing nothing, are the bloodstained corpses of an elderly man and a woman . . .

It is 6.30 p.m. on Sunday, 17 May 1980. Within an hour the handsome, detached villa at 2 Roseangle is sealed off and teams of detectives and forensic scientists are swarming all over it. For the four young footballers, all students at Dundee University on the opposite side of the road from the house with a commanding view of the Tay estuary, a Sunday-evening kickabout would never be the same again. Their grim discovery launched a murder hunt that would soon stretch the length and breadth of Britain, leaving a bloody trail and other dead victims of a crazed psychopath.

It all began more than twenty-four hours earlier, on the Saturday evening, when the occupants of the imposing villa – retired doctor Alexander Wood and his wife Dorothy (both 78) – heard noises coming from their basement. They entered to find a man with his back to them who turned, startled, at their entrance. It is difficult to know who was most surprised, but Dorothy reacted instinctively and stepped towards the intruder, who was aged about thirty. She shouted for her husband – disabled and with an artificial leg and who had been released from hospital only the day before – to call for the police, all the while pointing her finger in the face of the stranger in her home. He too reacted without thought and grabbed her arm. At the sight of this apparent attack on his distraught wife, Dr Wood moved forward to protect Dorothy and began lashing at the excited man with his walking stick. Dorothy tugged desperately at the stranger's hair and the man shouted that he didn't want to hurt either of them, but as the doctor struck him once more with his cane, that is exactly what he did.

Reason left the man and he turned to pick up a slater's hammer that lay in the basement. Screaming and shouting at the two old-age pensioners who had tried so gamely to protect themselves and their home, he lashed out, swinging the hammer-headed, hooked weapon and punching them at the same time.

Even the demented attacker did not know how long the frenzy lasted. The passage of time ceased for him as he rained blows on the helpless couple and his next recollection was standing gazing down at their dead bodies lying before him on the floor, covered in blood. He began to shake and simultaneously laugh and weep. Then he vomited and for the next two hours he sat on the floor beside the corpses.

But reason had not entirely left him. Remembering why he had entered the house through the basement window, the housebreaker-turned-double-killer made a quick search of other parts of the villa and loaded silverware and jewellery into one of the family's suitcases. He took rings and watches, necklaces and earrings and even a tea-set, a haul valued at £2,000.

Then he put on Dr Wood's raincoat to cover his own blood-soaked shirt and, glancing once more at his tragic victims, quickly left the house and hurried down Perth Road. He did not stop walking until he arrived at the railway station and seemed oblivious to the fact that he presented a noticeable figure, being dressed for rain on one of the warmest evenings of the year. A short time later, he boarded a train for London.

During the coming days, while the man sought refuge in various areas of the south coast of England and sold the stolen jewellery, police in Dundee tried to make sense of the savage attack which had stunned the city. Detective Chief Superintendent James Cameron, leading the murder hunt, had investigated his share of brutal killings in his time, but was clearly shaken at what he had seen in the basement of 2 Roseangle. Appealing for witnesses, he unusually broadened the call for assistance to include members of the Dundee underworld, stating publicly that the degree of violence was not normal for them and he was convinced that they would feel the same abhorrence as he did at what had taken place.

It was a plea that brought results and several housebreakers made contact to pass on points of information, at the same time expressing their distaste at the fate of the two helpless 78-year-olds. Yet there was nothing which gave the merest hint as to who might have been responsible. Door-to-door enquiries were stepped up and renewed appeals were launched through the media. A breakthrough seemed imminent when a local GP came forward to say she had been troubled by a fear that the dreadful slaughter might have been committed by one of her patients. She had racked her conscience and had decided it was her duty to pass on the name of the man she suspected. It was the kind of assistance the murder team was hoping for and the lead was immediately followed up – only for it to fall at the first hurdle when the suspect provided an impeccable alibi for the relevant times.

Among the other witnesses who came forward were several students who had lazed that sunny May afternoon on the lawns at Seabraes, the green oasis in Perth Road which almost forms part of the Dundee University campus. It was where the quartet of footballing students had played and where the always neatly trimmed grass adjoined the home of the Woods. The sunbathers told of seeing the old couple outside the house in late afternoon, waving off their dentist son Nicholas, who was travelling back to his home in Banchory. It was believed he was the last person – apart from the killer – to have seen the elderly couple alive, and that they had probably perished within an hour of his departure.

One of those who responded to the police appeals for help was a young woman who worked in the Labour Club, a short distance from the Woods' villa. She recalled that on the Saturday afternoon an 'odd-looking' man had arrived at the door of the club to ask for directions to the home of the Roman Catholic Bishop of Dunkeld, whose official residence was in Roseangle. She gave a good description of the strange visitor, whom she thought was aged about thirty, and remarked that he stood out because of the dated style of shirt with its large floral patterns that he wore. At the bishop's house, door-to-door enquiries revealed that a man fitting the same description had suddenly appeared in the garden there, but he had quickly departed after being confronted by the priest's housekeeper.

As these facts took their place in the growing murder log being compiled in the days after the discovery of the bodies, another, apparently unrelated topic surfaced. The latest edition of the *Police Gazette* arrived at police headquarters in Bell Street and a minor listing showed that Dundee-born Henry John Gallagher, sometimes known as Reid, had failed to return to Maidstone Prison after a home leave on 12 May. He was aged twenty-nine and serving a three-year sentence for burglary.

Bells began to tinkle. Detective Inspector William Hart recognised Gallagher as the man who eight years earlier had carried out a vicious assault on a Dundee minister, the Rev. Roy Hogg, minister of the High Kirk in Kinghorne Road and moderator of Dundee Presbytery. Gallagher had unexpectedly appeared one afternoon in June 1972 at the kirk manse in Adelaide Place, saying he was in great distress and apparently seeking spiritual advice. The minister was alone at the time but, having no reason to turn him away, invited the stranger in. Within moments Gallagher had demanded £20, saying that if he did not get it he would kill the cleric then go on to steal. In a prolonged ordeal, during which he tried four times to escape, Mr Hogg was severely beaten and kicked, then finally bound hand and foot by a dressing-gown cord. Gallagher ransacked the house before departing with a haul of silver.

He had no real hope of getting away with the attack. During his time in the manse, Gallagher had recounted a long tale of woe about his tragic life and had given his name and even an address. Despite his terrifying experience, the 67-year-old Mr Hogg was able to build an Identikit image of his attacker. This was then successfully matched to a police photograph taken during an earlier arrest of Gallagher, who had embarked on a life of crime as a schoolboy and who spent his first period in custody as a 12-year-old.

Quickly arrested for the assault and robbery at the manse, Gallagher was jailed for three years. He did not complete the sentence, however. Several months after his High Court appearance, he went on the run from Bridge of Earn Hospital, where he had been admitted from nearby Perth Prison to receive treatment for Crohn's disease (from which he had suffered since his teenage years). He vanished from the hospital wearing only pyjamas and a dressing gown.

The escapee eventually surfaced in Stockton-on-Tees and, after a period of sleeping rough and carrying out muggings, he once more decided to call on a clergyman for aid. He randomly chose the home of Father Donald Cronin, the 69-year-old parish priest of St Cuthbert's, and proceeded to unburden himself about his troubled life and the illness he had, which he repeatedly said would claim his life by the time he was thirty. The elderly priest listened but replied that he was unable to help, advising Gallagher to visit the local Social Security office. As he led his visitor out, Father Cronin took Gallagher's hand in his and remarked, 'God bless you, my son.'

This blessing seemed to ignite a suppressed rage within the prison runaway. He exploded with anger and set about the defenceless priest, striking him a dozen times with a club. Gallagher admitted later that he had no recollection of what had taken place, only that when his anger had subsided the room was a wreck, with table and chairs overturned and Father Cronin lying unconscious on the floor. Doctors were to say that only the unusual thickness of his skull had saved the clergyman's life. Gallagher fled to Harrogate, where he collapsed as a result of his illness. He was soon arrested. Once again, he readily admitted his crimes. This time he was given seven years.

When the Dundee murder team reacquainted themselves with Gallagher's background, it became apparent that he might well have returned to his native Dundee after going on the run from his latest stretch in Maidstone Prison. His fondness for attacking clerics also fitted perfectly with the circumstances surrounding the killing of Dr and Mrs Wood, as their assailant had apparently attempted earlier to locate the Roseangle home of the Roman Catholic bishop.

Armed with this thought, the detectives concentrated their inquiry on tracking him down. They learned from a Dundee prostitute that Gallagher had indeed recently been in town. They re-interviewed the helpful employee at the Labour Club in Roseangle and presented her with a selection of some ten photographs of men aged about thirty – among them Gallagher's. She had no hesitation in identifying him as the 'odd-looking' man in the flamboyant shirt who had called at the club a few hours before the Woods had so savagely been hacked to death. Detective Inspector Hart, showing the photographs to his namesake, Bishop Hart, the Bishop of Dunkeld, and the clergyman's housekeeper, received the same confirmation.

The murder detectives now knew without doubt who they were looking for, particularly since the brass nameplate on the doorway at 2 Roseangle could easily have been mistaken for the type found outside a manse.

In the days after the savage attack on the two 78-year-olds, police were involved in one of the biggest manhunts that Dundee had ever experienced. As word filtered out about just how viciously the helpless pensioners had been put to death, local people came forward with any scrap of information they thought might help. Witnesses told of a man in a raincoat and bloodstained hat making his way down Perth Road, carrying a suitcase, on the Saturday evening. The trail of witnesses led to the railway station and it became evident the killer had left the city by train shortly after his act of slaughter amidst the sunny, tranquil setting of Dundee's academic quarter. But where was he? With a twenty-four-hour start before anyone was even aware of his dreadful deed, he could be just about anywhere.

It was a week later before the public next became aware of Henry John Gallagher. The fugitive had found his way to Ramsgate – there he had fallen in with a couple who had promised, for a price, to provide him with false identification which would enable him to travel to France. Gallagher explained away his haste to leave the country by saying he was on the run from Scotland for drugs offences.

The double-killer then reverted to type, following an inexplicable but horribly predictable course of action. Desperate to cleanse his conscience before fleeing Britain, he stopped a woman in the street to ask for directions to the home of the nearest Roman Catholic priest. He was pointed in the direction of the residence of Father Paul Hull, a frail 88-year-old Benedictine monk, who lived with his 73-year-old housekeeper Maud Lelean in Hereson Road (next to St Ethelbert's Church in Ramsgate). He was seen entering the presbytery and then, a little more than an hour later, leaving it – and wearing a raincoat he had not previously had on.

On his arrival at the door of the manse, Gallagher had been welcomed by the white-haired priest with the kind face and he was immediately invited inside and given a seat. The caller said nothing for a few minutes, then hesitatingly disclosed that he had an important matter to confess, but would only do so if Father Hull promised never to reveal what he was about to be told. The priest agreed, but responded that if Gallagher did not trust him, he should not unburden himself. There was another prolonged silence, broken only when Maud Lelean entered with tea and buns for the pair. That, along with the patient, gentle coaxing by the old man seated opposite him, seemed to relax Gallagher and he finally uttered the words he had come to say: 'Father, I have killed two people in Scotland.'

That was as far as the confessor got. Father Hull sprang to his feet and rushed for the door, shouting to Maude who was returning to the room that the visitor was a murderer. Gallagher grabbed the cleric by the arms, blocking his route to the front door and pleading all the time that he should not repeat to anyone else what he had just been told. Maud, despite her terror and frailty, attempted to force the man who was attacking her kindly employer to release his hold. But she was quickly pushed away.

That was the point at which a veil once more descended over Gallagher's rationality, later to be described by him as 'like a switch being flipped'. He picked up the first thing at hand, the priest's walking stick, and in a demented rage set about the defenceless pair with unrestrained ferocity. His next conscious moment was several minutes later, when he found himself standing over their blood-covered bodies, shouting, 'Where's your God now? Tell me!' Then, in a further chilling replay of the ghastly events that had unfolded inside 2 Roseangle a week earlier, he searched the house for jewellery and silver, put the priest's raincoat on top of his blood-saturated clothing and fled the scene.

Some thirty minutes later, assistant priest Father Patrick Whealan called at the manse to discover the scene of horror in the blood-spattered study. He found Father Hull dead. Maud, seriously injured, was still alive, though unconscious. She was rushed to Margate Hospital and detectives began a bedside vigil in the hope of learning what had gone on in the house adjoining St Ethelbert's Church. However, she died three days later without regaining consciousness.

Gallagher, meanwhile, returned on the night of the murder to the Stag's Head pub for his arranged meeting with the couple who were going to arrange his false identification. There he gave them some of the stolen jewellery in exchange for a rent book and cheque book, which they assured him would allow him to make a day-trip to France. The couple noted that their new acquaintance was behaving oddly and queried several times if anything was troubling him, but accepted his reassurances that he was merely feeling a little under the weather. They also remarked to Gallagher that 'something big' must have occurred in Ramsgate, since the town was buzzing with police activity, including in the Stag's Head where two CID officer known to them had arrived shortly after they had. Since news of the bloodbath in the manse had not yet been made public, they were in no position to fit the jigsaw pieces together.

That night Gallagher stayed at the couple's home, but was unable to sleep for a single moment and chain-smoked his way through two packets of cigarettes. The next morning, as England awoke to the full horror of what had taken place in the home of the priest, the now-multiple killer knew he had to leave the area as speedily as he could. He boarded the first bus he came across. It took him to Canterbury and from there he went by train to London, where he spent the night.

Back in Dundee, the Woods murder squad had become aware of the fate of Father Hull and his housekeeper and immediately notified their police colleagues in England of their strong belief that they might all be looking for the same man. A nationwide hunt was launched, every police force in the country being alerted that a man who had almost certainly killed four times in crazed, psychopathic attacks on elderly people was on the loose and liable to turn up anywhere.

Henry John Gallagher, sometimes known as Reid, who had started his life of crime as a petty schoolboy thief, had leapfrogged the rest of the underworld to become the most wanted man in Britain and one of the most dangerous men police forces on both sides of the border had ever encountered. No one doubted that he was perfectly liable to slaughter again, his most likely victim being an elderly person living in a large house who was probably a minister of religion.

Bizarrely, although there was every possibility that he might next surface back in his native Scotland, the media there was prevented from using his photograph in connection with the deaths of Dr and Mrs Wood because his identification might infringe his right to a fair trial. This prohibition still exists in criminal cases, though in a slightly more relaxed form.

There were fewer scruples in England and Gallagher's photograph started to appear on the front of every newspaper in the country, alongside headlines such as 'Catch This Man' and 'Danger Man'. The fugitive began desperately moving from town to town, stealing £400 from a safe in a Salvation Army hall in Southend before making his way to Brighton. The town was packed with Bank Holiday visiting skinheads and Gallagher made a clumsy attempt at shaving his head so that he might disappear into the crowd. Instead, the cuts he inflicted on his scalp made him more noticeable than ever. Next, he wore a loud shirt, sunglasses and yellow and white cap and put a camera round his neck to pose as an American tourist. His amateur disguises did little to help conceal his true identity and the huge nationwide exposure being given to the hunt meant he was beginning to be recognised almost at every turn.

He spent a night in a guest house in Eastbourne but was forced to escape through a window when he heard the female owner tell her cook that she thought her guest with the strange haircut was the man police were seeking. From there he took flight on a bus making a day trip to Windsor Safari Park, but had to make another quick exit when a passenger started comparing his reflection in a bus window with the photograph of him on the front page of the newspaper in her lap. Gallagher realised his only chance of remaining at liberty was to keep on the move and he went next to Slough and Reading and then on to York after stowing away on board a train.

On the morning of 29 May, a week after he had battered Father Hull and Maud Lelean to death, the hunted man – somehow inevitably – turned up on the doorstep of the vicarage of St Chad's in York, just after breakfast. The vicar, Derek Hall, had just departed to give communion to sick parishioners and the door was answered by his wife, Dorothy. Gallagher, looking dishevelled and anxious after spending the night in a doss-house, asked if he could wash the family car. Instinctively, but almost immediately regretting it, Mrs Hall said her husband always washed his own car and, by way of further explanation, added that he was presently away from the house with it. As she spoke, she slowly started to realise that the uninvited caller was somehow familiar.

By the time she had closed the door and watched from a window while Gallagher walked away in the direction of York racecourse, Mrs Hall felt with growing certainty that she had just come face to face with the most wanted man in the United Kingdom, the deranged Scotsman who had brutally ended the lives of four people – and who preyed on clergymen. Ironically, the biggest clue to his identity had been the shaven head with its still unhealed razor cuts, the 'disguise' he had adopted in order to be less noticeable among the skinheads of Brighton. Mrs Hall at once phoned the police and began a systematic series of calls to the homes of every minister and priest she could think of.

One of those receiving a call was Father Hugh Curristan, priest of a church three-quarters of a mile away from the vicarage occupied by the Halls. Gallagher had arrived at the priest's house a few minutes earlier but Father Curristan, who had watched his arrival from an upstairs window, did not open the door because he did not recognise him as one of the regular tramps who came begging for aid. As Gallagher sat on the front doorstep, smoking, and while the priest continued to watch him from the window, the phone rang with the alert from Mrs Hall. Simultaneously, a police car passed the front of the house and Gallagher, panicking, hurried quickly away, but not without first attracting the attention of the officers in the car. They stopped him. However, as they started to question the multiple-killer, he took flight and jumped on to the back of a moving lorry. After a few hundred yards he leaped off, then fled over a railway line.

Police cars converged on the area and, in a scene reminiscent of a silent movie, the runaway killer was pursued through the streets and over fences by an ever-growing posse of policemen, at least one of whom was blowing his whistle as he ran. He was finally cornered in a back garden by Sergeant Arthur Snowden. When the end came, it could not have been more peaceful. The man who had terrorised two countries said simply, 'OK, you've got me,' before submitting quietly to his arrest by the sergeant.

News of the capture was passed to the murder team in Dundee and Detective Chief Superintendent Cameron immediately travelled south. In an interview Gallagher admitted to the murders of Dr and Mrs Woods.

The killer who could not stop confessing never stood trial for the Dundee killings, however. After pleading guilty to the manslaughter of Father Hull and Miss Lelean on the grounds of diminished responsibility, he was ordered to be detained in Broadmoor, the top-security English hospital, without limit of time. Several days later, the Lord Advocate in Scotland announced that in view of that disposal, no further action would be taken against him north of the border.

19

THE FIRST FOOT

Sandy Borland was one of life's nice guys. You never heard a bad word about him because nobody ever uttered one. He wasn't a saint, just the kind who would rather do a good turn than cause any harm. He didn't have much money because he was a jute worker who didn't earn a lot. What was left over he usually gave away. The man with the seemingly permanent smile was known as Little Sandy because he stood only a little over five feet in height. If they'd measured him by the size of his heart, they would have called him Big Man. He was born in Lochee and seldom strayed far from there and on the first day of 1957 that was where he died.

It made no sense then and, more than a half a century later, it still has no explanation. There didn't seem to be a single reason why Sandy Borland should die and every reason why that New Year's Day should have ended as happily as it had begun for the man who was one of his community's most loved figures. Instead, his life came to a savage conclusion only 200 yards from where he lived and the circumstances have haunted his home town ever since. Most disturbing of all is the probability that the two men who almost certainly held the answer to the riddle continued to live side by side with their baffled fellow citizens, quietly rejoicing that for 50 years they had got away with murder.

When they found 54-year-old Sandy, no one recognised him, not even his closest neighbours. He lay in a heap in the middle of Lorne Street, just down the road from where he lived with his

75-year-old mother Mary, and was so badly beaten his face had lost its features. Some thought he'd been hit by a truck. After his bloody corpse had been examined by experts down at the mortuary the consensus was as unexpected as it was incomprehensible. Little Sandy had been kicked to death, his body, like his face, bearing the evidence of a rain of vicious assaults by a booted foot, or, more likely, feet. In addition to the near obliteration of his features, several ribs had been fractured. He would have cried out when the first kicks were delivered but by the time they'd ended he would have been long silent, overtaken by the kind of death no one should have to suffer. Yet, right up to the moments before he met his maker, the ebullient little jute worker had been even cheerier than usual.

When he died he had been wending his way home just after 10 p.m., happily intoxicated after a period of drinking that had begun more than 24 hours earlier, on Hogmanay, and had resumed again early the next evening after a day's sleep. His traditional First Footing excursions round friends in Lochee had started immediately after New Year had been rung in. For a companion he had his 19-year-old niece Mamie, his brother Willie's daughter from London, who was experiencing her first Hogmanay in Scotland. He also had the company of two half bottles of whisky, bought in advance from the Corner Bar, one of his drinking haunts.

After celebrating for a few hours into the New Year, Sandy thought it wise to return Mamie to his mother's house, for he had more drinking to do and he considered an all-night session to be beyond a teenage girl, even one eager to enjoy the peculiar New Year customs north of the border. He then partied in a pal's house in Kerr's Lane until 6.30 a.m. before returning home once more, this time to fall into bed and sleep off the hangover that threatened to develop.

Later that afternoon, Sandy awoke, refreshed and ready to embark on a second round of First Footing. He decided he would visit the same friends he did most New Year Day evenings and take Mamie with him. It was then that fate intervened, seemingly insignificantly as such intrusions invariably are at first, but with devastating consequences for Sandy. Mamie declined the offer to recommence celebrations, believing a cold to be developing, but more probably still recovering from her participation in the unaccustomed festivities. Her uncle, being familiar with the feeling, did not press her. He set off alone – and almost certainly died as a result.

After visiting and sharing a few drinks with a long-standing pal who'd been under the weather the night before and not in the mood for First Footing, Sandy moved on. It was around 8 p.m. and the popular little reveller was in fine fettle. He had other friends he wanted to call on. At this stage, as one of his hosts was later to explain, Sandy was jovial – as usual – but still sober. However, two hours later and following more socialising, drink had overtaken him. Sometime around 10 p.m., after attending a party in a top-floor flat at the end of Lorne Street, Mrs Agnes Mack left her ground-floor flat in the tenement when she heard someone calling 'Aggie'. She found an under-the-weather Sandy seated on her doorstep and asked her husband to help her assist him on his way. The pair took the weary merrymaker a little way down the street, heading him in the right direction and advised him to go straight to his home at 123 Lorne Street. It was only after he'd departed that they noticed Sandy had dropped his whisky bottle. But rather than run after him with it, believing its owner might be tempted to consume more of its contents, they deposited the bottle in their home, knowing Sandy would better appreciate being reunited with it the following day. It was a drink he was never to take.

Within half an hour, the harmless bachelor who was everyone's friend lay dead on a freezing stretch of road just 100 yards away. From a short distance his huddled form seemed, to those who found him, more like a bundle of discarded rags than the body of someone who'd been at his happiest less than 60 minutes earlier. It was only when they came closer and the street lights revealed a pool of blood seeping away from the indistinguishable mass that they realised the clothing contained the crouched figure of a small man. His hands were up around his head, the way someone would hold them for protection. The defensive action had done their owner no good at all. Like the face they had tried to shield, both hands had poured blood from the flesh that had been opened up by the ferocious kicking.

The stunned locals could barely take in what had happened. Had it been anyone else, they accepted there might have been a drunken New Year's Day brawl, an event not entirely unknown in the city, particularly at that time of year. But there would never be physical conflict involving Little Sandy, of that they were absolutely certain. His lack of physique apart, it just wasn't in his nature to fight, no matter how many drinks he'd taken.

The police teams which swamped the area made little headway. They took statements from 70 people and carried out door-to-door enquiries at more than 100 addresses. But after widespread appeals, the nearest they came to making progress was when one or two witnesses came forward to say they had seen Sandy in conversation with two young men in the street a short time before he died. Despite the strong probability that they were his killers, the investigation progressed little further. The pair were never traced and those who lived in Lochee were convinced of one thing, they had to be outsiders because no who knew Sandy could have ended his life so savagely or pointlessly.

That they continued to walk the streets of Dundee without ever having to account for their despicable actions left a wound that never healed for the many friends of the little man with the enormous heart. But no one was more affected than his elderly mother, who never got over the cruel way one of her ten children had had his life taken away.

'He was such a cheery boy,' she used to say. 'He never harmed anyone. Why would they want to kill him?'

Why, indeed.

20

THE GIRL IN RED

The attractive teenager in the red mini-dress and knee-length black shiny boots hadn't a care in the world when she alighted from the late-night bus to walk the short distance home. The weekend was well under way and that evening, like most Fridays, she'd danced the night away in the J. M. Ballroom in the city centre. Now it was 1.30 on the Saturday morning and the dark-haired 16-year-old looked forward to a long lie-in before meeting up with her friends again later in the day. She smiled at the thought. Long-lies had become an enjoyable part of life since the start of the strike of General Post Office telephonists, of which she was one, even if she did have to take her turn on the picket line down at the exchange in Willison Street. It was anyone's guess how long the dispute would last, she thought, as she turned into the tree-lined drive that would take her to the multi-storey home in Pitalpin Court she shared with her parents.

At 5.30 a.m. the body of Diane Graham was found in the launderette area of the multi-block. Her red dress lay beside her and her black boots had been removed and taken away. She had been strangled with a ligature and her naked body bore the marks of match burns. The discovery had been made by the dead girl's next-door neighbour, who had gone to use the laundry before departing for work as a cleaner at Dundee University. Diane's parents, assuming their daughter had come home after they had gone to bed, then retired herself, knew nothing of her disappearance until being informed of the grim find in the launderette.

By the time the other residents of Pitalpin Court had come to their senses on the morning of 6 March 1971, the area was swarming with uniformed and plain-clothes police and the special incident room caravan of the City of Dundee Police was prominently in place in front of the tower block. Reporters were also on the scene and the first press conference of the day had taken place in time for the details to make the early editions of the evening papers. The attending journalists experienced the same feelings of revulsion and sorrow as the others who formed the wider cast of the murder hunt. But like the rest, they never forgot why they were there. Instinctively they knew there would be a big readership for the words they would write that day.

Murders almost always make the front page. On this occasion the ingredients made that certain, at least in Dundee. The victim was a pretty and carefree young girl. Her killer had apparently appeared from nowhere and had disappeared just as quickly. He could, on the face of it, have been almost anyone. It was good news for the reporters but bad for the murder squad detectives – random killings were the hardest to solve. As usual in these cases, the police would lean heavily on the services of the news reporters they would sometimes choose to shun.

Later that day *The Evening Telegraph* carried a full front-page 'splash' giving extensive details of the horrific discovery of the body and the events leading up to it. The story was accompanied by photographs of the victim, the murder scene and teams of detectives conferring at the mobile incident room. Prominent in the text was an appeal from the head of Dundee CID, who described how Diane had been dancing in the centre of town and might have been accompanied home at some point by a youth.

By four o'clock in the afternoon, the investigation was going nowhere. A picture of the movements of the dead 16-year-old on the evening before was being slowly built up, but it wasn't leading anywhere in particular. No one in Pitalpin Court had apparently heard or seen anything suspicious, though a girl in another multi-storey 100 yards away said she had detected screams at about 1.45 a.m. It was interesting but not particularly helpful. Nor was there any sign of the victim's boots, handbag and gloves, which had vanished. Although the local residents couldn't offer much information, they rallied round to provide soup, tea, coffee and food for the teams of police scouring that part of the Lochee area. It was appreciated – but not much consolation.

Things were considerably brighter for the publishers of *The Evening Telegraph*. Thanks to the timing of the tragedy, which allowed a complete account of the appalling circumstances to be recounted from the first edition onwards, the papers sold in high numbers throughout the city. Dundonians, like members of the public everywhere, are always intrigued by murders. Downtown sales rose by 25 per cent.

Among the readers that afternoon was a 17-year-old youth who devoured every word. He studied the photographs and read the account of the police hunt over and over again. Then he went to Pitalpin Court and made his way to the incident room.

'I'm the guy you are looking for,' he told Detective Chief Inspector David Fotheringham. 'I was on the bus with her.'

The chief inspector's first impressions were that the slightly built young man standing before him seemed remarkably young and inoffensive – and friendly. There was a complete absence of hostility and the dialogue between them continued amicably. His instincts told him to keep it that way, for he was certain there was much more to hear.

'We'd better have a chat away from here,' the policeman said softly. 'We'll go down to headquarters in Bell Street.'

The interview that followed came straight from the good cop–bad cop textbook. DCI Fotheringham, naturally easy-going and conversational, but one of the most productive interrogators in the force, probed gently and the story the youth had to tell slowly started to unfold. He identified himself as James Mullady, who lived in Kings Cross Place, on the other side of the wall which separated Pitalpin Court from the Beechwood estate. That night, he explained, he had been on the same bus as Diane and they had alighted at the same stop. He caught up with her and they had walked together and struck up a conversation. Then they had gone into the basement area of the multi-storey block and briefly 'kissed and cuddled' before he climbed the boundary wall to make his way home to Beechwood.

It was evident that his version of events had been only part of the story and the other detective sitting in on the interview slipped effortlessly into bad-cop mode, demanding loudly to be told the full story and showing none of the chief inspector's sympathy. He shouted and raged and in an apparent temper, stormed from the room. DCI Fotheringham leaned conspiratorially towards the 17-year-old sitting anxiously in front of him.

'Look, before he comes back, what really happened? 'he urged. 'I'm sure you didn't really mean to kill her.'

It was the key that unlocked a confession. In a tumble of words James Mullady explained that when he had approached Diane in the basement of the multi-block she had pushed him away, mockingly saying he smelled.

'Do you mean you had been drinking?' asked the chief inspector.

'No. It was my feet. I have awfy smelly feet and she said I was stinking,' said Mullady by way of explanation.

He quickly went on to disclose that after being pushed away by the 16-year-old in the red mini-dress, he had responded by shoving her in return, when she fell down. He wasn't sure what had followed but he slowly came to the realisation that she lay dead at his feet, the result of a terrible accident. Further coaxing by DCI Fotheringham brought the admission that he had stolen the boots, handbag and gloves – 'everything shiny' – because he imagined they might have had his fingerprints on them. The burns on the body had been caused, he explained, by matches he lit to locate the items he had removed. Shortly afterwards, he accompanied police back to Pitalpin Court and pointed out a drain near the tower block where he had concealed the stolen property. When his home in nearby Beechwood was searched, Diane's metal comb with her name scratched on it, was found under the mattress of his bed.

Six weeks later, at the High Court, Mullady pled guilty to a charge of murder and robbery. The proceedings lasted barely two minutes and the 17-year-old who had gone to 'help police' after reading in an evening paper that they were looking for him, was ordered to be detained during Her Majesty's Pleasure – the equivalent of a life sentence for someone his age.

Everyone connected with the case felt immense sympathy for the family of Diane Graham, who died for no other reason than that she happened to get on a particular bus. Among those most deeply affected was Chief Inspector David Fotheringham. Later he was also to admit to feeling considerable compassion for the youth who had been so willing to confide in him.

21

LITTLE BOY BLUE

Evil dwells in unlikely places. It takes no heed of geography or seasons and often announces its presence when least expected. It inhabits improbable minds and is no respecter of age. It penetrates the soul of the young just as readily as it infiltrates the psyche of the mature . . .

That bright summer's evening in 2001 it lurked at its most menacing – and most unforeseen. On the sunny slopes of the Law, dog walkers exercised their pets, children frolicked and couples meandered hand in hand. It was 6.30 p.m. in the middle of the trades holiday fortnight and the city was at play and at peace. No one spotted the powerful figure wearing the blue baseball cap and matching top and trousers who padded lightly through the undergrowth bordering the paths that criss-crossed the hill. He moved swiftly and silently and in his hand he carried a knife.

When he suddenly burst into view in front of the woman walking her dog, he paused for only a moment. Then he grabbed her, dragging her roughly back into the bushes from which he had unexpectedly emerged. He brought the knife swiftly across the throat of his petrified victim – then he started to swing it as though he was possessed by the Devil himself. He didn't stop until it had flashed twenty-nine times. By then the poor woman was dead. She lay on the ground bleeding profusely from wounds to her head, throat, face, chest, back, abdomen and an arm. She had not cried out, for the first thrust of the blade had severed her voice box. Before he departed, the figure in blue stamped on her face. Then he ran away down the hill, his urgent footsteps making no sound as he ducked and swerved through the heavy bushes.

It was some time before anyone became aware of the evil that had descended on the popular beauty spot that August night. The body of 34-year-old civil servant Anne Nicoll, whose home was only a few hundred yards away in Byron Street, lay undisturbed in the brushwood for almost an hour. At first she had the company of her beloved Sophie, the Airedale terrier she walked morning and evening on the Law, but the pet, distressed at the lack of response from his mistress, had finally retreated whimpering from the scene. Sophie remained in the vicinity and was still there when Anne's partner of four years, 33-year-old Gordon McKenzie, anxious at their failure to return home, came looking for them, retracing their usual route. The terrier led him through the woods to the thicket where Anne lay crumpled and bleeding on her side.

He did not know that, as he desperately tried to revive the woman he loved, his every move was being watched by a figure crouching behind a bush a short distance away. The silent observer no longer wore blue, for after he had run from the hill the disciple of the Devil had hurried to his home nearby and showered. Then he returned to watch and await the discovery of his handiwork.

The savage and apparently motiveless killing stunned the city. It was murder at its most wicked. The victim was liked by all who knew her, a decent woman who took pleasure from the simple things in life and who never had a bad word to say about anyone. Police were only too aware that anyone who could take a life so randomly and with such unbridled ferocity was perfectly capable of repeating the act. Dog walkers deserted the hill and children were kept indoors.

More than a hundred detective and uniformed police officers swamped the area in the following days, with reinforcements being brought in from a neighbouring police force. Hundreds of people who frequented the Law or lived in the area were interviewed. The response from the public, outraged by the indiscriminate attack, was unprecedented. Four days after the fearsome stabbing, Detective Chief Inspector Andy Allan announced a breakthrough. One of those who answered the press appeals was an elderly lady who had also walked her dog that night and had been alarmed after an encounter with a stranger. The 68-year-old told how she had spotted a figure in a brilliant blue tracksuit and baseball cap flitting through the woods. Then he had suddenly appeared on a path in front of her and instinctively she had said 'Hello'. He did not return the greeting, but had grunted and stared at her. After he passed, she turned to find that he too had turned and was continuing to look at her.

The woman, who had walked her dog on the hill for eight years, became frightened and hurried away. Describing her encounter, she said: 'I thought to myself, "I had better get out of here quick". I don't know why.'

Police immediately issued a nationwide appeal for information about the 'man in blue'. It brought instant results. Others came forward to say they too had become anxious after sighting a suspicious figure in a corresponding outfit – except it wasn't a man but a youth. An 11-year-old girl told how she had been on the hill with her 12-year-old cousin when a teenager clad in blue suddenly came out of the trees to appear behind them. He started to follow the children and the 12-year-old, frightened and apprehensive, keyed the 999 emergency number into his mobile phone, keeping his finger on the 'call' button ready to connect the call in case anything happened. A 15-year-old, who had been walking his dog with two other teenagers, told how they too had become afraid when a menacing figure in blue had passed them on the hill, moving fast and constantly looking behind him. Crucially, one of the trio said the stranger seemed to be aged about 15 or 16 with red or blonde hair, and with a pierced eyebrow. It was a major lead. Police had suspected from the moment the murder hunt had been launched that the perpetrator probably lived locally and knew the hill intimately because of the apparent ease with which he had moved across it. The likely age of the person who had become their prime suspect indicated he may even be one of the teenagers from the area who used the thickets of the Law as a gathering place for assorted activities, including the consumption of drugs and alcohol.

Police concentrated their investigation on the movements of youths who frequented the area. Among them was Robbie McIntosh, a 15-year-old schoolboy who lived in Kenmore Terrace, less than 200 yards from the murder scene and in a house whose window looked directly into the home of victim Anne Nicoll's father. He had red-blonde hair and a pierced eyebrow. His mother was a social worker at HM Young Offenders' Institution, Castle Huntly, Longforgan, a few miles from Dundee, and he was the dominant figure in a gang of teenagers who roamed the hill. Locals knew him as a sullen troublemaker who became difficult when he didn't get his own way. Some said he had an evil streak.

The burly teenager had been among the first people the murder team had spoken to after the discovery of the mutilated body. He had been part of a group of ten youths who gathered on the hill to spectate as police taped off the death scene. All had their names and addresses taken as potential witnesses and in the following days McIntosh, among others, was interviewed on several occasions. He became of particular interest after eyewitness descriptions of the 'man in blue' began coming in, and his status changed from important witness to prime suspect.

McIntosh admitted to having been on the Law prior to the discovery of the body, but each time he was questioned he gave a different account of his movements on the night of the killing. He described how he had seen Anne Nicoll walking her dog and watched as she had a conversation with another woman who had also been exercising her pet. He told of a man sitting on a bench near the spot where the corpse had been found. Later, he said, he saw a well-known 'junkie and weirdo' who sniffed gas from a canister. Each interview brought a new explanation of his movements and variation in timescales. He spoke of a suspicious figure he had spotted while he strolled the hill in early evening.

Finally, he confessed to having gone to the Law to smoke a joint of cannabis.

Police decided to round up all the young witnesses and interview them individually again, this time simultaneously so there could be no exchange of stories. They called at McIntosh's house at 7 a.m., only to learn he had departed for Glasgow Airport to bid farewell to his sister who was returning to her home in Canada after holidaying in Scotland. Uncertain about whether he might return to Dundee, detectives rushed to the west and brought him back from the airport for interview at police headquarters. He was arrested the same day.

Nine days later, McIntosh appeared before a sheriff to be judicially examined by a procurator fiscal, a procedure which allows an accused person to give an account of any circumstances relevant to the case, such as a plea incriminating someone else for the crime, or that the accused had acted in self-defence or had some other justification for what may have happened. McIntosh was advised that if he did not answer any questions at that stage, but later said something at the trial which he could have disclosed at the examination, that this omission could go against him. Citing the advice of his solicitor, the teenager declined to answer any questions. By the time the long-awaited trial opened at the High Court in Forfar the following April, McIntosh had turned sixteen and his protected status as a juvenile had expired, allowing him to be publicly identified.

Being charged with murder did nothing to lessen his arrogance. On his first appearance in court he laughed and joked all his way to the dock. During his journeys to and from court, he blew kisses to photographers and when his friends took their seats in the public benches he greeted them with a grin, acknowledging their presence with a knowing nod of his head. Nor was he overawed by the solemn majesty of the High Court. While some of the teenagers who gave evidence against him were in the witness-box, he fixed them with a brooding, unwavering stare. At one point, the proceedings had to be interrupted after McIntosh sat making obscene gestures to a young witness under the pretext of moving his hand round his face.

Some of the young witnesses related how the swaggering McIntosh had arrived in the vicinity of the Law at around the time the body had been found with a 'red and puffy' face and had explained that away by saying he had just showered. Staff in a chip shop recounted how he had appeared in the shop that evening to tell them that a woman had been stabbed to death on the nearby Law, a seemingly inconsequential remark – except that it had been made before any member of the public could possibly have known. Police had meticulously checked the timings, even down to the running time of the TV programme *EastEnders*, which a witness in the shop had been watching, and examined the movements of emergency vehicles in the area, to conclude that McIntosh had jumped the gun with his news. The case against him was slowly building.

Then came a bombshell. In his plea of not guilty at the outset of the trial, McIntosh had lodged a special defence of incrimination, naming as the killer one of his friends, a 16-year-old former classmate who looked not unlike him and who also had a pierced eyebrow. The incriminated youth was called to give evidence and described himself to the jurors as a meat technician, which most assumed meant a butcher.

He described how he had been at his grandmother's home between six o'clock and nine o'clock on the night of the murder, but admitted he had gone to the Law later to watch the police activity. He also revealed that on the day after the murder he had been drunk and had boasted that he had been the killer. On top of that, he confessed to having had a homemade knife in his possession, before and after the attack, and that his mother had disposed of the knife down a drain following the launch of the murder hunt.

Cross-examining the 16-year-old, Peter Gray QC, McIntosh's counsel, suggested to him that he and McIntosh had met that night and had gone to part of the Law known as Dead Man's Cliff where they had smoked cannabis together. While they were in the midst of preparing a joint, Anne Nicoll had passed by and, seeing what they were doing, threatened to tell their mothers.

'You were not happy and as she walked past you, you took your knife out of your back pocket, you came up behind her and drew it across her face, and then you butchered her, didn't you?' posed the QC.

The teenager denied every part of the suggested scenario and explained that it would be of no consequence to him if someone told his mother they had seen him smoking cannabis, since she already knew he did so.

Later, an 11-year-old boy, shielded by special screens round the witness-box, revealed that he had met the trainee butcher on the night of the attack and noted that he had a bruise on his cheek and a cut lip. He also had a 'shiny thing' in his back pocket. It was almost possible to feel the current of excitement which ran along the packed public benches in the courtroom. Folk leaned forward to catch every word. They gasped inwardly when the 11-year-old went on to say that he met the 16-year-old the following day. Then he told the court: 'He pulled out the knife and said, "It was me that killed Anne Nicoll." '

It was all startling evidence and completely changed the complexion of the trial. Now the jury were aware that two teenagers, friends who were remarkably similar in appearance, had one way or another admitted to being near the murder scene that night. One of them – and not the one in the dock – had apparently even announced to young acquaintances that he was the murderer. But which, if either, was actually the killer?

A strong indication that it was McIntosh came, as it so often does, with the presentation of the forensic data. A meticulous search of his house had not unearthed any blue top and matching bottoms – but it had produced a baseball cap and rolled-up sock, both bearing minute specks of blood. DNA tests revealed that the blood on the sock was, with a billion-to-one certainty, Anne Nicoll's. The trace of faint bloodstaining on the baseball cap was less conclusive because the sample was incomplete and showed a mixed profile – but it was still a thousand-to-one probability to have been a mix of McIntosh's and Ms Nicoll's.

Before the jury retired to examine the enormous amount of evidence they had heard over the eleven days of the trial, they were invited to consider a possible explanation for the presence of Ms Nicoll's blood on the accused youth's belongings. Defence counsel suggested that he might have been at the scene, and close enough to have picked up specks of the dead woman's blood, but only as a spectator while the friend he had accused carried out the murderous onslaught. It was an intriguing proposition.

McIntosh himself was unprepared to shed any light on what had taken place on the Law that summer evening, exercising his right not to give evidence and declining to go into the witness-box.

The jury retired with a lot to think about.

What they did not know was that before going out onto the hill that evening, McIntosh had spent twenty minutes on his home computer accessing a number of pornographic sites depicting torture and violent sexual acts of rape, where the victims included children. McIntosh had tried to remove the images, but specialist forensic computer unit police officers were able to retrieve the sickening pictures. Significantly, they were also able to extract data showing that in the months leading up to the slaughter on the hill he had visited sites referring to stalking and rape. The prosecution had hoped to lead evidence during the trial about what had been found on McIntosh's computer, but it had been ruled inadmissible on the basis that there was a material difference between viewing violent sexual conduct and being a perpetrator of it. Furthermore, there was no indication that the attack on the unfortunate Anne Nicoll had been sexually related.

Others who knew McIntosh could have told the jurors it wasn't surprising he found himself in the dock of a High Court – especially a neighbour who five months before the slaying of Anne Nicoll had warned that he was on a course to commit an 'unpleasant' act against someone. The fearful resident had even penned a letter intended for McIntosh's mother, but it had been placed through the wrong letterbox, arriving instead at a neighbour's. The recipient passed it to a local councillor, who forwarded it to the police. The text of the anonymous letter read:

> I think it's about time something was done about your son. He has brought nothing but trouble to this street.
>
> Him and his friends make people's life a misery, running through people's gardens, closes, etc, vandalising the park and people's cars. The language is terrible. I have heard they take ecstasy tablets on Friday afternoon. Check out the condoms in the park along with the drink cans.
>
> Someone is going to end up getting something done to them and it won't be pleasant.
>
> People are wondering how you managed to get a house in this street. Other people wait years. Your son is an unsociable tenent (*sic*). We need to petition to get you out.

Other residents in quiet Kenmore Terrace, where McIntosh lived with his mother, shared the letter-writer's unease about the youngster in their midst. One householder described him thus: 'He is evil. I said that laddie was evil before anything happened.'

His schoolteachers could speak of him as a 'walking nightmare', a swaggering thug who insulted staff and bullied smaller and younger pupils. He had had no interest in learning and was unreceptive to any kind of discipline. At Harris Academy, which he attended for a few years, he was frequently sent to a special windowless room for misbehaving where there were only two desks and two chairs – one for the errant pupil and the other for a supervising teacher. The regime removed contact with other children, except during the lunch-break, and the time was spent in solitary study. Most pupils sent there seldom returned after a single day in the 'cooler.' McIntosh was a regular occupant, put there repeatedly for offending and apparently unperturbed by the harsh routine. Eventually, he was expelled from the school and moved to the city's special unit for disaffected secondary pupils.

He had also become a growing menace in his neighbourhood in Kenmore Terrace, where he had gone to live with his single-parent mother four years earlier. He led the local gang and they terrorised much of the community, rampaging through gardens and breaking fences. On the local bus service he would lead other teenagers in loud chants about sex. Those courageous enough to challenge him were met with a sneering torrent of abuse.

None of that information was available to the jury, however, when they retired to consider their verdict. No one save the jurors themselves ever knows the precise directions a jury's deliberations take, but anyone who sat through the eleven days of evidence of the high-profile trial would have been bound to ponder long and hard over the claims by McIntosh that the frenzied attack had been carried out by the youth he named. Uppermost in most minds was that the two youths looked remarkably similar, with the same hairstyles and even pierced eyebrows. Then there was the apparent boast by the incriminated youth – a meat technician – that he had been responsible for the fearsome knife attack.

As the minutes ticked by while the packed courtroom waited for a verdict, a few seasoned veterans of previous trials began to contemplate the possibility of the fence-sitting 'not proven' decision. After more than four hours the jurors returned. None of them looked for more than a moment in the direction of the 16-year-old who sat glowering at them.

When the foreman stood to announce the jury's findings, the only sound to penetrate the silence that had descended was the shuffling of feet of some of the teenagers who sat in the public benches. Finally, after the formal pronouncements of the clerk to the court, the foreman delivered a verdict of guilty – by a majority decision.

Passing sentence, Lord Bonomy looked with barely concealed disgust at the powerfully built teenager standing before him. Recalling the appalling attack on Anne Nicoll, he told him:

One witness described her as being butchered and no better description can be applied to the way in which she met her death.

It was a dreadful way for anyone to lose their life and for that conduct there is no explanation and I think I can say nothing in the surrounding circumstances that might be considered in mitigation.

Telling the expressionless McIntosh that he took into account the extremely violent nature of the attack, the judge ordered that he be detained without limit of time but with a recommendation that he serve at least fifteen years.

Although the trial had lasted eleven days, no one connected with the case was any wiser about the motive for the senseless slaughter. The circumstances of the crime horrified the city but, equally, it baffled a community who could not comprehend what would drive a 15-year-old boy to attack so mercilessly an inoffensive and decent woman who had done him no harm.

No one was more bewildered or outraged than Gordon McKenzie, the victim's partner, who had gone to accompany her home from the hill she loved to stroll but instead found her mutilated body. As the callous young killer was led sullen-faced from the dock to begin his sentence, Mr McKenzie called out to him from the public benches, 'See you when you get out, you bastard!'

22

THE MANSION HOUSE MYSTERY

Whatever way it was viewed, the lady who lived alone in the mansion house could never be described as an ordinary Dundee spinster. Miss Jean Milne was eccentric but friendly, well read, fluent in foreign languages and something of a traveller. She was extremely comfortably off and the 23-apartment house she had quietly occupied for much of her life was set in its own grounds in an exclusive area of upmarket Broughty Ferry. Although she was sixty-nine years of age, she preferred to dress colourfully and youthfully and there was an occasional glint in her eye that hinted at more adventurous living on the frequent holidays she spent in London and on the continent. Those who believed she led a double life were not mistaken. When she came to die, it somehow wasn't all that surprising that her passing was surrounded by mystery and intrigue, as baffling today as it was in the genteel period of her killing in 1912.

In the October of that year she suddenly went missing. She had last been seen around the middle of the month, but then she just vanished. No one was particularly surprised, or worried, for she had spoken of returning to London once more before the year was out. Most of her friends and contacts assumed she had just departed a little earlier than intended. On 2 November the postman was unable to insert mail into the letterbox of her mansion, Elmgrove, which stood in tree-filled splendour on a two-acre corner site where Strathern Road met Grove Road, because of an accumulation of letters already there. That puzzled him, because on her travels away Miss Milne always made arrangements to have her mail redirected, even sending a card to post office headquarters when she was due to return. He informed the police.

An officer called at the mansion late that evening but received no reply. Reluctant to force an entry in case Miss Milne was indeed at home but sleeping, and because a fellow officer had been reprimanded for doing precisely that on a previous occasion, he left. The next morning at 9 a.m. he returned with Mr Coullie, the local joiner, and they broke in through a window. The silence that enveloped the freezing house was broken by the gasps of both men at what confronted them.

Miss Milne lay dead in the hall two feet from the bottom of the carpeted staircase leading to the upper rooms. She was dressed in a skirt and blouse and her feet were bound together with curtain cord. The stairs, floor and walls were splattered with blood and, beside her body, which had been partially covered with a white sheet, lay a bloodstained poker with hair attached. Garden shears, which had been used to cut the telephone wires, had been discarded nearby. Despite her age and fragile frame, it seemed Miss Milne had made a determined effort to fight off her attacker, which was consistent with the reputation she had among her acquaintances for being 'plucky'. Furniture was upset and a glass vase had shattered. Further along the hall lay her straw hat with its lining soaked in blood. More blood stained a gas lamp high up on a wall. Her false teeth were also broken.

A post-mortem revealed that the 15-inch poker had been used to inflict a number of blows, but none of them particularly severe or by themselves likely to have been the sole cause of death. It was concluded that she may have been left alive by her assailant but had died from the shock of what had taken place. Certainly, it seemed unlikely that whoever had wielded the poker had set out to commit murder, otherwise the feet would not have been tied together or the phone cables cut. It looked as though robbery had been behind the attack, for the house also had the appearance of having being ransacked. All the doors and windows were locked, but since the front door had a check-lock it would have closed up behind anyone passing through.

When news of the gruesome find spread through the refined, leafy suburb, those who knew Miss Milne were shocked, but not hugely surprised. It was no secret that she had money. Her brother, a tobacco manufacturer, had died nine years earlier and she had continued to live in the vast house, enjoying an annual income of £1,000 from the considerable sum he had also left. At that time, two years before the outbreak of the First World War, that amount of money facilitated an exceptionally comfortable lifestyle, similar to the sort that around £100,000 would provide a century later.

Friends had advised against her remaining in the mansion, particularly after she had dispensed with the services of a servant maid and a gardener, but she had shrugged off their concerns. Some said she was absolutely fearless.

She was also happy to flaunt her wealth. Apart from her travels at home and abroad, she enjoyed attending concerts in Dundee and frequently travelled into town to shop and dine in the best restaurants. Sometimes on these journeys she carried significant amounts of money, a practice she never attempted to conceal. On one occasion, she told a fellow traveller on a tramcar that she was carrying eighty sovereigns in her purse. She would do the same in shops.

Those who knew her best described her as an 'agreeable creature' but with 'indefinable peculiar habits' and an oddly contrasting lifestyle. In many ways she lived economically, making many of her own clothes and allowing the extensive grounds at Elmgrove to become overgrown. Yet she adored expensive jewellery, spent considerable sums on her numerous trips and holidays and gave generously to her church.

Socially, she was equally contradictory. She could be withdrawn and reclusive and although she had visitors, she seldom paid return visits. On her jaunts outwith the city, however, it seemed she mixed freely, made friends easily and would correspond with them.

At that period Broughty Ferry was not yet formally part of Dundee (that came the following year) and the area had its own police force. The first action of Chief Constable J. Howard Sempill was to call in Detective Lieutenant John Trench of Glasgow Police, an experienced and celebrated detective who had been engaged in the famous Oscar Slater case four years earlier. In a remarkably similar set of circumstances, Slater had been convicted of murdering a wealthy spinster in Glasgow.

Trench arrived in Dundee the day after the discovery of Miss Milne's body and immediately went to the scene with Chief Constable Sempill where the pair carried out a detailed examination of the interior of the house. The following day they returned to do the same in the grounds and round the exterior of the mansion. Trench determined that since there was no sign of a forced entry, Miss Milne had probably come upon a chance thief who had entered while she was in the garden and had died at his hand after tackling him. He further deduced that robbery was the motive because three purses found in the house contained no money.

Such a scenario ignored most of the evidence. In the bedroom where one of the empty purses had been located, Sempill had found another purse and this contained 17 sovereigns (worth about £1,700 today). Apart from a single missing ring, nothing appeared to have been stolen. Indeed, Miss Milne still wore a considerable amount of expensive jewellery, including six rings, a watch, ear-rings and neck-chain, all made of gold. Other valuables lay openly elsewhere in the mansion. An opportunist thief who took the time to rifle three purses was unlikely to have missed the easy pickings they provided. The initial observation that the apparent upheaval in the house was due to a ransacking was admitted by Trench himself to have more probably been the result of the confused manner in which Miss Milne led her life – for although her mansion had many rooms, she lived almost entirely in only one of them, reading and teaching herself foreign languages. She dined on a corner of a large table, the remainder of which was piled with books and magazines, which also lay in dis-array on chairs amidst other scattered objects. The lack of a forced entry was also just as indicative of the likelihood that the dead woman had known her killer, or least had been happy to admit him or her, than it was of an opportunist thief slipping in unseen while she was in the garden.

Intriguingly, it seemed she may also have had a recent visitor for in the room a tray had been set with a cup and saucer and teapot. A half-eaten meat pie was on a plate. A cigar stub was also found in the fireplace.

Trench was informed of another find. A two-pronged carving fork, smeared with blood, had been discovered in the hall, lying close to the victim. Although this might have seemed an important piece of evidence, scant significance was attached to it by the two specialists who carried out the post-mortem. Dr Sturrock, a local doctor who was also the Broughty Ferry Police Surgeon, and who made the initial examination of the corpse at the scene, pointed out two small puncture wounds on the side of Miss Milne's chest, but these were dismissed by the two experts as maggot holes. When Dr Sturrock suggested an inspection be made of the victim's back, they merely lifted one of her shoulders and, after a cursory look, said that only 'post mortem marks' were present.

The existence of the carving fork and its apparent connection to Miss Milne's death continued to trouble Dr Sturrock, however, and some two weeks later he pressed Trench and Sempill to have Miss Milne's clothing closely examined. This revealed a series of twin holes corresponding to the size of the carving fork and consistent with it having been used to stab her about twenty times through her clothing, mainly on her back but also on her breasts and wrist. Traces of blood were found on parts of the cloth-ing indicating that it had come from some of the wounds. Although any injuries were clearly not life-threatening, their full extent and part in Miss Milne's ordeal were never established, for by that time she had been buried and permission was not given for an exhumation.

The post-mortem had indicated that the petite spinster might have met her end some two to three weeks before she was found, giving a possible date of death around the middle of October. Enquiries revealed that Miss Milne, a regular church-goer, had attended a service on 13 October, but not since, and had also been seen two days after that. However, a church elder delivering Communion cards had called at the large house on 16 October but had received no answer. It seemed Miss Milne had met her fate earlier that day. A copy of *The Courier* found in the house had apparently been read, but *The Evening Telegraph* of the same date was unopened. The actual date of her death was to prove crucial.

The enigma of the mansion house murder, and the widespread press coverage of the subsequent investigation guaranteed enormous interest in Dundee and further afield. On the following Sundays, hundreds of trippers travelled from the city into Broughty Ferry to peer intently into the Elmgrove grounds, hoping for a glimpse of police activity or one of those on the periphery of the inquiry. The early announcement of a £100 reward for information leading to an arrest added to the allure. The money, a significant sum at the time, also helped produce a steady procession of witnesses.

James Don, a dustman, had a particularly material piece of information to impart. He told Detective Lieutenant Trench that he had been sweeping in Grove Road in the early hours of 16 October when he saw a man emerge from the gateway at Elmgrove at 4.30. On seeing the street-sweeper, the figure withdrew back into the shadows, only to reappear a moment or two later before walking briskly away, looking neither right nor left, coughing slightly but failing to acknowledge the presence of Mr Don. The observant dustman described the secretive stranger as being dressed entirely in black and wearing a bowler hat and overcoat. He said he was about 5 feet 8 inches in height, aged thirty to forty and sharp-featured with a fair moustache. A man of the same description, but with 'piercing eyes', was said to have boarded a tramcar which departed from nearby Ellislea Road at 5.30 a.m. to take workers into Dundee. Then a taxi driver came forward to say he had picked up a similar male in Dundee the prior evening and had dropped him in the vicinity of Miss Milne's mansion.

Neighbours spoke of having seen an open-top four-seater car parked near Elmgrove on the evening of 15 October. Its lamps had been left burning and it had remained in the street without its driver for about an hour before vanishing at around 9 p.m. The same people said they had noticed a light shining from an upstairs landing window of Elmgrove during the same period.

Of even greater interest to the police, however, was the picture that started to emerge of an unexpected side to the church-going and reclusive Miss Milne. It transpired that on her trips away from Broughty Ferry she led a distinctly different type of existence from the almost solitary one she had at home. The elderly spinster who preferred to dress in youthful, almost gaudy clothes, revelled in the attention of younger men and made numerous acquaintances among them. Several wrote to her, some even sending poems.

The unlikely femme fatale did not trouble to hide her double life from her acquaintances. She would return from a holiday to speak at length about the gentlemen she met, although she never mentioned names, and would giggle girlishly when discussing them. 'She was more like a young girl on holiday than a woman nearing her allotted span,' was how a lady friend acidly put it. After one visit to London, Miss Milne excitedly told a neighbour how she had become acquainted with a 'college-bred' man and was considering inviting him to Broughty Ferry.

Two women who knew her observed Miss Milne in action for themselves. A few weeks before her violent end, Miss Milne was spotted by them enjoying a sailing holiday on a cargo steamer in the Scottish Highlands accompanied by a good-looking man of about thirty-five. They had seen her with the same man in Glasgow the previous week, when they had all attended a meeting of shareholders of Caledonian Railways.

A maid in a large house overlooking Elmgrove also had an intriguing tale to tell. She revealed how, in the second week of

October, she had looked into the garden of the mansion from an upstairs window of her employer's home and was startled to see a man in evening dress pacing back and forth. She was especially surprised because it was mid-forenoon. The inappropriately dressed figure seemed unaware that he had been spotted, for he was deep in meditation and continued to walk about, hands in pockets, for more than ten minutes. The astonished maid told police that the stranger was about six feet tall, aged between thirty and forty and 'very handsome'.

A young boy also came forward to say he had witnessed a man in a tall hat entering the grounds of Elmgrove in the period leading up to the day when the spinster was probably killed. Another of those with a story was a gardener who had been inside the mansion on 19 September when a man arrived on the doorstep. Miss Milne became coy and said it was the friend she had been expecting. The gardener explained that the visitor sounded German when he spoke and he assumed him to be the man Miss Milne had previously been so animated about when she revealed how they had met on one of her lengthy stays in London.

All of this was naturally of deep interest to Chief Constable Sempill and Detective Lieutenant Trench, but it did not point to a single suspect, for the descriptions and circumstances of the men differed in some cases. It did, however, give a useful indication of the extent of Miss Milne's associations away from home and the part younger men played in the life of the elderly murder victim. Like the picture of Miss Milne's double life that began to emerge, the identity of a possible suspect became more confused.

The investigation was made even more complex by an officer from the dead woman's church who described to police how he had called at Elmgrove on 21 October to collect a charitable donation from Miss Milne. She did not answer the door, he said, but he was certain he had seen her standing at an upstairs bedroom window. When he called back later the same day, he again received no reply. However, he noted that on this occasion the shield on the front door keyhole was lifted when it had not been earlier. If the church officer was correct, it completely contradicted the evidence that Miss Milne had perished on 16 October. On the other hand, if he had indeed seen a woman, but who was not Miss Milne as he had naturally assumed her to be, that opened up the possibility that the killer may have been a woman, or that there was a female accomplice.

Chief Constable Sempill travelled to London to liaise with Scotland Yard and enquire into the spinster's activities there and any friends who may have visited her during her stays in the Strand Palace Hotel. The continuing investigation and detailed coverage it was given daily in the press had built up major interest in the goings-on in the Broughty Ferry mansion house. Police forces across the land had also been alerted to the hunt for the killer. Ten days after the discovery of the body, police in Maidstone in Kent took more notice than their colleagues elsewhere after they arrested a Canadian for obtaining board and lodgings by fraud. Described as well educated and handsome, he appeared in some ways to match the description of a man sought for the Elmgrove killing, although there was no known connection to the events in Broughty Ferry. The man, Charles Warner, was jailed for fourteen days and as he went off to prison a phone call was placed to the investigating officers in Scotland. At the same time, a photograph of Warner was sent north.

Although the picture was of relatively poor quality, five of those in Broughty Ferry who had seen males in and around Elmgrove at the vital times said they believed Warner was the same man. Amidst great excitement, the five – three women and two men – were put on a train for England to see if they could make a positive identification. When they alighted from the overnight express in London, they were met by a large throng of sightseers, reporters and photographers, for by now the case had also attracted the interest of Londoners.

The next day Warner was taken into the yard of Maidstone Prison and one by one the Broughty Ferry group entered to view a line-up of prisoners. Four of the five picked him out; one of the women said she was uncertain. The tall Canadian was led away protesting his innocence and accusing the witnesses of having colluded.

A few days later, after the conclusion of his short sentence on the minor fraud charge, Warner was met at the prison by Chief Constable Sempill and Trench and arrested for the murder of Miss Milne. He was manacled and taken away in a cab to journey north on the next train to Scotland. A large crowd was at the prison gates to witness the departure. Bizarrely, the cab was stopped en route to the railway station at a nearby bank and Warner, handcuffed to Trench, was allowed to enter to collect money which had been wired to him. As he re-entered the taxi after the transaction, he told reporters who were following in close pursuit, 'You know they have arrested an innocent man.' At the railway station, where the air was heavy with smoke and the smell of magnesium from the flash cameras, he continued to inform the large posse of newsmen that he was blameless. News of Warner's arrest spread north and when his train pulled into Dundee a crowd of more than a hundred people, plus a large contingent of police, waited on the platform for a sight of him – although it was 5.30 in the morning.

Not everyone was convinced of his guilt. The only evidence against him seemed to be that he was handsome and vaguely fitted the description of a man seen around Elmgrove at the material times. The witnesses had made their first identifications from a poor photograph and it was not unnatural that they would want to seem helpful, especially since they had become something of celebrities in their own right. Witnesses in London who were acquainted with Miss Milne had never seen him in her company. More importantly, Warner protested that he had been on the continent at the time she was supposed to have been murdered. As supporting evidence, the Canadian recalled that he had pawned a waistcoat in Antwerp on 16 October and even managed to produce the ticket.

Chief Constable Sempill departed at once for Belgium, taking the pawn ticket with him. Following the instructions given to him by Warner, the policeman located the shop and found that the pawnbroker's records confirmed the accused man's account. Next, Semphill travelled to Amsterdam to check another part of Warner's story – that the British Consul there had issued a passport to the Canadian on 17 October. That, too, was established beyond doubt. The case against the protesting man being held in jail in Dundee dissolved. A short time later he was released.

That was as close as the police came to solving the mystery of the mansion house murder in Broughty Ferry. After Warner had been set free the investigation floundered, all impetus gone, and one of the most celebrated murder mysteries of the 20th century stuttered to an inglorious end. Although much of the evidence suggests that the spinster with the widely contrasting lifestyles died on 15 or 16 October at the hands of some stranger she met on her romantic expeditions away from home, that is by no means certain. The lightness of the blows which hastened her end could have been inflicted by a female, and one witness, the church officer, was emphatic he had seen a woman standing at an upper window five days after that. What if she had been the killer? The proposition that a woman might have been the attacker fits with the fact that none of the poker blows were severe enough to have killed Miss Milne. And the curious infliction of what apparently amounted to 'prods' with the carving fork could hint at a form of torture rather than an attempt to kill. No-one ever explained either why a flower vase full of urine was found on a back stairway, despite the mansion having several toilets and bathrooms. Additionally, the floor of the hall close to where Miss Milne lay dead was littered with spent matches. What was their significance?

Much of that may support the notion subsequently whispered by locals that the dastardly deed was the work of a demented young woman whose parents lived close by. It was said she was usually detained in the Dundee lunatic asylum but was occasionally released for "holidays" with her wealthy family. Could she have visited and returned again after initially attacking Miss

Milne? It was also claimed that after the murder she was never again permitted home.

Detective-Lieutenant John Trench endured his own form of torture after the case against Warner collapsed. When the Canadian had been arrested, the detective promptly abandoned his 'strong' chance-thief theory, switching to a conviction of Warner's guilt.

This appeared to have less to do with actual evidence than personal prejudices and the fact that the man they detained in London had a nomadic lifestyle and used a variety of aliases.

In his official statement, previously held privately by the police for almost a century, it is revealed that Trench had rapidly come round to the idea the murder was of such a brutal nature that it was likely to have been the work of a 'maniac or foreigner.' In a further demonstration of 'impartiality', he describes Warner as being 'very, very coarse and vulgar.' And, oblivious to the opinion of witnesses that the man they'd seen was handsome, stated that the suspect 'has a particularly repulsive face.' More bizarrely still, Trench disputed that Warner was a Canadian, claiming he had 'all the peculiarities of an accomplished American crook who had probably served many terms of imprisonment on the Continent or in America.' Just to round things off, he confided that Warner struck him as a 'particularly bad man who, I would say without hesitation, was capable of committing any crime.'

To Trench's credit, he returned to Glasgow disappointed but contrite, subsequently agonising at length about how he had jumped to conclusions and how he and Sempill had arrested a perfectly innocent man for a murder which had taken place when the accused was hundreds of miles away in a foreign land.

It may have been these thoughts which prompted him to consider again the case of Oscar Slater, the man he had helped convict of the murder of the Glasgow spinster four years earlier. Trench had long felt uneasy about the quality of the evidence which had put Slater in the dock and after returning from Dundee he was even more convinced that an injustice had been done. He played a prominent part in demanding a review of the case and his agitation caused so much trouble he was thrown out of the police, eventually being reinstated. He died with Slater still incarcerated in Peterhead Prison. Sadly, he never knew that the information he had passed to a journalist led to the publication of a book which ultimately forced the authorities to re-examine the circumstances of the murder of the Glasgow spinster. They found that Oscar Slater had indeed been innocent and after almost nineteen years in prison he was freed, his conviction quashed.

Miss Jean Milne's unsavoury and untimely demise is likely to forever remain a mystery but, as far as Oscar Slater at least was concerned, it was not entirely in vain.

On her death, Elmgrove, the mansion where she lived and died so mysteriously, was bequeathed to the Church of Scotland and, under a new name, eventually became a care home for the elderly. Miss Milne's sole heir to her financial estate was her closest relative, Frank, a nephew. He was also a young man who lived in London and during that last summer she spent there he visited her twice at the Strand Palace Hotel. He was such a favourite of his aunt that earlier that year she had bought him a car.

23

BRIEF ENCOUNTER

They had never set eyes on each other before their paths crossed in the centre of the city that fine summer evening. Window-shoppers still strolled Murraygate in the fading August sunshine of 1977 and, in Dundee's downtown pubs, the Thursday-night regulars had been joined by a stranger from Montrose.

At 8.45 p.m., in a flat tucked behind some of the shops, Linda Batchelor volunteered to fetch carry-out meals for herself and her boyfriend, whom she'd gone to visit an hour earlier. The pretty 19-year-old clerk departed with a cheery 'Bye for now!' and set off for a Chinese restaurant 200 yards away in St Andrews Street.

At exactly the same moment, 18-year-old Brian John Mearns walked out of a bar in that street and turned into Murraygate.

They met at the doorway of Richards, a fashion store with a short arcade of off-street window displays that provided shelter when it rained and privacy from those passing along the street. No one knows for sure if the two teenagers even spoke to each other, but within moments of them first coming face to face, Linda was fighting for her life in the concealed corner of the arcade.

She did not win. A few minutes later a passer-by saw Mearns emerge from the entrance, wiping his face. His demeanour aroused the suspicions of the man, who just before had heard noises coming from the precinct. He ran into the arcade and found Linda dying from injuries which were later described as 'utterly horrifying'. She was naked from the waist down, apart from socks, and had suffered serious head injuries. A broken pick shaft had been driven so far into her body through her private parts that it had all but disappeared.

The observant pedestrian who made the dreadful find rushed back into the street to summon aid, then followed in the direction her attacker had taken, hoping to apprehend him. He never saw him again. The 18-year-old who, minutes earlier, had committed such a savage and random murder had quickly disappeared into a restaurant in St Andrews Street, where he asked to use the toilet. As he desperately sought to remove his victim's blood and straighten his appearance, his description was being broadcast over the police radio network.

Among others, it was heard by PC David Martin, who was on patrol duty in the city centre.

At 9.15 p.m. he was in Commercial Street when he spotted Mearns approaching and noted that he matched the description of the subject of the all-points bulletin. As the young fugitive came closer, PC Martin also detected what appeared to be bloodstains on his shoes and damp patches on his trousers. The constable's heart beat faster, but he remained composed. Making no reference to the vicious attack that had been carried out a short distance away, he merely asked Mearns where he was going. The untidy teenager replied that he was about to make his way back to his home in Baltic Street in Montrose. Then, out of the blue, he asked, 'How is the lass?' As incriminating remarks went, it was about as damning as they come. Taken to police headquarters, the 18-year-old made other statements which clearly involved him in the crime.

Experienced detectives, well used to lengthy murder inquiries and the frustrating brick walls that can be encountered in the hunt for the perpetrator, were taken by surprise at the suddenness of the events of the evening, for the circumstances were unique. In the space of just thirty minutes, two young people – total strangers, as far as anyone knew – come face to face utterly by accident; on the spur of the moment, one is viciously killed by the other, who takes flight; then, just as much by chance, the suspect walks into the arms of the police and immediately implicates himself.

The murder stunned the city but, even after the completion of the court formalities, no one was any closer to understanding what had brought on such a frenzied, sadistic and random assault. When Mearns appeared at the High Court in Dundee eight weeks later, the two men at the heart of the proceedings were advocates who in later years would become judges in the supreme court. That day, however, they could shed little light on the nauseating drama that had played out in the heart of a city on that peaceful summer evening.

After Mearns pled guilty to the murder, Advocate Depute John Wheatley, prosecuting, recounted the bizarre circumstances of the killing and said the accused man had previously appeared to have had normal relationships with girlfriends, although he also seemed to have something of a drink problem. On the day of the murder, 'for reasons that were obscure', Mearns had decided to travel from Montrose to Dundee, where he had visited two bars. Mr Wheatley explained that although there were sexual injuries inflicted in the assault, there were no signs of intercourse.

Andrew Hardie, the defending advocate, said that because of the nature of the assault, psychiatric reports had been obtained about Mearns, but they gave no indication that his responsibilities were substantially diminished, Nor did they indicate that he required any psychiatric treatment.

Pressed by the judge, Lord Wylie, to provide an explanation for the killing, Mr Hardie said he had tried to determine one, but Mearns had either been unwilling or unable to provide a reason. Jailing Mearns for life, with a recommendation that he be detained for at least fifteen years, His Lordship told the unemotional teenager standing quietly before him, 'This is about the most horrible murder I have come across in all my years on the bench and at the Bar.'

It was not the last the public was to hear of Brian John Mearns, however. Exactly twenty-two years later, while serving out the last months of his life sentence, he failed to return to Saughton Prison in Edinburgh from an outside work placement while training for his eventual release. He had gone on the run to London with a 25-year-old woman he had become involved with while carrying out service with a charitable group as part of his freedom preparations programme. A week after absconding, he was found unconscious in a street in Shrewsbury after taking a drugs overdose. It seemed he and his female companion had argued the day after arriving in London and she had immediately returned to Scotland. Mearns was admitted to hospital in a critical condition and spent some time in an intensive care unit before being taken back under guard to Saughton to resume his sentence. He was still detained at the time of writing (2005).

His decision to flee baffled members of the Scottish Prison Service, who could not understand why he should choose to escape when his official release had been so imminent. It made no sense at all – just like the appalling crime which sent him to prison in the first place.

24

REPENTANCE

Saturday afternoon in Hilltown. A distant cheer carrying on the icy February wind sweeping over the tenement blocks told of a goal at nearby Dens Park. Few who bent into the breeze as they went about their business cared very much. Those who supported Dundee FC were already at the game and the rest were more interested in the betting shops or purchasing something for that evening's tea.

The agitated figure who thrust his way into a side-street phone box was least interested of all. His head was near to bursting with what consumed him and all he could think of was shouting it out and finding some peace. He dialled 999 and asked for the police. Then he told his extraordinary tale to the female operator, 'I've killed my father. You'd best come and get me.'

He was still unburdening himself when the policeman who had been alerted by the switchboard staff at headquarters in Bell Street a mile away arrived outside the telephone box. The caller hung up and, turning to the officer, exclaimed, 'Aye. It was me. I killed him. I put a pillow over his face.'

The next few hours that afternoon in 1974 were among the most bizarre of the detective's entire career. The man identified himself as 42-year-old Joseph Gibson, who lived in Rosebank Street with his 81-year-old father, and he invited the officer to go home with him to see for himself what he had done. When they went to the ground-floor flat together the old man was dead, sure enough. He lay serenely on a bed, dressed in his best suit and with cotton wool filling his nostrils. He had clearly been visited by an undertaker and the funeral was just as obviously imminent. Death, it appeared, had been as a result of perfectly natural causes.

What began as routine checks, however, produced some startling facts. The man who had been so anxious to confess his guilt knew all about killing. Fourteen years earlier he had been sent to Carstairs State Institution without limit of time after strangling his mistress, with whom he lived, with a scarf. He had been detained for twelve years before being released on licence. A telephone call to the dead man's family doctor revealed that the GP had not examined the corpse of Mr Gibson senior and a death certificate had been issued purely on the basis of the man's medical history, which indicated that he had suffered from several potentially fatal diseases. A hasty post-mortem by the police surgeon told a different story. Mr Gibson's life had ended after suffocation, most likely by a pillow or something similar.

Three months later, when Joseph Gibson sat in the dock of the High Court in Dundee and admitted a charge of culpable homicide, Lord Stott was informed that had it not been for the phone call the accused man had made to the police, the killing would never have been discovered and the arranged funeral would have gone ahead as planned. He also heard that, although Gibson had done his best to care for his elderly father, some ill-feeling had developed between the two and the suffocation had occurred on a night after the old man had locked himself out. The amount of force used to kill him had been minimal and frail Mr Gibson was already 'at death's door'.

His Lordship, after expressing some surprise that the authorities had not decided to treat Gibson as a medical case, took a lenient view. He sent the son who had confessed to prison for three years, commenting, 'This was perhaps the minimal culpable homicide that one could perceive.'

*****

By calling the police to desperately admit to a killing, Joseph Gibson's actions are far from unique. He is just one of a long line who have been so overwhelmed with the magnitude of their crime that they can think of nothing else until the outpouring of their guilt has been completed – as though admission gives them exoneration.

Two years after Gibson's 999 call, another son in another part of the city dialled the same number with similar matters to get off his chest.

The New Year of 1976 was less than three hours old when 16-year-old schoolboy Barrie Michael Seabright contacted police to admit to a double murder in the family home. Unsurprisingly, given that it was New Year's morning when drunken calls to police headquarters are not particularly unusual, PC Alexander MacDonald and Sergeant Peter Brown were not entirely sure what to expect when they went to the house in Balunie Crescent. They walked in on a scene of unimaginable horror. A badly injured man lay in a bedroom bleeding profusely from a number of wounds. In the hall, a woman, also with several severe lesions, was pinned to the floor with a three-foot sabre through her stomach. Both were barely alive and blood saturated many parts of the house. The male, defying expectations, survived his dreadful injuries but the female died a short time afterwards.

The story that unfolded seemed to come straight from the pages of a paperback on Satanism. The schoolboy killer-confessor explained that earlier that morning he had brought New Year in with his father, Frederick, and his father's partner, Barbara Brown. He had then gone for a walk and, after returning home, had been compelled by voices urging him to kill. Watching, as though through someone else's eyes, he said, he had taken an ornamental sabre to hack down his father and then Barbara Brown. Throughout it all, the voice in his ear repeated over and over, 'Got to kill. Got to kill.' and he swung the sabre again and again.

When he was done, he picked up the phone, and recounted to a startled operator what had taken place.

Although he was considered sane and fit to plead, Barrie Seabright was said to have been suffering from diminished responsibility at the time of his fearsome attacks and the original charges of murder and attempted murder were dropped to be replaced by culpable homicide and assault, to which he pled guilty. His defence counsel, Donald Macaulay QC, described the circumstances as unusual and disturbing, saying Seabright had not previously evinced any animosity to either of the victims.

'It was completely irrational and out of character,' he said. 'He had apparently been taken possession of by some force which motivated him to kill for no apparent reason.'

The 16-year-old himself admitted that at the time he would have killed anyone, even the first person he saw. His father told the authorities that he and his son had been interested in black magic, though he did not know if this had any bearing on the New Year's Day events.

Lord Dunpark listened intently to reports from psychiatrists before ordering that Seabright be detained in a young offenders' institution for twelve years. He said the 'bizarre accounts' of the teenager's mental condition meant he should be subject during that time to periodic mental assessment.

*****

Another youth to use a telephone kiosk as a confessional box was 18-year-old Walter Robert Donachy, who visited one immediately after killing the uncle he had been named after, in an axe attack. The baby-faced 5 foot, 2 inch teenager had gone to live with Walter Williamson, his mother's brother, after being discharged from the army a few months earlier because of an ear complaint.

The relationship between the two had been reasonable enough, except when 47-year-old Walter senior had taken drink. Then he would turn on his diminutive nephew and arguments would rage. The one that erupted on a bright May evening in 1971 had its customary roots in drink. The pair consumed two bottles of sherry and some beer between them and the usual pattern ensued when Uncle Walter began to pick on the teenager – only this time he lifted a poker and moved towards the youth.

Fearing for his life, the 18-year-old reached out for an axe which had been left on a sideboard after his uncle had finished chopping firewood. He caught the advancing figure of the older man several times on the head, inflicting fatal wounds.

Moments after the dying man sank to the floor, reason abruptly returned for little Walter Donachy. He gazed unbelieving at the body at his feet and the blood spreading in a crimson pool across the floor. The axe seemed to be held in a hand which was not his. He opened his fingers and it dropped beside the body where all movement had ceased. Then, as though slowly awakening from a dream, he put on a jacket, locked up and walked from the tenement flat in Fintry Crescent.

He continued his unhurried journey for almost two miles until he found a phone box. When he spoke to a policeman the words were as explicit as they were extraordinary. The whole story was recounted in detail and after he had finished, the incredulous officer asked him to remain where he was.

The killer with the boyish looks and slender frame waited patiently outside the telephone box in the fine evening sunshine until a constable arrived a short time later to take him away.

When his time came to stand trial, the 18-year-old denied the murder, pleading self-defence. It was not a submission that convinced a sufficient number of jurors. After retiring for only thirty minutes, the jury foreman announced that they had found Walter Donachy guilty as libelled by a 10–5 majority. As he walked from the dock to start his life sentence wearing his favourite brown, fringed cowboy-style jacket, he paused and turned towards his mother, who sat sobbing in the public benches. Looking at her with tears in his eyes, he called out, 'It's OK, Mum. They canna shoot us.'

*****

When George Glennie's turn came to confess, it was a more gradual, but in the end, equally urgent process. While detective teams scoured Dundee and beyond for the person who had strangled and stabbed to death a 45-year-old spinster in her own home, he lived with the knowledge of his actions for three days, outwardly appearing his usual relaxed, untroubled self. Inwardly, however, he was in turmoil.

His journey to repentance for the most wicked of all crimes began, if not innocently, certainly not especially unusually. In November 1985 he was aged twenty-eight, in a loving and happy marriage and in steady employment. During the six years of their union he had never displayed any violence towards his wife and their relationship was strong and apparently fulfilling. They had two young sons, on which their father doted. George Glennie considered his marriage to be the most important thing in his life.

At work – he was a packer in a city textile factory – he was described as popular and cheery, well liked by his colleagues, who found him easy-going and uncomplicated. Among those to develop a fondness for him was 45-year-old Rhoda Allan, a winder at the Tay Spinners plant in Arbroath Road. Other workmates knew her as a 'quiet, religious woman'. She was also lonely.

When the young father told her his wife worked on permanent night shift, Miss Allan apparently invited him to visit her at her home in Bridgend Street any time he wanted company. He declined the invitation at first, but after it had been repeated on several occasions, he eventually paid her a call. They had sex. Other requests to make follow-up visits were declined, until one Sunday evening after Glennie had spent the day decorating at home. He phoned Miss Allan, then travelled the short distance from his own house to hers. Again they enjoyed intercourse.

It was while they lay together in bed that life began to unravel for George Glennie. Overcome by guilt at what had taken place and reflecting that he had left his loving wife and two sons at home, he told his companion that he would not be making any more visits. Angry words were exchanged and it seems the woman at his side became distraught, furiously threatening to inform his wife of his infidelity. It was not an entirely unexpected reaction, for Miss Allan was not always stable. In the previous six years, she had been a regular caller to the Dundee Samaritans and only the evening before had contacted them because she felt unhappy. She confessed that she had been so low she had taken six sleeping tablets.

Glennie was to say that he had little recollection of the immediate aftermath of their quarrel. His first clear memory of events after the shouted row was when he found himself standing beside the bed with a knife in his hand. His mind had apparently erased the fact that in the preceding minutes he had used his trouser belt to strangle the woman he had gone to visit, then stabbed her a total of twenty-seven times – eleven in the neck and sixteen in the chest.

The unlikely killer returned home and, for the rest of the day and all of the next, acted as though life was continuing to run its easy and uneventful course.

By the Tuesday morning, however, and after another night without sleep, he could no longer maintain any pretence of normality. When it came time to make his routine call home from work to his wife at 8.10 a.m., he blurted out the details of his actions that Sunday evening. In shock, his wife hung up. Four times more he called to repeat his story, saying he was about to give himself up. His parting words to the stunned woman he loved were, 'Say cheerio to the bairns.'

A short time later, in the centre of town, George Glennie walked up to a police constable who was on traffic points duty in Cowgate to tell the startled officer, 'You'd better take me to headquarters. The murder – it was me.'

With more than a little unreality surrounding his actions, the policeman asked the man who had just confessed to a brutal killing to wait on the pavement while he summoned a replacement to take over traffic-directing operations. When they finally started to make their way to headquarters in Bell Street, Glennie's legs buckled beneath him and he had to be supported for the remainder of the journey.

The High Court proceedings that followed the bizarre confession were uncomplicated. The accused man denied murdering his mistress, but was prepared instead to admit to culpable homicide on the grounds that he had no memory of what had taken place and that he had been provoked by his victim's threat to inform his wife of their relationship.

The jury did not agree with his proposition. An hour and a half after retiring, they decided by a majority that his uncharacteristic conduct in the bedroom that Sunday evening amounted to murder. He was given the mandatory life sentence. Ten years later, almost to the day, he was released on licence, one of the shortest periods anyone will serve after being convicted of murder.

*****

Edward Burns, a 43-year-old father of nine, wasted no time in confessing to his deadly deed. Indeed, he was so swift with his admission he had shot and killed his rival in love that police were not even aware murder had already come calling.

It was a simple and not unfamiliar scenario that figuratively and literally triggered the dramatic chain of events of 14 November 1967. Several months earlier, his wife had walked out of their home in Devon to go off with David Horsburgh, a family friend with whom she had been involved in a romantic liaison for some time. The pair found their way to Scotland, eventually settling in a rented semi-detached villa in Tullideph Road, Dundee.

Burns, desperate for a reconciliation and demented by jealousy, eventually tracked them to the city but had no knowledge of where they had set up home. Knowing that 40-year-old Horsburgh was a bus driver, the jilted husband waited outside the main coach depot in town until he spotted his rival coming off shift. Then he followed him back to Tullideph Road.

As Horsburgh was putting his key into the lock of the front door, he heard his name being called. Turning, he was confronted by Burns, who was waving a shotgun and demanding to know why his life had been so devastated. Seconds later, a blast of gunfire brought neighbours rushing to their windows. By the time they had pulled their curtains apart, the Englishman who had recently moved into the street lay prostrate in a pool of blood on his doorstep. Even as they observed the scene, a white car pulled away from the pavement, disappearing in the direction of the city centre.

Behind the wheel, Burns drove sedately but purposefully. Less than ten minutes later, he parked the hired Ford Anglia car in front of police headquarters then calmly walked up to the desk of the charge-room.

'You'll be looking for me shortly,' he told PC Neil Alexander, who was coming to the end of his shift. 'I have just shot someone.' Then he related how he had followed his victim from the bus station before coming face to face with him outside the neat semi-detached villa.

'He messed up my life. His name is Horsburgh,' he said by way of explanation for what had taken place, adding that the weapon they would be looking for was under the dashboard of the Anglia sitting outside.

When charged, his admission was frank: 'Yes, I did it. He broke up my family.'

By the time the man who had driven hundreds of miles with a gun in his car to seek revenge appeared in court, his story had a significant addition. He explained that he had presented the gun merely to frighten Horsburgh enough to make him terminate the relationship with Mrs Burns. The fatal shot had been fired accidentally only when the victim had attempted to push the barrel away.

It was an unconvincing tale and failed to convince a single member of the jury. Less than an hour after they had retired to consider their verdict, Edward Burns, the man who had confessed to a killing the police had no knowledge of, was on his way to start a life term.

25

THE TEMPLETON WOODS MURDERS

In life, their paths never crossed. They were almost the same age and lived in the same city, but they could not have been more different. In death, they became inextricably linked, their names forever bound together. More than quarter of a century after they met their maker they are still spoken of in the same breath. And still no one knows if they had anything in common at all – except perhaps the last person ever to see each of them alive.

The tale of their posthumous introduction began on the afternoon of 21 March 1979 when a couple walking in the snow in Templeton Woods on the outskirts of Dundee came upon the body of a young woman. She was naked and had been strangled. A huge murder hunt was launched but it led nowhere.

The investigation had all but petered out when 11 months later two men hunting rabbits in the same wood discovered the body of another young female. She too had had been asphyxiated and all of her clothing had also been removed. The locations in the forest where the two corpses had been found were only 150 yards apart.

From that day hence, the hellish fate of the two young women, who never knew each other, has joined them together like sisters, their untimely passing creating the most enduring murder mystery their home town has ever known.

Did they perish at the hands of the same serial killer? Or were their deaths, like their lives, disparate and unconnected? Judge for yourself . . .

CAROL

When the car eased to a halt at the pavement corner in the centre of town, the young woman in the black velvet jacket who stepped out of the shadows to open the passenger's door exchanged few words with the pale-faced driver.

'Are you looking for business?' she asked with a mixture of nervousness and defiance.

'Aye,' the driver replied, nodding an invitation for her to take the seat beside him.

The 18-year-old slid thankfully into the warm interior of the vehicle, saying no more but glad to escape the freezing cold of the March night. Moments later the car was clear of the Red Light area and was lost in the mid-evening traffic in central Dundee. The two occupants only spoke again to discuss the teenager's range of services and their cost. Then they headed out of town towards Templeton Woods on the northern edge of the city where lovers found romance in secluded lanes and strangers performed love-less acts of intimacy, with money taking the place of passion.

Nobody, except the man who took her on that emotionless jour-ney, knows exactly what happened next. But Carol Lannen never returned to the streets of Dundee or the three-month-old baby son she had left at the home she shared with her sister.

The following afternoon, a young couple strolling through the snow-covered woods found her unclothed body 150 yards into the forest, her last breath of life having been throttled out of her.

No one would have believed then that the grim discovery on 21 March 1979 would launch the most intensive and long-lasting murder hunt the city had ever known, with more man-hours being devoted to its solution than any other homicide before or since. More than a quarter of a century later, after scientific advances gave the investigation fresh impetus, detectives were still sifting evidence, still seeking witnesses – and were still no further forward in tracking down her killer.

Yet it had not seemed in the first days of the inquiry that the case would prove particularly baffling or find a prominent place in the record books of Dundee's black museum of violent death. When Carol Lannen stepped into the car at the corner of Exchange Street and Commercial Street at 7.50 p.m. to be driven quickly away, her movements had been noted by a fellow prostitute. 'Working girls' know only too well that their chosen profession places them in the front line to become the victims of men who find pleasure in attacking women who sell their services, so the band of sisters who walk the streets look out for each other. They take casual note of the cars each of them depart in and if there is a dodgy punter on the prowl the word is put around. It isn't much, but it's a safety net of sorts.

That night, one of the girls paid particular attention to the driver who anxiously pulled away from the pavement with Carol seated next to him. She was later to describe him as being aged between 25 and 30, of thin build and with a pale complexion, short dark hair, short sideburns and a moustache which needed trimming. The description led to the murder team issuing a photo-fit picture of the man, the first time police in Dundee had ever released such a picture.

This information was better than the detectives might have hoped for. By definition, prostitutes and their customers operate in a shadowy, anonymous world of false identities and fleeting encounters, where there is a brief exchange of cash and carnal activity before the participants disappear back into the night. They seldom swap business cards and even 'regulars' don't give much away.

Unexpectedly perhaps, the witness was unable at first to offer much assistance about the type of car the man had driven. That was as frustrating as the fact that snow had fallen later that night, causing difficulties for forensic specialists hoping to take casts of footprints and tyre tracks in the wood. The evidence they sought melted away almost as fast as the fresh snow. Tracker dogs growled and sniffed but trotted in aimless circles in the sodden conditions. In addition, the victim's clothing and handbag, which might have yielded clues, were missing.

The random nature of how the two people who had gone together to Templeton Woods that night, had met, made it vital for police to find some kind of clue to the make and colour of car the couple had shared.

The helpful fellow prostitute was questioned at length but little progress was made. She knew more about faces than automobiles. Finally, she agreed to submit to hypnosis by a local dentist who used the technique in the treatment of some of his patients. It produced the result that the woman believed the car was red and possibly a Ford Cortina estate.

That formed the linchpin for almost the entire police inquiry. Scores of detectives were drafted in to track down the drivers of such vehicles. Registration records were minutely examined and in the weeks that followed more than 6,000 men all over the country, who drove that type and colour of car, were questioned. The exhaustive research drew a blank. So did the offer of confidentiality for kerb crawlers who were invited to come forward with information.

Eleven days after the launch of the murder hunt, events took an unexpected – and in many ways – unwelcome turn. Carol's handbag and some of her clothing were found 85 miles away on the banks of the River Don near Kintore, 17 miles north of Aberdeen. That added a new dimension to the inquiry. No longer could it be assumed that the killer was probably local. Now the investigation had to be widened, and significantly. It was never established how long the bag, which contained money and a family allowance book, had lain before being found, but some reports suggested the items had been seen there at least a week earlier. That fitted. Reasonably, police assumed the killer would have disposed of them soon after the murder since he would have been reluctant to drive around with such incriminating evidence for any length of time. The question was raised that the hunted man may have had strong links in the north, for unless it had been an elaborate red herring, he would have been unlikely to have driven 85 miles in heavy snow and on difficult roads just to dispose of the bag and clothing. Could he have been a worker in the oil industry, which linked Dundee and Aberdeen in so many other ways? Or could he have been a taxi driver, say one who had taken a fare – perhaps an oilman – north and used the distance to dispose of the incriminating items in his boot?

Yet, despite the minor breakthrough of the riverside find, it yielded nothing of assistance to the investigation. It served only to widen and complicate the murder hunt.

The slaying of the 18-year-old mother was not the first killing in Dundee to go undetected. But it was the first to be the subject of such a prolonged and meticulous hunt for the person responsible. Within weeks, more than 7,000 people had been interviewed and every hotel, boarding house and bed and breakfast establishment in the city had been visited by police officers. The inquiry attracted national media interest but nothing produced the breakthrough that had initially appeared to be so imminent.

As the months passed and the leads dried up, the size of the operation was scaled down. It regained impetus twice within the space of a few weeks some 20 months after it began, first with the discovery of a woman's blood-stained clothing in a lay-by on the outskirts of Aberdeen, seemingly deposited by the driver of a red Ford Cortina. Then, a woman reported that she had been picked up in the centre of Aberdeen and assaulted, but not injured, by someone said to be driving a red car.

Those heading the Dundee murder hunt were alerted to both incidents. But, once more, seemingly promising developments dissolved into nothing as quickly as they had materialised. Every other unsolved murder of young women across the country brought inevitable comparisons and close scrutiny for similarities. None yielded the unmistakable fingerprints – actual or metaphorical – to confirm the killing was part of any serial spree.

After several years passed without a breakthrough, some began to question the wisdom of allowing almost the entire focus of the Carol Lannen inquiry to be devoted to finding the driver of the red Ford Cortina estate car, who was widely assumed to have been the killer. Since there was little else for police to go on, such a concentration on the ownership of the vehicle was understandable. But what if the categoric description of the car by a fellow prostitute, probably no expert in car identification, under hypnosis, had been wrong, perhaps drawn from her by well-meaning but untrained interrogators? It meant that the drivers of anything but that model and colour of vehicle were unlikely to have a policeman knocking at their door.

Despite the passage of time, the mystery continued to attract headlines and every newspaper article or TV broadcast surprisingly brought forth fresh scraps of information and new witnesses with tales to tell or fingers to point in particular directions.

A television documentary featuring the case 25 years after Carol's naked body was found lying in the forest snow produced a flood of more than 100 phone calls to the hastily reconstituted incident room. Astonishingly, 17 people provided possible identities for the photo-fit picture of the driver who had taken the young mother on her final journey.

The new murder squad pursued every lead – and met with the same lack of success as their dogged predecessors.

Unusually in such a sustained and intensive inquiry, not a single serious suspect emerged. Given the detailed description of the pale-faced man who prowled the red light district that night, the vast number of car drivers interviewed, and the finding of the victim's belongings 85 miles from the murder scene, these things by themselves make the case particularly remarkable.

It didn't help that there was no obvious motive. Prostitutes are easy prey and a distressing number meet their end at the hands of a certain type of man who simply finds gratification in killing women. Those driven to murder on these occasions frequently cannot stop at a single victim – in which case the man who drove into Templeton Woods that cold winter night, may have succumbed to the same irresistible urges before or since. If he wasn't one of these unfathomable people, what other reason could he have had for so brutally ending the life of a young woman? Did his victim recognise him and threaten to expose him, or was there an accompanying blackmail demand that required a violent response? Police considered these possibilities but there was no one, at least then, who fitted the profile.

ELIZABETH

When Elizabeth McCabe stepped out into Union Street from Teazers nightclub around 12.30 a.m. that freezing February morning in 1980, an air of despondency hung over her. A weekend that had promised so much had ended with her having a tiff with her best friend and in a few hours time she would be back on duty at Law Nursery where she was an assistant. It was another Monday and nearly a week would pass before her next night out. She pulled up the collar of the short jacket that covered the blue V-neck jumper she had bought on the Saturday afternoon, smoothed her matching denim jeans and walked slowly away, the bright lights and dull beat of the discotheque fading behind her as she threaded her way through the knots of other late night stragglers. Within seconds she was lost to the sight of other revellers filtering out of Teazers.

From that moment on, she simply vanished. Not a person on earth has ever come forward to positively say they saw her again, though, for one person at least, her final movements will be the most indelible memory of their life.

Despite the 20-year-old disappearing into the night, her non-arrival at home did not immediately sound alarm bells. When her mother Anne went to rouse her for work at 6.30 that morning and found her bed still freshly made, she was concerned but not overly worried, believing she had probably stayed the night with Sandra Niven, the friend she had gone clubbing with the previous evening. But by teatime, having phoned the nursery to be told Elizabeth had not turned up for work and that none of her pals, including Sandra, had any idea of her whereabouts, she was filled with apprehension. With growing anxiety, she went with her husband Jim to their nearest police station to report their daughter missing. The details of Elizabeth's last movements were noted, mild assurances were given that she would likely re-appear soon and officers promised to be in touch if there were any developments. Beyond that, not much happened. Young women not turning up for a day or two after a night out was not particularly unique. Besides, there was nothing to suggest she might have come to harm. It was an understandable reaction from the police, even if her parents were convinced their daughter's failure to return home was far from ordinary.

Two weeks passed without any hint about what might have happened to the attractive student nursery nurse. Family and friends were recruited to tour the pubs Elizabeth was known to visit and customers were asked if they had seen her and requested to look out for her. Nightly, her distraught father trailed the city streets in search of his vanished daughter while her mother sat fearfully by the phone awaiting the call which would end their misery. She prayed it would come from Elizabeth, but as the days passed she knew in her heart that was unlikely. Her missing girl was the first-born of her four children and was a responsible, considerate daughter who had never caused her any trouble. There did not seem the least likelihood that she would stay away from home without any kind of explanation or contact. Nor was there any possibility that she might have taken her own life. Elizabeth enjoyed her work and the Dundee social scene and had been excitedly looking forward to her 21st birthday in a few days time. Her disappearance made no sense at all.

Frustrated by the apparent inaction of the police, who in fairness had nothing but a missing person report to go on, Mrs McCabe called the offices of *The Courier* newspaper to enlist their aid in running appeals for anyone with information to come forward. Seasoned journalists instinctively knew this wasn't just the usual anxious mother whose wayward daughter had decided to stay away from home for a few days. None of the customary pieces fitted. Elizabeth, almost 21, had never gone absent before, always kept the family informed of her movements and had no obvious reason for disappearing. They ran the story of the troubled family and their growing fears that something terrible had happened. Despite several articles highlighting the mystery, no one came forward to offer the slightest clue about what might have occurred in the early hours of 11 February, or any time afterwards. It was as though the nursery assistant had never existed.

Around noon on Tuesday 26 February, the day before Elizabeth would have celebrated her special birthday, the situation dramatically changed – and a never-ending nightmare began for the McCabes.

Two rabbit hunters exercising their dogs in Templeton Woods pushed their way through a dense crop of small fir trees and emerged into a clearing where one of the dogs was sniffing at a pile of branches. When they investigated and pulled the tree cutting away, they were faced with something they had never expected to see. Before them lay the body of a young woman. She was naked and clearly very dead. In addition to the branches covering the lower part of her torso, a blue V-necked pullover had been placed across her shoulders,

It was a sight the pair would be unlikely ever to forget. It was also one which the first police officer on the scene, Sergeant David Gibson, knew would remain with him forever. As he took in the horror of what confronted him, the sergeant reflected that whoever had disposed of the body might, unusually, have experienced pangs of conscience at what he or she had just done. It seemed to him that the laying on of the jumper on the naked corpse might not have been so much an act of attempted concealment as one of concern, the jersey having been placed where it was to afford a degree of dignity, perhaps even warmth, to the violated woman underneath. On the other hand, perhaps it was the officer's own compassion which prompted such thoughts. Seeing a murder victim at close quarters can stir unexpected emotions.

Within an hour of the grim find being announced, the same journalists in the newsroom of *The Courier*, who days before had intuitively suspected a distressing outcome, began writing the first of the hundreds of thousands of words that would ultimately follow. The files on the other Templeton Woods victim were hurriedly retrieved and the 11-month unsuccessful hunt for Carol Lannen's murderer was back on the front pages, alongside the account of where and how Elizabeth had finally been found.

For the first time, the city was alerted to the chilling possibility that a serial killer might be loose in the city. The link has been made ever since.

On the evening leading to her disappearance, a Sunday, Elizabeth and her friend Sandra Niven, a nursery workmate, had visited a few pubs before ending up in Teazers discotheque. But, as the night wore on, the pair, who were considering sharing a flat together, had a minor disagreement. They seemed to have resolved it, but later, as closing time approached, Elizabeth was nowhere to be seen. Sandra went in search of her chum and found her with her jacket on and about to descend the exit stairs. The two exchanged a few friendly words then Elizabeth departed, apparently alone and presumably to find her own way home.

It was around 12.30 a.m. and it was the last time the two friends ever spoke to each other.

No one – except her killer – knows what happened to the reserved 20-year-old after that. Despite extensive inquiries and appeals, not a soul came forward to say they had seen the petite figure her making her way home along the two-and-a-half mile route to her home in Lyndhurst Avenue in Lochee. Some believe she may have travelled in a taxi, or what she took for one, or that she had accepted a lift from someone she knew. Family and friends said that Elizabeth, a quiet but intelligent girl, would never willingly have entered the car of a stranger, especially after an incident on a previous night out in town when she had allowed herself to be driven away from the city centre by someone she had mistakenly believed to be a taxi driver. Describing the incident to Sandra Niven afterwards, she said simply that she had been taken 'to the back of beyond' but gave no details of anything that may have occurred. She had, however, been upset by the experience.

Whatever had taken place, it had been enough to make her wary and after that she would only travel in taxis with official roof lights. It was a practice that was to have considerable future significance.

Practically all of Dundee's 700 taxi drivers were questioned, some at length, along with kerb crawlers and other late night drivers who operated in the city. By the end of the first week, statements had been taken from more than 1000 people, among them regulars from the nightclub and bar scene in the central area.

As the hunt intensified, the head of the CID in the city advised women not to make their way home alone at night. It was a natural but needless warning. With the bodies of two women who had vanished from the city centre having being found inside a year, and their killer or killers still on the loose, a climate of fear descended every time darkness fell. Overnight, the relatively common custom of unaccompanied women accepting lifts from strangers to save a taxi fare came to an end.

A female town councillor, worried about the safety of lone women, and concerned for the reputation of her city, launched a reward scheme. Others contributed and within days £5,000 was on offer to anyone who could help trace and convict the person who had ended Elizabeth's life. It was never claimed.

Within days of the body being discovered, much of the victim's clothing was found at three different locations in the city, all within a short distance of Camperdown Park, which is close to Templeton Woods, but it did little to assist the investigation.

Because of the condition of her body, there was a feeling among some experienced police officers that Elizabeth – unlike Carol – might not have met her end in the forest but that her corpse had been taken there some time after her death because it could be easily disposed of in the woods.

Like every police inquiry, those involved in the two murder hunts approached their investigations with open minds, though it was easy to recognise the similarities between the two killings. The most marked was the location of the bodies – 150 yards apart in the same woodland on the outskirts of town. The victims were practically the same age and both had last been seen in the city centre, also at spots only a few hundred yards apart. They had simply disappeared after apparently being willingly driven off. Each had been stripped and strangled and had their clothing removed from the scene. Even the time of year was similar.

But these parallels were not so striking as to present an absolutely compelling case, conclusively indicating a common killer. There were no trademark features pointing irresistibly in a single direction, no unmistakeable message that the same killer had come calling.

There were also marked differences. Carol had actively been seeking the company of unknown males, and not for conversation or romance. Elizabeth, keen to advance her career and looking forward to her 21st birthday, would have been unlikely to have allowed herself to be driven away by a stranger.

Police found themselves frustrated by the dilemma. The idea of a serial killer being responsible had a natural appeal for the media. It made a 'better read' and helped sell papers. But the press treatment of the cases also assisted the murder squads. It guaranteed headlines and kept the cases in the public eye long after any single slaying would have featured. Senior officers were in no doubt, however, that the understandable desire by the media to tie the two murders together might also be counter-productive. The more the killings seemed connected, the more potential witnesses might have been convinced the same person had to be responsible for both deaths. If a member of the public suspected a person's link with one killing, but knew they could not have been involved in the other, would they simply have disregarded their suspicions and kept quiet?

Yet publicity was vital. If people continued to speak about the twin murders, the better the chances were of a conscience being stirred and the desperately awaited breakthrough occurring.

There was no lack of effort by the media. They stoked up interest with every morsel of fresh information, but as the days slipped into weeks, then months, without any kind of outcome, the story inevitably dropped off the front pages, then out of the papers entirely. It seemed to the public that the killer of Elizabeth McCabe, like that of Carol Lannen, might stalk the streets of Dundee indefinitely.

They were not to know, however, that for some on the murder team, the disappearance of Elizabeth did not seem the unfathomable mystery it might have appeared. They entertained their own suspicions about what could had happened to her after she walked away from the city centre nightspot and also who she might have been with. It would take the passage of many years, however, before the anxious and baffled citizens of Dundee would learn anything of that.

VINCENT SIMPSON

Shortly before breakfast time on the morning of 15 July 2005, a convoy of police vehicles drove slowly into leafy Longlands Way, in Camberley, Surrey, the upmarket commuter town 30 miles from London. Two of the cars drew to a gentle halt outside the front of one of the houses in the row of smart family residences, but the occupants did not alight. It was only when they were sure that the team of officers, in the three vans that had carried on to the rear of the house, was in position that they left their vehicles and walked up the garden path to ring the doorbell.

Inside, the 59-year-old owner of the £300,000 house wondered who could be calling at such an early hour. Vincent John Simpson answered the door – and his worst nightmare began. The callers informed him they were investigating the death of Elizabeth McCabe more than 25 years previously in a Scottish city some 400 miles away and they required his assistance.

Within a few hours the bespectacled, balding window cleaner was taken to Woking police station and formally charged with murdering the student nursery nurse by striking her on the head and strangling her some time between 10 and 26 February 1980. Later that same morning in Dundee, when news of the arrest broke in the *Evening Telegraph*, all those who recalled the quarter-of-a-century-old murder hunt were stunned at the unexpected announcement. The trail had apparently become so cold it seemed to have petered out for good.

Vincent Simpson, however, did not altogether share their surprise.

Unknown to the public, he had been identified as a prime suspect in the very first days by some to those hunting Elizabeth's killer. Convinced that she was likely to have travelled in a taxi for her homeward journey after leaving the nightclub, the murder teams concentrated much of their efforts in tracking down all those who had been driving cabs in and around the city in the early hours of that February morning. Special questionnaire forms were compiled and a plea went out for members of the taxi community, who had been on duty, to come forward. Among those who willingly responded was Simpson, a taxi owner and part-time window cleaner from Newtyle, a small village a few miles beyond the north-west outskirts of Dundee. He and his Dundee-born wife Gillian, a nurse, and their three children had lived in Camberley until a year earlier but moved to Newtyle because her parents in Dundee wanted to see more of their grandchildren. To facilitate the move north, her folks purchased the taxi business for the couple, who had met when Simpson was treated by Gillian for a leg injury, sustained while playing football on a trip to Scotland.

Around the same time as the Newtyle cabbie was completing the police questionnaire, a couple from Carnoustie on the other side of Dundee were reflecting on whether or not to answer police appeals for assistance by informing them of an unusual encounter they'd had around 12.30 a.m. on 11 February, the date when Elizabeth had gone missing and whose ultimate fate was filling the papers. Driving home after a visit to friends, they were approaching Templeton Woods when a taxi emerged at speed from a side road leading into the forest and turned in front of them without stopping. The man was particularly interested in the model of the taxi as the vehicle was the latest Ford Cortina model, a Mark V, which he was a familiar with and dreamed of owning. But other things also drew the couple's attention. The interior light of the taxi was on and the driver appeared to be controlling the vehicle by his wrists. Later, after deciding to report their experience to the police, the Carnoustie couple described how it had seemed the man behind the wheel was scanning his vehicle for something.

'It was as if he had dirty hands and was afraid to touch the steering wheel. It was as if he was looking for something to wipe his hands with,' they were to tell detectives.

When the murder squad cross-checked with data already held, they found that one of those who owned a Mark V Cortina was Simpson. He had also admitted to having been working that night. Furthermore, the sign on its roof was identical to the one described by the Carnoustie couple. He was immediately taken in for questioning.

In the days that followed, he was interrogated on repeated occasions, sometimes being roused at his home at 5 a.m. and held at police HQ until 11 p.m. the same day, the rules on limited questioning of suspects having still to be introduced at that time.

Detectives would later explain how, during one interview session, Simpson admitted that he would occasionally visit Templeton Woods, which was on his route between Newtyle and Dundee, to spy on couples having sex in the open or in their cars. On these Peeping Tom expeditions he would often take his dog with him as an excuse for being near the vehicles.

Questioned about his movements on the night of Elizabeth's disappearance, the officers recounted how the cabbie had willingly confessed to having gone twice to the woods that evening. On the first occasion, he told them he had seen a dark coloured car moving up and down as though the occupants were engaged in intercourse. When his dog jumped up on the car he called it off and went home. Later that night, he returned to the forest. The car he had watched earlier had gone but another one was present, though he could see no sign of activity. He decided to leave the woods but after driving a short distance he pulled over in the side road leading to the main highway and had begun to masturbate. When he drove off a few minutes later he continued in the act and ended with semen on one of his hands. He could not find a tissue and used his cash bag to wipe the fluid off. In the process, he switched the interior light on to see what he was doing and to check if his trousers had been stained. The officers claimed that Simpson related how he had then driven into Dundee and, after picking up several fares, had returned home at around 2.45 a.m. and gone to bed.

By any definition, police were entitled to think they had made a breakthrough in the case. Persuaded by the statements of those who knew Elizabeth McCabe best, it was reasonable for them to assume she had taken a taxi home, but only one bearing an official sign. Witnesses had seen such a car leaving Templeton Woods around the crucial time and a person who owned the precise model of vehicle they had observed had admitted that he had been twice in the forest that evening when he engaged in sordid sexual activity. As murder inquiries went, they appeared to have a more than reasonable case for identifying Vincent John Simpson as a suspect.

Regrettably, from their perspective, suspicions were all they had. No other useful evidence was available which might have incriminated him further or, indeed, which might have eliminated him entirely, for at that time forensic science had not reached the sophisticated levels that were to follow.

Yet he was not the only individual to occupy the minds of detectives. The movements of others with links to Elizabeth were also being examined in some detail and at least three other people were classified as 'people of interest'. But it was to be another 25 years, and only after Vincent Simpson had been taken from his home in England to stand trial in Scotland, before such information would come to public light.

His elevation from suspect to accused happened only after fresh advances in the analysis of DNA samples allowed matches from hitherto unimaginably minute quantities of the cellular material.

A spot of sweat, or a piece of biological matter as small as a millionth of the size of a grain of salt, for instance, were now sufficient to establish ownership.

It was this scientific advance which opened up a major cold case review of the 2004 Templeton Woods murders. Ironically, Simpson's arrest came about as a result of a special crime squad's attempts to prove that someone else – later found to be completely unconnected with the case – had killed the nursery nurse.

At that time the murders of six other young women in Scotland in the late 1970s and early 1980s also remained unsolved. Because of loose similarities in the eight deaths, a nationwide detective team was assembled to review the cases under the code name Operation Trinity. Much of the inquiry was to focus on determining if DNA matches could be made from low copy number – smaller, poor grade – samples taken from the possessions of the victims. Similarities and differences were put under the microscope, figuratively as well as literally, to determine if all the homicides had been the work of the same person, specifically Angus Sinclair, a serial rapist who had been convicted of causing the deaths of two females and jailed for life.

As it turned out, Sinclair was swiftly eliminated from the Dundee murder inquiries, for the very good reason that he had been in prison at the material times. However, the forensic re-examination of clothing and other items belonging to Elizabeth McCabe and Carol Lannen was already underway. That study produced what police believed to be a major development in the case of the young student nursery nurse. The new techniques had discovered DNA traces on the new blue jumper she had worn that night and which had been used to partially cover her naked body. Since Sinclair could be discounted as the source of the genetic material, police set about trying to trace its owner. It was decided to obtain a sample covertly from Vincent Simpson by then living in England. The result produced a strong match. In addition, tests on a hair found on a black plastic sheet used in the mortuary examination of Elizabeth also indicated that it belonged to the

Newtyle taxi driver. That, and the information about Simpson already held in the McCabe murder file from 1980, was enough to convince prosecutors they had a strong case. They ordered his immediate arrest.

But even after his dramatic apprehension hundreds of miles away, there was still to be no speedy conclusion of the case. Extraordinarily, almost another two-and-a-half years would pass from the time of Simpson's arrest to his eventual trial in the High Court in Edinburgh; a period he spent free on bail after being released from custody, permitting him to once more return to Camberley.

Although such a lengthy gap between arrest and trial was highly unusual, so were the circumstances that brought it about. The comparatively recent introduction of low copy number DNA profiles into court cases meant that, in many respects, it was evidentially untested. Nor was it without controversy. Many believed the technique to be flawed because it was appreciably less exact than the established profiling procedures and carried a significant risk that samples could be easily contaminated. These were factors Vincent Simpson's defence team would spend many pre-trial months exploring. They also devoted countless hours considering if others might have had more of a case to answer than their client.

The length of time taken to finally start proceedings was not the only remarkable aspect of the trial. On the opening day in October 2007, Mr Mark Stewart QC, who headed Simpson's legal team, lodged two special defences – firstly, that the accused man had an alibi because he was elsewhere at the material time, and secondly, on the grounds of incrimination. To support the latter, the young QC claimed that if the crime had been committed it had been carried out by one or more of 13 other individuals, all of whom he named to the court.

Unsurprisingly, the trial extended far beyond the normal duration of capital cases. It lasted for seven weeks and from start to finish fascinated the Dundee public who had waited 27 long years to learn what had happened to the pretty young nursery nurse about to celebrate her 21st birthday.

From the outset, the daunting challenge facing the defence was to disprove the apparent evidence of their client's DNA being found on Elizabeth's clothing and what seemed to be his hair having been located on the mortuary sheet covering her body.

Until the start of the trial, juries across the country and further afield had come to believe that DNA proved an infallible link to its owner. Thanks to numerous high-profile cases that spawned an endless series of films, TV thrillers and books, the public were extremely familiar with how successful the identification of the genetic material had been in tracing and convicting everyone from serial killers and rapists to small-time housebreakers. It was more available than fingerprints and a thousand times more damning. But such success was the result of the examination of large, high grade and comparatively fresh samples, producing matches that were mathematically impossible to reasonably contradict.

The advent of the new lower grade specimens was a different matter entirely and not something the public was particularly familiar with. The problem for the first defence teams facing this new evidence in court was to persuade juries that this poorer quality material was much less likely to produce conclusive proof than the prime quality DNA, which had brought dramatic convictions in the celebrated cases.

Another major plank in the bid to have Vincent John Simpson acquitted was the task of presenting an acceptable hypothesis that someone else, who would be named, might be responsible for the killing of Elizabeth McCabe. While it is no part of the defence's job to prove another's guilt, claiming incrimination by suggesting it might be a particular other person is a recognised strategy that can be sufficient to sway an undecided jury. Simpson's plea was highly unusual because 13 other individuals had been listed as possible perpetrators of the act which had brought about Elizabeth's death.

In order to present this aspect of the defence, it was necessary for Mark Stewart QC to introduce evidence about the victim's sexual history, which didn't exactly fit with the public perception that Elizabeth had been a timid and fairly straight-laced young woman with little interest in the opposite sex. Within the space of a few days, and after hearing from a number of witnesses, a picture emerged in court of someone who had experienced her first sexual encounters in relatively casual circumstances. Most specifically, she had lost her virginity to one of the 13 named on the indictment, a man around her own age who had been a boyfriend of her friend Sandra Niven, the companion she had been with at Teazers discotheque on the night she went missing. The court heard that a few months before that fateful evening, the two friends had been in town but had had a disagreement. Elizabeth had then 'stormed off' to go home alone and on the way had stopped off at the flat of Sandra's boyfriend, which was on her route. Elizabeth later told Sandra she had slept with him. Further evidence was given that the nursery nurse had gone to the flat on other occasions, by Sandra recounting how, on one of these visits, she had followed her chum to find out where she was going.

Sandra described in court how, on their last night out together, the two had been joined at their table in Teazers by two male friends, but one of them, who was in a relationship, left to go home alone. Elizabeth felt she was left playing 'gooseberry' and had started to cry in the toilet, saying she was upset because 'no one liked' her. After placating her, Sandra told how she had loaned her friend £1 so she might buy another drink. Sandra agreed that in an interview with police after the discovery of her friend's body in the woods, she had recounted how Elizabeth had explained during their toilet conversation that one of those who 'hated her' was Sandra's former boyfriend, adding that the reason for that was because she had been 'annoying him'.

The court also heard from Sandra that she had seen Elizabeth and the male in question in conversation in one of the bars they had visited before going to Teazers and, although the pair seemed to be on friendly terms, the man appeared at one point to be 'shooing her away'. Sandra said that after it was learned Elizabeth had gone missing, she had suggested to her anxious parents that her chum might have gone once again to the man's flat on her way home.

Before giving evidence himself, the man was advised by Lord Kinclaven, the trial judge, that he need not answer any questions which might suggest he had committed a criminal offence, nor need he say anything else which might incriminate him. During his long spell in the witness box, the man vehemently denied being responsible for Elizabeth's death, saying he had been interviewed by police 19 times when attempts had been made to 'fit him up with it.' He agreed he had a history of violence and had been sentenced to three years' imprisonment after being convicted of serious assault and that a local sheriff had once described him as a 'fighting machine'. He also admitted that on the night of Elizabeth's disappearance, he had been looking for sex and some time after midnight had left his house to phone a female acquaintance in the hope of finding it. He acknowledged, too, that Elizabeth's handbag and some other possessions had been found near his flat and that her clothing had been disposed of a mile and a half away. Admitting that on the day she had vanished he had not gone into work until the afternoon, he said this was a 'common occurrence' after being out at the weekend. However, he strenuously denied the suggestions of Mr Stewart that he had met up with Elizabeth late at night, shared a fish supper with her and had then taken her back to his flat.

During heated exchanges from the witness box, the man repeatedly protested his innocence, exclaiming: 'There's no way I murdered that lassie. Twenty-five years ago there was no way the police could prove I murdered her. Twenty-five years later they still haven't found my forensics on that lassie's body.'

He was not the only person called to give evidence about his sexual connections with Elizabeth. One of the man's friends also went into the witness box to explain how his semen had been found on the crotch of the jeans Elizabeth had been wearing on the night she was killed.

He told the court that he and the 20-year-old had formed a relationship after meeting some six to nine months before she disappeared. They eventually had sex together but the last time had been a number of weeks before she went missing. He explained to the jury that their association had not been 'like boyfriend-girlfriend going to the pictures' and that they'd had only two 'romantic encounters'. He had been surprised when police told him his DNA had been found on Elizabeth's jeans because he knew her to be 'a clean girl who would have washed her clothes'. He described in court how the first time they'd been intimate it had been at the flat of his friend – the boyfriend of Sandra Niven – and she had worn her jeans.

Questioned about his movements on the night Elizabeth vanished, he said he had left home at about 11 p.m. for a midnight start at the downtown railway depot in Dundee where he was a shed man. He rejected suggestions by Mr Stewart that he had commenced work earlier or might have 'sneaked away' from the rail-yard, explaining his absence would have been noticed and a search carried out. He elaborated further that, in the event he had not been found, police would have been informed.

Another of the 13 men listed as one of those who might have committed the murder was a city taxi driver who had been on duty at the time of Elizabeth's disappearance. He told the jury he had gone to the police to volunteer information after reading press appeals but their attitude to him had been 'terrible'. One detective inspector had even openly accused him of her murder, he said. He went on to describe how, at around 12.45 a.m. at the taxi rank at City Churches a few yards from Teazers, he had picked up two men and a woman. He dropped one of the males and the woman in Dryburgh, Lochee, then dropped the other man off in nearby Menzieshill. When he saw a photograph of Elizabeth, he thought she and his passenger that morning were the 'exact same girl'.

The cabbie said that subsequently, police searched his home, taxi and personal car. He had been 'horrified' at his treatment and he, and taxi-driving colleagues, were of the opinion that police were convinced a taxi driver had been responsible for the girl's death.

Police witnesses gave details of two others listed among the 13 on the incrimination list, explaining how they had drawn up a catalogue of names of people known as 'nominals of interest' to the murder inquiry and from whom DNA samples had been taken. Among them was a young man who had lived a matter of yards from Elizabeth McCabe's home and who, three years after her death, had broken into a neighbouring house. Once inside he had murdered the woman of the house then raped and assaulted her daughter (see The Not So Ordinary John Smith).

Another on the list was a young man who had been interviewed by the inquiry team in 1980 and who had admitted to being in Teazers that night and speaking to Elizabeth there. He had also admitted to picking up females in the nightclub and then taking them to Templeton Woods for sex. Police agreed that around that time the man had been convicted of abducting a nurse. He had also initially lied to police about his movements on the night of Elizabeth's disappearance.

Medical experts explained to the court how an examination of Elizabeth's body at the time had revealed that she been manually strangled, possibly as a result of a disruption to the vagal nerve in her neck, which connects to the brain stem and regulates breathing and heartbeat. A small bruise consistent with a thumb mark had been found on the neck and it was likely Elizabeth had suffered 'a fairly quick death, probably within 30 seconds'. She had not 'struggled for life' and there were no defensive injuries indicating she had tried to protect herself.

Pathologists had established that the nursery nurse had had sexual intercourse in the 12 hours leading up to her death and it was quite possible she had been killed in 'an explosion of temper' during the act of intimacy when a hand on her neck could have triggered a reflex stopping her heart and breathing.

Partially digested food was found in her stomach and the

alcohol level in her blood was 110 mgs, an amount which would not have resulted in her being incapacitated. The court also learned that, depending on the actual ground temperatures when she was killed, Elizabeth's body could have been stored somewhere cold before being later taken to Templeton Woods and left.

Much of the trial centred naturally on the suggestion that Vincent Simpson's DNA fatally connected him to Elizabeth McCabe. No one disputed that without apparent evidence of that link, he would never have been charged, far less put into the dock of the High Court. His principal scientific accuser was Dr Jonathan Whitaker, a world expert based at the laboratories of Forensic Science Service in Yorkshire who had previously testified in a number of high profile cases in Britain and abroad, including the celebrated Australian Outback murder of English backpacker Peter Falconio.

Altogether the doctor spent four days in the witness box of the High Court explaining how low copy number samples found on the victim's blue jumper and the hair root from the mortuary sheet identified them as almost certainly coming from Vincent Simpson. He described how three partial profiles which had been removed from the neck area of the jumper – where someone might have grabbed it – produced odds of one in 8.9 million that they could have come from anyone but the accused. Put together with the hair root findings, he claimed the combined odds of them belonging to someone unrelated to Simpson were one in 40 million.

He used graphs and charts to help present his case and it's fair to say the evidence was of considerably greater complexity than jurors would normally have to grapple with.

Mr Mark Stewart and his defence team set about dismantling the DNA findings methodically, blazing a trail others would inevitably follow in the testing of this new scientific evidence. By careful cross-examination of Dr Whitaker and a number of police witnesses who had been involved in the case 27 years earlier, he established how the samples could easily have been contaminated because of poor police handling techniques. Much of the unsatisfactory care of various exhibits was a result of the limited stage forensic science was at in 1980. Scenes-of-crime investigations were unaware then of the demanding, sophisticated protocols that would one day follow for the essential preservation of evidence, and it was normal practice for crucial areas to be examined by squads of people wearing just their usual outdoor clothing. Vital productions, and even the bodies of murder victims, would be handled in comparatively casual circumstances, there being no concept of the ease with which invisible traces of genetic material could be transferred or mixed by people touching two separate items. Under cross-examination, Dr Whitaker admitted that secondary transfers of DNA could create difficulties and agreed with Mr Stewart that the condition of some of the evidence before the court posed 'a real, not theoretical problem.'

Other aspects of police protocols were shown to have been shoddy, even by standards existing at the time, such as when productions from the Elizabeth McCabe and Carol Lannen cases were placed together. None of the bags used to store evidence had been sealed and items belonging to Vincent Simpson had been placed alongside some of Elizabeth's possessions. It wasn't contested either that some of the McCabe items were stored beside departmental Christmas decorations, nor that others had been used for training purposes. Some pieces of evidence, such as Vincent Simpson's cash bag, on which he told police he had wiped his soiled hands after emerging from Templeton Woods, had simply become lost over the years. So had hair, blood, urine and saliva from Elizabeth's body, along with her tights and underpants.

One police officer, detailed to examine and catalogue the evidence during a case review in 1998 had stated in his report: 'The condition of productions is poor and given the manner in which they were stored over the years, it is highly unlikely any court could accept their integrity.' It was a damning indictment of his own force's inept procedures and far from helpful to the prosecution case.

Perhaps most frustrating of all was the unexplained disappearance of four vaginal swabs which had been taken from Elizabeth after her body had been found. During a cold case review in 2004 one of them had been discovered, almost by accident, in a folder kept in a cabinet. But although earlier examination of the swab established the presence of semen, it had been tested to destruction and, along with natural deterioration, the integrity of the sample had been degraded to such an extent that the extraction of a helpful, identifying DNA profile was impossible. Had the other swabs – likely to have been far less closely scrutinized – been properly retained, conventional and completely reliable DNA might have been found which could have proven who had had intercourse with Elizabeth prior to her death; a potentially crucial link to who might have killed her. Considering that one estimate of the cost of subsequently examining the low copy number samples was put at £1 million, the loss, or disposal of the original vaginal swabs was a major economic, as well as fatal, shortcoming in the Crown case.

Mr Stewart exposed other prosecution weaknesses in the case against his client, among them the evidence which had made Simpson a suspect in the first place after the apparent sighting of him emerging from Templeton Woods in his taxi around the time of Elizabeth's disappearance. The couple driving home who spotted the cab were positive that this had occurred between midnight and 12.30 a.m., practically the exact time other witnesses had said they had seen Elizabeth setting off from Teazers in the centre of town. If all of them were accurate in their timings, it meant she was still alive at the time the taxi was leaving the woods.

Referring to a detailed examination of Simpson's taxi, the defending QC also pointed out: 'Not one fibre, not one hair, not once piece of evidence linking Elizabeth McCabe with Vincent Simpson was recovered.'

The jury did not have the benefit of hearing from the accused man himself. He, along with his wife Gillian who attended the court daily, declined to testify, as was their right, and Lord

Kinclaven properly stressed that no inference should be taken from their refusal to enter the witness box.

However, the detective inspector who had gone from Dundee to Camberley to arrest Simpson told the court that in interviews conducted at Woking police station the accused man had resolutely denied any connection with Elizabeth McCabe. He had also been adamant in repeated denials that he had visited Templeton Woods that night and suggested his supposed statement in 1980, that he had gone to the woods with his dog to watch couples having sex, was something that had been inserted into his statement by detectives. He denied even having a dog at that time. When police officers told him that they had him 'bang to rights' he had replied, 'In that case then bang me up. Let's go to court – let's do the business. I have got nothing to hide.' The detective inspector admitted that the police car used to take Simpson back to Dundee after his arrest in Camberley had been fitted with concealed listening and recording devices in the hope he would say something incriminating on the journey north. Nothing of the kind occurred.

When Mr Alex Prentice QC, the prosecuting advocate depute, rose to his feet to sum up the Crown case seven weeks after making his opening remarks, few would have envied him his task. His entire case hinged on the acceptability of the vital scientific DNA evidence and he admitted as much to the jurors. He invited them to view the lengthy proceedings as a 27-year-old jigsaw puzzle which, although containing missing pieces, could still be fitted together to create an understandable picture. A main component was the evidence of the couple who had seen the taxi emerging from Templeton Woods being driven 'bizarrely' by someone they could accept was Vincent Simpson. He dismissed the contradiction in the timings as simply being an honest error in their precise recollections.

The advocate depute conceded that there had been contamination of the mortuary sheet containing the hair root. However, even if they rejected this part of the Crown case, they should accept the expert findings of the DNA on the victim's jersey. Not only had three partial profiles been recovered, they had been found in an area of the neck where experts would have expected someone to have grabbed the jumper.

'Remember, Vincent Simpson rejects any suggestion he was in contact with or ever met Elizabeth McCabe,' he stressed to the jury. 'This is not a case where it is suggested she was in a taxi and he might have helped her out or anything like that.'

In contrast to the less than satisfactory presentation of conclusive evidence by his colleague, QC Mr Mark Stewart had built a formidable case indicating his client's innocence. Over the long weeks of the trial, and with the precision of a surgeon, he had systematically dismantled the scientific evidence, exposing the possibilities of its contamination and the slack police work surrounding it.

However, he did more than just demolish the forensic case. He also introduced other scenarios as to what might have happened after Elizabeth walked away from Teazers that cold February morning, saying the circumstantial evidence was stronger against several other individuals. Although he pointed out it was not the job of the defence to prove another's guilt, he suggested it was more likely that the nursery nurse had visited the flat of Sandra Niven's one-time boyfriend, where she had gone before to engage in sex. Then, after having something to eat, she again had consensual sex before a 'sudden violent explosion', which resulted in her death. Mr Stewart said he was not even sure the Crown had proved Elizabeth had been murdered and that the crime may have been one of culpable homicide.

Pointing to the absence of injury on her body, he said any young woman in Dundee would have been aware at that time of the shadow cast by Templeton Wood after the finding of the body of Carol Lannen there months earlier. But if Elizabeth had been taken unwillingly in a taxi past her street towards the woods, she would have had six minutes in which to defend herself. There was no evidence that anything of that kind had occurred.

Mr Stewart accused police of being blinkered in their investigation and suggested Vincent Simpson had become a suspect only because he was a taxi driver. Having discredited so much of the vital scientific evidence, as well as advancing possible alternatives to what had happened to Elizabeth on her journey home, the QC crushingly used four words to describe the investigation by Tayside Police and the subsequent prosecution. They were 'not fit for purpose,' he said.

It was a view apparently shared by the jury. After an absence of only three hours, a relatively short time considering the volume of seven weeks of evidence, they returned a majority Not Guilty verdict.

The bespectacled 61-year-old in the dock, who throughout the trial had surprised many with his relaxed, friendly demeanour, sat with his head bowed as his fate was announced. When he finally looked up, his only reaction was to reply, 'Thank you very much.' He then departed quickly through a side door, his nightmare over at last.

Like every other unsolved murder, the files of Carol Lannen and Elizabeth McCabe will remain forever open. Taken together, the separate inquiries, the intermittent cold case reviews, the costly analysis of the low grade DNA samples and the long trial of Vincent Simpson, has meant the expenditure of millions of pounds. Although the sums of money involved are unprecedented in the history of Dundee policing, that would be no deterrent if fresh evidence emerged to point the way to likely conclusions leading to the final closure of the murder logs. Justice is beyond value in an orderly society and those who suffer at the hands of the wicked deserve to have the price of achieving it paid, whatever the cost.

Nevertheless, the prospects of ever winning convictions for the Templeton Woods murders diminished significantly with the presentation of the case against Vincent John Simpson. When Mark Stewart QC and the others in his all-Dundee defence team of advocate Ashley Edwards and solicitor George Donnelly demolished the Crown case so expertly, they effectively made it far more difficult for any future prosecutions to succeed. Forensic science will continue to advance, probably to levels even more unanticipated than the major breakthrough of DNA, but nothing will ever change the police procedures of 1979–80 and beyond, when officers, unaware of what lay ahead, innocently contaminated their own evidence.

Thanks to that and the continuing passage of time, no one, except the person or persons who took the last breath of life from two defenceless young women, is likely to ever know for sure if they were sisters in death or just strangers whose resting places simply happened to be 150 yards apart.

The tantalising, yet inconclusive, coincidences which attach to the murders will always ensure a continuing fascination with the cases, however, and legitimate theories pointing to possible scenarios will continue to be advanced.

There may be food for thought, for instance, in other pages of this volume. Some nine years after the discovery of Carol Lannen's body in Templeton Woods, a walker in another forest on the opposite side of the River Tay also came upon the body of a woman who had been strangled. She was identified as Lynda Hunter, the wife of depraved social worker Andrew Hunter, who was subsequently jailed for life for her murder (see Collared).

During his trial, it emerged that he too trawled the city centre for prostitutes. At the time of Carol Lannen's death, the slimly built Hunter was aged 28, pale-faced and with a moustache. The photo-fit of the Templeton Woods murder suspect, said to be slim, moustached and aged 25–30, also bore a striking resemblance to how he looked at that time. Hunter used the services of a number of call girls, among them a 22-year-old drug addict who apparently committed suicide the day after his wife's corpse was found in the Fife forest. The pair enjoyed sex sessions in his home, before and after he murdered his wife, and it was later learned the two had become acquainted when Hunter met the young woman in his role as a social worker. Could he also have been a social work contact of the unfortunate Carol Lannen? Was there a possibility they may have formed an association and that she had perhaps threatened to expose him?

He may not have had any particular connection with Kintore where the handbag and clothing of the 18-year-old were found, but neither did he have business in Manchester where he took such elaborate steps to throw police off the scent by abandoning his wife's car after taking her life. Anything the resourceful social worker might have known about the teenager who perished in Templeton Woods, however, went to his grave with him. He died in Perth Prison five years into his life sentence.

The contrasting lifestyles of the two unfortunate young women is the principal reason many of the police officers involved in both cases believed they met their deaths at the hands of different people. Yet, why should that necessarily eliminate the possibility of a single killer? Many men who keep the company of prostitutes lead perfectly normal lives and have ordinary relationships with decent women they are attracted to, some of whom may also be reserved and ambitious. Being interested in ladies of the night does not preclude a simultaneous interest in pretty nursery nurses, nor the ability to communicate with, and be attractive to, both of them, though for differing reasons.

Many questions thrown up during the trial of Vincent Simpson were left unanswered. An intriguing factor to emerge during the long hours of evidence, but which was not probed further, was that there were reasonable grounds to believe that Elizabeth might not even have been in a position to have hired a taxi to take her home in the first place. In a passing reference to how upset the victim had been in Teazers when she had felt like a 'gooseberry', her friend Sandra Niven had recounted how she had lent Elizabeth £1 for a drink. If she was without money for a cab, why had she declined the offer of a lift from Sandra and her male friend? Upset at feeling left out, and imagining she was disliked by male acquaintances, what had been in her mind when she stepped out into the night from the club? It did not seem she was in a particular hurry to go home. Is it possible she had made other arrangements about how she was to spend the next part of her night out?

Whatever her intentions, the one undisputed fact is that Elizabeth was last seen in the centre of her home town before she suddenly vanished into the night. The final, certain sighting of her was at a spot in town just a few hundred yards from where the other young murder victim, with whom she was to be forever linked, was also seen for the last time before she, too, simply disappeared.

The trial of Vincent Simpson produced another curious fact about their final movements.

When Carol Lannen was last glimpsed it had been when she stood on a street corner outside the Occidental Bar. On the evening before Elizabeth McCabe met her maker, she had gone to the Occidental for a drink but left in embarrassment after having been mistaken for a prostitute by a male drinker.

In all probability, it was just one more coincidence in their widely differing lives. Or perhaps not.

SOURCES

Books

Christie, J. B. W., 'Crime', in *Third Statistical Account of Scotland: City of Dundee*, Herald Press, 1979

Hamilton, Judy, *Scottish Murders*, Lomond Books; Geddes & Grosset, 2001

Millar, A. H., *Haunted Dundee*, Malcolm MacLeod, 1923

Skelton, Douglas, *Blood on the Thistle*, HarperCollins, 1994

Magazines

Bonner, John, 'The Dundee Strangler', *True Crime Monthly*, February 1982

MacPherson, Euan, 'Jack the Ripper in Dundee', *The Scots Magazine*, January 1988

Melville, William, 'Blood Group Determination', *The Police Journal*, October–December 1971

Reid, Henry John, 'Real Lives', *The Guardian Weekend*, 26 March 1994

Newspapers

The Courier
The Daily Express
The Daily Mail
The Daily Record
The Evening Telegraph
The Glasgow Herald
The Scotsman
The Sunday Post

LAWLESS

By Alexander McGregor

The gripping novel from the bestselling author of THE LAW KILLERS

When investigative reporter Campbell McBride arrives in his old home town to sign copies of his true crime bestseller, he is confronted about one of the murders he has covered. It seemed routine - a tempestuous relationship, boyfriend murders girlfriend, case closed. But there's something that McBride can't figure out.

Then he receives the first of the messages, baiting him, ridiculing him. But how do they know where he is, what he's doing? With his old newspaper rival and sparring partner Richard Richardson also taking a close interest in McBride's decision to stay in town and interest of another kind in DI Petra Novak, McBride gets to work. And the more he digs, the deeper he gets. Not just into an investigation which puts his own life in danger, but into the ghosts which haunt him in the place he once called home.

Fast-paced and acutely observed,
Lawless *confirms Alexander McGregor as*
a major new force in crime writing.

Available from
BLACK & WHITE PUBLISHING
Price £10.00 Hardback ISBN 978 1 84502 109 2

LAWLESS

It's cold in Dundee. But not as cold as the trail being left by a murderer - a trail so cold even the police don't know it exists ...

1

He'd seen his name in print often enough above newspaper stories but it looked different on the spine of a book. He still wasn't entirely convinced that he and the Campbell McBride described on the jacket were the same person. According to the blurb, he was a distinguished investigative reporter and an authority on crime. Now he'd turned author and, what was even more unlikely, the book had become something of a best-seller. OK, maybe it wasn't *War and Peace* but thousands had seemed to want to read his account of the catalogue of murders that had taken place in Dundee, the town he used to call home.

During that afternoon of the signing, he had worked his way through an unexpectedly long line of people wanting his name on their copy of *The Law Town Killers*. Some were old acquaintances – even a couple of ex-girlfriends – a few were amateur detectives but most were just curious. Maybe they thought that getting the author's signature would make the book more collectable.

McBride saw it differently – sign as many as you can and that way they're less likely to lend the book out to friends who should be buying their own copy. At least that was the theory. But they could be a bit contrary in that city of contradictions.

As the queue gradually evaporated, McBride became aware of a middle-aged man hanging back, waiting to be last. He was small and spruce, his salt-and-pepper beard close trimmed. Not carrying any extra weight. Clothes sensible, matching. Not cheap – maybe expensive. He held the paperback protectively to his chest – not like a reader, more the way a professor would before he delivered a lecture. Perhaps he wanted a long chat about forensics or a complicated dedication. Either way, he was going to take up time.

When there was no one else left, the precise, uncluttered figure approached and his body language definitely wasn't that of a fan. He was controlled but agitated. There was none of the usual uncertainty of what to say, no half–smile or hesitant attempt at a handshake. Spreading the book open, he held his fingers over the start of one of the chapters.

'Your book's shit and this is the biggest pile of it – just like yourself.' The words were chiselled out but the voice was measured, soft – just loud enough for McBride to take in but not for anyone passing the table. 'You couldn't be bothered doing any proper research, could you? Or were you just talked out of it by your pals in the police?'

Before McBride could look up or think of a sensible response, the troubled man had turned away and was walking towards the main door of the store. Ten seconds later, he had vanished into the throng of shoppers that packed Murraygate every Saturday afternoon.

Even if he'd been inclined to, McBride knew there was no point going after him. That part of town was the commercial backbone of the city. The shoppers always came at you like a football crowd and, with seven days to go before Christmas, sanity had deserted them. It was said that, if you stood under H. Samuel's clock long enough, everyone in Dundee would pass you by. That day, they seemed to be going round twice.

McBride had prepared himself for possible confrontations with the family or friends of some of those he'd written about. It was inevitable, he reckoned, that he'd cause offence somewhere. He'd revived a lot of old memories that some would have struggled to bury and his resurrection of the facts wasn't going to make him the most popular guy in the country as far as they were concerned. He would have felt the same if he'd been one of them and he'd resolved to be apologetic and sympathetic. He would respond with unaccustomed gentleness. But, when the simmering anger spilled from the man at the end of the queue, there hadn't been an opportunity for saying even a holding, 'Sorry you feel that way.' How could he placate someone who apparently didn't want to listen?

When he looked at the book still open in front of him, he was surprised to discover that the chapter wasn't among those he'd mentally noted as the ones most likely to stir up trouble. In fact, if he'd been forced to choose the least offensive, the chapter staring back at him would probably have been it.

It was textbook straightforward – young man strangles girlfriend after argument . . . abundance of evidence . . . arrested within hours . . . jailed for life . . . end of story. The killing had only made it into the book because the victim had been a policeman's daughter. If such a thing as an open–and–shut murder existed, the death of Alison Brown and the subsequent despatch to prison of Bryan Gilzean for her slaying constituted it.

So why had the brief episode with the troubled man who had come to Waterstone's bookstore to make a point left him with such an irrational feeling of unease? He told himself it was because he would have preferred a longer, less considered outburst – something he could have dealt with, apologised for.

The world is full of bampots, he reflected. Forget it. But he knew he wouldn't.